IN THE STRENGTH OF THE Lord

IN THE STRENGTH OF THE *Lord*

TALKS FROM THE 2009 BYU WOMEN'S CONFERENCE

DESERET BOOK

SALT LAKE CITY, UTAH

Library of Congress Cataloging-in-Publication Data

Women's Conference (2009 : Brigham Young University)
In the strength of the Lord : talks from the 2009 BYU Women's Conference.
    p. cm.
Includes bibliographical references and index.
  ISBN 978-1-60641-228-2 (hardbound : alk. paper) 1. Mormon women—Religious life—Congresses. 2. Church of Jesus Christ of Latter-day Saints—Congresses. 3. Mormon Church—Congresses. I. Title.
  BX8641.W73 2009
  289.3082—dc22   2009042223

Printed in the United States of America
Publishers Printing, Salt Lake City, UT

10 9 8 7 6 5 4 3 2 1

CONTENTS

CONTENTS

GOSPEL LIVING

IN THE STRENGTH OF THE LORD

Sandra Rogers

In August of 2008, when our committee began planning the 2009 conference, we hoped to find a theme that provided encouragement to rely on the Lord in all things, in good times and in times of uncertainty and challenge. In August 2008 the Dow Jones Average was still above 11,000. Massive layoffs had not taken place across the United States. The U. S. housing crisis and subsequent foreclosures were just showing the tip of a terrible iceberg. The good Saints in California had not yet faced the venom of the campaign on Proposition 8 and its vicious aftermath. Those in Fargo, North Dakota, had yet to fight the rampaging Red River. We knew that a severe and perhaps prolonged recession, political barbs, and natural disasters were not the only challenges nor the only uncertainties that you and your families would be facing. We felt drawn to a theme that would be an anchor for anyone facing any challenge of mortality.

I do not plan to dwell on the breadth and depth of what can be just plain tough about mortality. I do want to point out why mortality is the way it is. The Lord taught Moses that "worlds without number have I created; and I also created them for mine own purpose. . . . [and] this is my work and my glory—to bring to pass the immortality and eternal life of man" (Moses 1:33, 39). Fundamental to achieving an immortal life like

---

Sandra Rogers is a daughter, sister, and aunt. She is the international vice president at BYU, and was dean of the College of Nursing from 1993–1999. She serves as a ward Sunday School teacher.

God the Father and His Son have, with the family relationships they enjoy, and with the characteristics of Godliness they possess, was the principle of agency. To become like God, His children had to be free to choose. And in order to be able to choose, there had to be opposition. As Lehi explained, if we did not have opposition there could be no righteousness and there would have been no purpose for our creation (see 2 Nephi 2:11–12). God gave us commandments so that we could return to Him, develop His traits and His capacities, and become like Him. As we use our agency to obey those commandments we will stand proven to the Lord (see Abraham 3:25).

This magnificent plan was explained to us in the council in heaven, including the fact that we could all very well stumble, trip, fall, falter, crumble, faint, or fail during this mortal test. But we were assured by Him who cannot lie (see Titus 1:2) that we could be rescued from our spiritual clumsiness by a Holy Redeemer, filled with perfect charity, who would "go forth, suffering pains and afflictions and temptations of every kind; . . . [taking] upon him the pains and the sicknesses of his people. And he will take upon him death, . . . and he will take upon him [his people's] infirmities, that his bowels may be filled with mercy, . . . that he may know according to the flesh how to succor his people according to their infirmities" (Alma 7:11–12).

Someone with plenty of talent and plenty of intelligence, a supreme example of the natural man, someone dazzling and charming enough to be called a "son of the morning" (Isaiah 14:12) offered to fill the role of Redeemer for us. His plan had two major errors that demonstrated his disregard for eternal laws and his amazing arrogance. Lucifer would get us through the test of mortality, all right. All we had to do was give up our agency while Father gave up His glory (see Moses 4:1).

We are all here because we chose the Holy One of Israel. We saw through the smoke and mirrors of Satan's devious and disobedient offer. We chose Christ. When He said, "Father, thy will be done, and the glory be thine forever" (Moses 4:2) and "Here am I, send me" (Abraham 3:27), we "shouted for joy" (Job 38:7).

Satan then began his continual war against Christ. Because we used our agency to choose God, His Son, and their plan, we are here, right now, having this mortal experience. Truth is, we have been opposing Satan for a long time. His goals are simple: Thwart the plan of God, make us as miserable as he is; bind us captive when we give our agency to him (see 2 Nephi 2:27); laugh at our distress when we are in his chains (see Moses 7:26); desert us if we choose to follow him (see Alma 30:60); and reign with blood and horror on the earth.

But Christ did come. He did complete the atonement. He did suffer for us. He did rise from the tomb and He did appear to Joseph Smith. President Eyring has taught, "We have trials to face because our Heavenly Father loves us. His purpose is to help us qualify for the blessing of living with Him and His Son, Jesus Christ, forever in glory and in families. . . . The restored gospel not only teaches us why we must be tested, but it makes clear to us what the test is. . . . 'And we will prove them herewith, to see if they will do all things whatsoever the Lord their God shall command them' (Abraham 3:25)."[1] President Eyring also explained that we will need more than our own strength to keep the commandments—a strength that will come to us in any circumstance we face because of the Atonement of Jesus Christ. President Eyring said that "because the Atonement of Jesus Christ is real. . . . we can become stronger for the tests of life. We then go in the strength of the Lord . . . [and] He goes with us. And in time we become His tested and strengthened disciples."[2] Mortality is a test with opposition, to see if we will choose the Lord. Satan is here to heckle, distract, shove, kick, and gouge us along the way.

Mortality is like taking a very difficult final examination in the most important course of your degree program, with people yelling obscenities in one ear and whispering sweet nothings in the other, kicking your shins, poking their fingers in your eyes, turning the lights on and off, making the room either blazing hot or freezing cold, telling you that you'll never succeed and should not even try, and playing your least favorite music loudly in the background. Mortality, with its normal losses, sorrows, sicknesses, disappointments, torments, weeds, mistakes, errors, sins, and other afflictions would be a reasonable test in and of itself. But throw in Satan and his minions and now we have a test of faith and obedience that will ensure the Lord knows what we are made of.

You know this is true because you're out there taking mortality's exams. But there is another, even greater truth. And that is the message of this Women's Conference. During all this testing and trying in mortality, remember what we rejoiced about in the Council in Heaven. We have a perfect friend beside us to buoy us up; to steady our feet; to put starch in our feeble knees; to enlighten our minds; to lead us, guide us, and walk beside us; to bear our burdens and our griefs; to take our stripes when we have been in error; to "take our lickin'" for us when we have sinned; to face the bullies with us; to wipe our fevered brow in sickness; to mourn with us when we lose the people we love the most—and the things we probably shouldn't have loved so much; to steady us when the job is lost; to reassure us when our hearts are troubled or sore afraid or lonely; to ease our pain; to stand with us when we have been falsely accused; to carry us when we are tired and weary; and to comfort us through a betrayal of trust. We have a Savior and a Redeemer. When we rely on His strength we can ride out the storm, complete the test, fight the good fight, finish the course, and keep the faith (see 2 Timothy 4:7).

In Psalm 27:1 we read, "The Lord is my light and my salvation; whom shall I fear? the Lord is the strength of my life; of whom shall I be afraid?"

Paul testified, "I can do all things through Christ which strengtheneth me" (Philippians 4:13).

At a time when chaos and confusion encircle us, when disappointments and pressures mount, when even our strictest obedience doesn't seem to be rewarded in the ways we might have hoped, we can be assured that through the Atonement of Christ we can endure well all that we face, and come off more refined in Christ's image, more true in our discipleship, and more content in our hearts.

As I have examined stories in scripture and Church history that demonstrate how people have relied on the strength of the Lord in very challenging mortal moments I am impressed with common themes.

Those who rely on the strength of the Lord understand the purpose of life and its adversity. Because they understand what the test is all about, they don't get confused. They understand the difference between the normal tests of mortality which require faith, obedience, and endurance and the "wages of sin" which require faith, obedience, and repentance. They keep their eyes on eternity. They understand life isn't about getting as much as we can of power, or honors, or stuff. Instead, it is about becoming like Christ in integrity, humility, and charity. They recognize that adversity refines us as it turns our faces and hearts to the Lord. They know, as

Elder Oaks said, that "adversities can be the means of obtaining blessings unobtainable without them."[3]

In 2008 I had the opportunity to travel with the BYU Folkdance Ensemble to Eastern Europe. At a fireside in Bratislava, Slovakia, I met a white-haired woman who radiated pure joy. Sister Valeria Žišková was the last person baptized in what was then Czechoslovakia before the missionaries were pulled out of the country just before World War II. She had been quite ill but insisted on being baptized. The next day the missionaries left and were gone for decades. From her childhood to her very mature adulthood she was without the Church organization but she grasped tightly to its divine truths. Despite the terrors of the Nazi occupation and the brutal repression of the Communists, especially directed to those with ties to the West, she kept her faith and raised her family with that faith. How she rejoiced when the Church returned. She knew the purpose of life, and she had relied on the strength of the Lord through many difficult circumstances.

People who go forth in the strength of the Lord know the character of God. They know that He is omnipotent, omniscient, and filled with charity. He knows the end from the beginning. His arm is stronger than any arm of flesh. They know He is the Mediator, the price-payer, and the "foundation whereon if men build they cannot fall" (Helaman 5:12). They know that He atoned for the sins of the world, and that through repentance and obedience we can be snatched from the Devil's captivity and be born of God (see Alma 36:17–23 and Mosiah 27:29). They are valiant in their testimony of Jesus Christ.

The Lord chastened Joseph Smith after the loss of 116 pages of the Book of Mormon manuscript, with these words: "For, behold, you should not have feared man more than God. . . . you should have been faithful; and he would have extended his arm and supported you against all the fiery darts of the adversary; and he would have been with you in every time of trouble" (D&C 3:7–8). Because of Joseph's sincere repentance, the Lord also extended to him what is, to me, the most charitable form of His strength. Following His chastisement of Joseph Smith, Christ offered this bright beam of hope, "But remember, God is merciful; therefore, repent of that which thou hast done which is contrary to the commandment which I gave you, and thou art still chosen, and art again called to the work" (D&C 3:10). I love those words. I love what they represent. When I have fallen short because I, like Joseph, have mistakenly relied either on my own strength of the strength of others, I love the hope I find in them.

Zeniff and his people prevailed against the Lamanites because they "did go up in the strength of the Lord to battle. Now, the Lamanites knew nothing concerning the Lord, nor the strength of the Lord, therefore they depended upon their own strength. Yet they were a strong people, as to the strength of men" (Mosiah 10:10–11). We will face many circumstances where our challenges (by individuals or by circumstances) are compounded by the "strength of men." That strength could seem overwhelming and sometimes very persuasive unless, like David with his small stones against the immensity of Goliath, we have drawn on the strength of the Lord (see 1 Samuel 17:32–51).

Going forward in the strength of the Lord requires us to trust Him, to trust His messengers, and to be willing to hear and follow counsel. Such trust and willingness to be counseled comes more naturally to those who are meek, humble, teachable, and obedient. Unfortunately we can, at times, steadily rely on the strength of the Lord until we are caught in a moment of pride or weakness. In the same moment we can too easily forget that the Lord's strength sustained us before and imagine that we truly "did it all ourselves." Sometimes we can think we have been following long enough and that now we can do it all on our own. I learned this important lesson in a decisive way.

In 2005 I traveled to the Dominican Republic with a good friend to pick up her son from his mission. We wanted to meet the people he knew and loved. We rented a car in Santo Domingo, which I drove. The night before we were to leave the country I was struggling to map out the way to the airport. I was inspired to hire a taxi to guide me to the airport, as I had absolutely no idea where the airport office of the car rental agency was.

At four A.M., I strategically placed the Spanish-speaking missionary and his mother in the guide taxi with instructions to drive slowly and not lose the "gringa" following behind. The plan was to drop off the missionary's mother and our luggage at curbside. The taxi would lead me to the car rental return location, wait while I checked in the car, and then return the missionary and me to the airport.

Everything worked as planned. I followed the taxi driver with exactness. We arrived at the airport, unloaded the luggage and the missionary's mother. I was happy and relieved. I followed the taxi out of the departure lanes and away from the airport and then, for some inexplicable reason, I was overcome with a fit of pride. I saw a sign saying "rental cars" with an arrow pointing off to the left. When the taxi driver ignored this sign and kept driving straight ahead, I thought at that moment something like, "Gee, I just saw a rental car sign at an airport where I have never been before in my life. I must surely know better than that native taxi driver who has been to this airport a million times." I decided to follow my own counsel instead of the wisdom of the local expert, an expert I had hired because he knew the way. I still cannot explain why I had that prideful, conceited, dumb moment. But it happened. I just ignored the guide and went off on my own to the left.

What a mess. I hadn't gone in the correct direction at all. I was completely in the dark, both figuratively and literally. I made it back to the road the taxi had taken, but I couldn't find it anywhere. I passed rental returns for every company except the one I needed. I ended up back on the freeway headed to Santo Domingo. Large concrete barriers made it impossible for me to reverse direction. I imagined how lost I would be once I arrived back in the city.

I clearly knew how desolate it was to be left to my own weak wisdom and puny strength. I started praying a desperate prayer, begging the Lord for forgiveness for my pride and stupidity. I noticed a gas station that serviced both sides of the freeway. I drove in, held up the rental car agreement and asked the workers in broken Spanish, "ayuda mi por favor, ¿donde esta Nacional?" but they couldn't help me. I ended up back at the airport and went back down the road the taxi had taken with the same result, turning around again at the gas station and paying toll charges both times. Naturally, the missionary and his mother were also very worried. I had the airline tickets so they couldn't even try to check in.

I had now spent more than an hour driving around without success. The sun was starting to come up and it wasn't long before the plane was scheduled to leave. I was an emotional wreck. I promised the Lord I would never be so dumb again if He would just help me out this time. The third time around the airport I felt impressed to try a road I hadn't seen before.

I ended up in a rental car return, but not the one I needed. Still, the good workers there took pity on me and were willing to go with me to the correct car rental agency. Then they took me to the airport. I had been saved from my own idiocy by their generosity and kindness, and God's mercy.

I had an entire flight back to Utah to meditate on the lessons I learned from that experience. I thought about how foolish I was to have followed the taxi driver so carefully for so long and then, suddenly believing I didn't need guidance anymore, go off on my own. I recognized that no matter what you think you know, you never want to put yourself in the position of thinking that on this one issue, or in this one situation, "I certainly know more than the Lord does and I certainly do not need to follow Him or to rely on His strength."

Those who go forth in the strength of the Lord understand that the winds of mortality will still blow against them. Yet because they understand the plan and have a testimony of the Savior, they rejoice even in the midst of their afflictions and press on in obedience. Rather than focus on the lone and dreary world, they express joy in the great plan of redemption. Mormon described the many trials of Alma and Amulek and then commented, "Yea, and [the Lord] also gave them strength, that they should suffer no manner of afflictions, save it were swallowed up in the joy of Christ" (Alma 31:38).

In 1833, almost 1,200 Saints had built homes, planted farms, established a school, and were publishing a newspaper in Jackson County, Missouri. W.W. Phelps was at work printing *The Book of Commandments*.[4]

But the idyllic Zion so hoped for by the Saints lasted only a few brief months. The neighboring Missourians were incited to violence, and a campaign of abuse and falsehood began. On July 20, 1833, a council of Missourians voted to eject the Mormons, "peaceably if we can, forcibly if we must."[5] They demanded that the Mormons leave the county, close the press, and halt any future emigration of Mormons to the area. Mobs numbering between 400 and 500 men came down on the Saints. They tore down the two-story building in which the printing press was housed and destroyed the press. The Phelps family lived in the same building. Sister Phelps and her sick baby were driven into the street amidst the broken furniture. Bishop Edward Partridge and another brother were tarred and feathered. Other brethren were scourged. The mob served notice to the

Saints that every man, woman, and child would be whipped and scourged if they did not leave.

When the cold of November came that year, the Saints were forcibly removed from Jackson County. After the Mormons had surrendered their weapons as a token of good faith, the mob attacked, whipping the men, and driving the women and children from their homes at gunpoint, then setting fire to the houses. The banks of the Missouri River were lined with pitiful Mormon refugees, many without clothing, food, or any means of shelter from the winter storms. Some died from exposure, and "the fleeing multitude left, in the frozen stubble" of the fields, "a trail of blood from their lacerated feet."[6]

It was during this period, not in the early, more peaceful days in Missouri, that W. W. Phelps wrote the hymn "Now Let Us Rejoice." He didn't write this hymn when things were going well. This great and grand hymn of the Restoration was penned at a time of defeat at the hands of a mob, a time of frustration, homelessness, suffering, death, privation, cold, wet, and hunger. Those terrible afflictions produced a hymn of rejoicing that gave hope and strength to the Saints.

I confess that I haven't always appreciated this hymn—I thought the alto part was boring. But now I will never sing it without remembering W. W. Phelps and the other Saints who, while facing great hardships, still had cause to rejoice and bear testimony. Is it any wonder that this hymn became a favorite of the Saints? It was sung in Kirtland at the temple dedication. It was sung in Far West, in Nauvoo at the first meeting of the Relief Society, in Winter Quarters, in Nebraska and Wyoming, in Utah, and in every Latter-day Saint settlement of the West. It is one of the first hymns translated into new languages. Now when we sing it, we know we join with generations of valiant Saints here and abroad who bear record that in the strength of the Lord, all things can be met with joy.

Those who rely on the strength of the Lord also understand the effort it takes to draw near to the Lord. They understand the power of making and keeping covenants with God. They know that sacrifice brings forth the blessings of heaven. They know that faith, testimony, and trust in God must be nurtured and nourished every day through service, study, and prayer. They know that obedience in small, seemingly inconsequential things can make the difference in large, very consequential things. They know that the fruit of the tree of life is sweet beyond comprehension and no filthy water, nor mist of darkness, nor scorn from those in the great and spacious building will keep them from it (see 1 Nephi 8).

Esther understood this principle when she determined to go into the King in hopes of saving her people, but only after she had asked her fellow believers to fast for her (see Esther 4:16).

The woman who pressed through the crowd to touch the clothing of Jesus and was healed when His virtue and strength passed to her because of her faith and her effort believed this principle (see Mark 5:25–34).

Emma Smith knew this principle when she hid the manuscript of the Joseph Smith translation of the Bible in special pockets in her petticoat and then bravely walked through winter wind and icy snow from Far West to Quincy, with a babe in her arms and small children clinging to her skirts.[7]

Sister Lucille Sargent, a Latter-day Saint living in what was then called Peking, China, in the 1970s acted on this principle. At that time, there were no other Latter-day Saints living in Peking. She was not married. She sent her tithing envelope regularly to Church headquarters. She had been in the Foreign Service for more than twenty years, living in remote areas, most of the time alone.

When President Faust and his wife, Ruth, met Sister Sargent, Sister Faust asked how she managed to maintain her spiritual strength when she was all alone. Sister Sargent replied, "I always pray aloud, and on Sunday I would sing some hymns and pray aloud and read the scriptures." She said that when she was considering her assignments, she would tell her supervisors, "I can take these difficult posts. I have special help."[8]

Sister Sargent had learned, like Paul, that "all things work together for good to them that love God," and that "in all these things we are more than conquerors through him [meaning Jesus Christ] that loved us" (Romans 8:28, 37).

I have always loved the compelling story of the people of Ammon. When they were converted, they relied completely on the strength of the Lord. Their conversion infuriated their wicked Lamanite brethren, who slaughtered them in their meekness because the people of Ammon had made a covenant to never again take up their weapons of war.

When so many of their people were brutally destroyed at the hands of the Lamanites, they did not bitterly turn on Ammon, accusing and berating him for teaching them the gospel and making them vulnerable. They didn't demand to know why their obedience wasn't being rewarded with protection. No, instead they asked Ammon to inquire of the Lord what they should do. Ammon was told to lead the people to Zarahemla. Remember, the Nephites in Zarahemla had suffered much at the hands of the Lamanites, so the people of Ammon were justifiably apprehensive about going there. Yet, relying on the strength of the Lord, they took their families out into the wilderness toward the land of Zarahemla. Ammon himself must have been anxious about how the Anti-Nephi-Lehis would be received in Zarahemla because he went ahead to sound out the Nephites. Not only did the good Saints in Zarahemla welcome the repentant, converted Lamanites, but they gave them their own lands and offered them protection. The Anti-Nephi-Lehis relied on the strength of the Lord to go to Zarahemla. The faithful Nephites relied on the strength of the Lord in meeting their former enemies with open arms and forgiving generous hearts (see Alma 27).

500 B.C. was the season for relying on the strength of the Lord for Esther and her people. The season for relying on the strength of the Lord for the Anti-Nephi-Lehis and the people of Zarahemla was 80 B.C. The season of strength for W. W. Phelps and the other Saints in Jackson County was A.D. 1833. Sister Sargent's season of strength was the 1960s and 70s. And our season for strength is right now, today and tomorrow, and the next day.

Let us do all that we can do to increase our faith in and reliance on our Savior so that we can say, like Alma, "give us strength according to our faith" (Alma 14:26). And on the days when we feel our faith is lagging, let us be like the father with the child possessed by a spirit, who, when "Jesus said unto him, If thou canst believe, all things are possible to him that believeth . . . cried out, and said with tears, Lord, I believe; help thou mine unbelief" (Mark 9:23–24). Let us make the Lord our hope and our strength (see Joel 3:16). Let us follow Him with exactness. Let us draw near to Him (see D&C 88:63). Let us put our trust and our love in the true and living God because His strengthening grace is, and always has been, and always will be, sufficient in every season of our need (see Moroni 10:32). [9]

NOTES

1. Henry B. Eyring, "In the Strength of the Lord," *Ensign*, May 2004, 16.
2. Ibid., 19.
3. Dallin H. Oaks, "Adversity," *Ensign*, July 1998, 9.
4. George D. Pyper, *Stories of the Latter-day Saint Hymns,* 3rd edition, (Salt Lake City: Deseret News Press, 1948), 188.
5. Joseph Fielding Smith, *Essentials in Church History* (Salt Lake City: Deseret Book, 1973), 132.
6. Ibid., 132–139.
7. See Joseph Smith, *Joseph Smith* (manual). In Teachings of the Presidents of the Church series (Salt Lake City: The Church of Jesus Christ of Latter-day Saints, 2007), 369.
8. James E. Faust, "Married or Single: Look beyond Yourself," *Ensign*, March 1980, 35.
9. See Bible Dictionary, s.v. "Grace," 697.

STRENGTHENING RELATIONSHIPS

Nourishing and Protecting the Family

Julie B. Beck

Since the 2008 BYU Women's Conference, we have met with many thousands of sisters throughout the world, and it has been at times very emotional to see you. I feel emotional now as I look in your faces and realize that among you are women who have had experiences that span all possible mortal experiences. You are each unique and precious, and Heavenly Father is teaching and preparing you for the blessings of eternal life.

In our presidency, we have talked about three lifelong responsibilities that Latter-day Saint women have to help them prepare for the blessings of eternal life. First, we are to increase in faith and personal righteousness. There has been much spoken about that at this women's conference. Second, we have a responsibility to strengthen families and homes, and third, we have a responsibility to seek out and help those who have needs—any kind of needs. We are a *relief* society and that is what we do. We provide relief from all that hinders the joy and progress of women and all of Heavenly Father's children.

Julie B. Beck is the general president of the Relief Society, and was serving as the first counselor in the general Young Women presidency prior to receiving her call to direct the Church's organization for women. As a child she learned to speak Portuguese when she lived in Brazil while her father served as mission president. She is a graduate of Dixie College and Brigham Young University. She was a full-time homemaker prior to her service in the Young Women and Relief Society general presidencies. She and her husband, Ramon Beck, have three children and twelve grandchildren.

As I have pondered this assignment for many months now, I have read and studied more than you want to know about. I have a fat folder full of ideas and thoughts, and many of these things I scribbled down in the middle of the night, reminding myself not to forget to say this or that. I have a big stack of books, talks, and messages from prophets that I have studied and pondered to learn how to nurture my own daughters and help others nurture their families.

I have thought about my own daughters and my daughter-in-law, about how hard they work and what their assignments are, and about my granddaughters, who will be growing up before very long. Our oldest granddaughter is about to turn twelve, and that means she will enter the Young Women program and start preparing to be a woman. That happens fast. I have thought of a lesson my mother taught me. She actually learned it from the Winder family—Sister Susan W. Tanner's family. The Winder family was a dairy family, and one time when my mother was visiting at the Winder farm, they were displaying a new strain of milk cows to their visitors. They said, "We bought these wonderful Jersey cows, and our aim is that every mother produces a superior daughter." My mother caught hold of that idea. She said, "That's the job of a mother. Every mother should produce a superior daughter."

Today I would like to focus on the doctrine of the family and then talk about some of the things that are threatening the family. I will then discuss some of the responsibilities that Latter-day Saint women have regarding the family in our day. When I think of this responsibility, I am not thinking only of those who are married or have children or those who have children now in their homes. When it comes to the family, we have responsibilities similar to those of sailors on a ship in a storm—it's all hands on deck. That is what we need in our day.

First of all, let's talk about the doctrine. We have "The Family: A Proclamation to the World," which was read in a general Relief Society meeting in 1995 by President Gordon B. Hinckley, who was representing the First Presidency. This proclamation summarizes the doctrine in a very succinct way, but a study of it reveals a rich depth of understanding in regard to the doctrine of the family. At the time when the proclamation was given, President Hinckley said that it was a declaration and reaffirmation of standards, doctrines, and practices relative to the family, and that prophets, seers, and revelators of this Church have repeatedly taught these things throughout the history of the Church. So when the proclamation was read, it was not anything new. It was a restatement and reaffirmation; the doctrines are tied to the very beginning of the Restoration.

In this Church, in the restored gospel of Jesus Christ, we have a theology of the family. We call it the plan of salvation, the plan of happiness. It is a theology of the family, and that is important for us to know. I will tell you about the three pillars of that theology.

First is the Creation, the time when the family unit was formed. The Creation was not just about creating an earth—it was about creating an earth upon which a family could dwell. In the family unit was a male and a female—Adam and Eve. The scriptures call her "our glorious Mother Eve" (D&C 138:39). Adam and Eve were each given specific responsibilities in the Father's plan.

The second pillar of our theology is the Fall. The Fall provided a way for the family to grow—not just in numbers, but in experience, which would help them increase their faith and righteousness.

The third pillar of our theology regarding family is the Atonement, which ties families together forever and gives us an opportunity for eternal growth and perfection. That is our theology. That is the Restoration. Families were in it from the beginning.

If we know our theology, we know who we are. In the proclamation on the family, we learn that "all human beings—male and female—are created in the image of God. Each is a beloved spirit son or daughter of heavenly parents. . . . In the premortal realm, spirit sons and daughters knew and worshiped God as their Eternal Father and accepted His plan by which His children could obtain a physical body and gain earthly experience."[1] That is a key part of our doctrine, and key words are *parents*, *sons*, and *daughters*.

President Spencer W. Kimball said, "We have always understood that the foundations of the family, as an eternal unit, were laid even before this earth was created!"[2] We know that we received our "first lessons in the world of spirits," as the Doctrine and Covenants tells us (D&C 138:56). We were prepared to come to earth for this experience. We knew about the plan of the family before we were born.

Now I want to talk about another important part of the proclamation on the family, which is marriage. The proclamation states that "marriage between a man and a woman is ordained of God and that the family is central to the Creator's plan for the eternal destiny of His children."[3] Soon after the proclamation was read, Elder Robert D. Hales of the Quorum of the Twelve spoke at the 1996 BYU Women's Conference. This is what he said: "The family is not an accident of mortality. It existed as an organizational unit in the heavens before the world was formed; historically, it started on earth with Adam and Eve, as recorded in Genesis. Adam and Eve were married and sealed for time and all eternity by the Lord, and as a result their family will exist eternally."[4] Isn't that a beautiful teaching?

Both Adam and Eve had leadership roles in their family. They received their responsibilities by virtue of their celestial marriage and sealing. President Ezra Taft Benson said that this was an order of the priesthood: "This order is . . . described in modern revelation as an order of family government where a man and woman enter into a covenant with God—just as did Adam and Eve—to be sealed for eternity, to have posterity, and to do the will and work of God throughout their mortality. . . . This order of priesthood has been on the earth since the beginning, and it is the only means by which we can one day see the face of God and live."[5] So that marriage, celestial marriage, was an order of the priesthood, and they needed that marriage in order to one day see the face of God and live (see D&C 84:22). They were preparing for the blessings of eternal life as they began their family.

Now some people wonder about the responsibility of Eve in that order of the priesthood and that marriage. Elder Dallin H. Oaks said of Eve: "Her act . . . [was] eternally a glorious necessity to open the doorway toward eternal life. . . . Some Christians condemn Eve for her act, concluding that she and her daughters are somehow flawed by it. Not the Latter-day Saints! Informed by revelation, we celebrate Eve's act and honor her wisdom and courage in the great episode called the Fall."[6] Eve had a leadership role in choosing to bring children to the earth in order to teach them and give other children of our Heavenly Father opportunities for the blessings of eternal life.

Elder David A. Bednar taught us two reasons why marriage is essential: "Reason 1: The natures of male and female spirits complete and perfect each other, and therefore men and women are intended to progress together toward exaltation. . . . Reason 2: By divine design, both a man and a woman are needed to bring children into mortality and to provide the best setting for the rearing and nurturing of children."[7] These are two important reasons why marriage is absolutely essential to fulfilling God's plan for His children.

I love what President Boyd K. Packer said about this plan: "The great plan of happiness (see Alma 42:8, 16) revealed to prophets is the plan for a happy family. It is the love story between husband and wife, parents and children, that renews itself through the ages."[8] He also said, "Nothing is more important to the Church and to civilization itself than the family!"[9]

I want my daughters and my granddaughters to know why we teach and talk about families. We have a granddaughter in middle school in California, and she had some experiences this last year in learning about the family and learning to defend the doctrine of the family. It was a beginning for her—sometimes painful—but she learned things that are essential for her to know.

How early did the Prophet Joseph Smith know about the doctrine of the family? Was it something that was revealed to him as he went along? The words in section 2 of the Doctrine and Covenants were given to seventeen-year-old Joseph Smith on the evening of September 21, 1823, when Moroni visited him. These are the only words from that visit that are included in the Doctrine and Covenants. Other teachings of Moroni are included in Joseph Smith's history, but these words Joseph Smith formalized and put as essentially the first section of the Doctrine and Covenants. Section 1 is an introduction to the Doctrine and Covenants. So the first revealed section of the Doctrine and Covenants and the first principle recorded there is as follows:

"Behold, I will reveal unto you the Priesthood, by the hand of Elijah the prophet, before the coming of the great and dreadful day of the Lord. And he shall plant in the hearts of the children the promises made to the fathers, and the hearts of the children shall turn to their fathers. If it were not so, the whole earth would be utterly wasted at his coming" (D&C 2:1–3).

What priesthood was the Lord revealing by the hand of Elijah the prophet? It was the priesthood that prophets, seers, and revelators have taught us about. It was the priesthood that seals a man and a woman together and prepares them for the blessings of eternal life. If it were not so, the whole earth would be wasted. This points directly to the temple. Joseph Smith was taught about the blessings of the temple when he was seventeen years old. Isn't that wonderful? He started right off knowing about the theology of the family.

Now let's review briefly some of the things that are threatening the family. In Ephesians chapter 6, it says, "We wrestle not against flesh and blood, but against principalities, against powers, against the rulers of the darkness of this world, against spiritual wickedness in high places" (v. 12). That is what we are fighting against. President Thomas S. Monson recently taught: "Just a few short generations ago, one could not have imagined the world in which we now live and the problems it presents."[10]

We see evidence everywhere of the decline in the importance of the family. We know that marriage rates have declined. There is an increase in unmarried couples living together. Divorce has increased. Out-of-wedlock births have increased. Twenty-five percent of pregnancies worldwide—and this was a number of years ago—end in abortion. One-fourth! There are probably more abortions now. Low birthrates are reported, and they are dropping every day. Children are less valued; families are less valued.

Marriage and family should be about "us" and "we." The doctrines being preached by the world today are about "I" and "me." These worldly teachings are not new. If you look in Alma chapter 1, you read about a man named Nehor, who caused a lot of trouble by teaching a doctrine about "me," that I am important and that I should get paid for what I do. He taught that it does not really matter what we do, as long as we make ourselves happy. One of the people who believed him was Korihor. Korihor was called an anti-Christ because he said there would be no Christ. As recorded in Alma, he asked: "O ye that are bound down under a foolish and a vain hope, why do ye yoke yourselves with such foolish things? Why do ye look for a Christ? For no man can know of anything which is to come" (Alma 30:13). Does this sound familiar? Have you heard these kinds of things preached? Have you read them in popular writings?

Korihor also said: "These things which ye call prophecies, which ye say are handed down by holy prophets, behold, they are foolish traditions of your fathers. How do ye know of their surety? Behold, ye cannot know of things which ye do not see; therefore ye cannot know that there shall be a Christ. Ye look forward and say that ye see a remission of your sins. But behold, it is the effect of a frenzied mind; and this derangement of your minds comes because of the traditions of your fathers, which lead you away into a belief of things which are not so. And many more such things did he say unto them, telling them that there could be no atonement made for the sins of men, but every man fared in this life according to the management of the creature; therefore every man prospered according to his genius, and that every man conquered according to his strength; and whatsoever a man did was no crime" (Alma 30:14–17).

I hear this all the time. This is the gospel that is being preached popularly in the world. In Book of Mormon times, Korihor led away "the hearts of many, causing them to lift up their heads in their wickedness, yea, leading away many women" (Alma 30:18). I found that interesting—"many women." This is the doctrine about "me" and "I" and what I do doesn't affect you—I should be able to do what I want. Why would I want to tie myself down with a family? After all, a family is a burden to society. We hear these kinds of phrases in the world today.

Now, Nehor and Korihor thought they were originals, and the people who are preaching these things today also think they are being original and clever. They are not original or clever; their teachings are pirated from the leader of darkness and are taught by failed leaders. Nehor and Korihor were failed leaders who did not prosper. They are called "anti-Christs." We should never forget, sisters, that anti-Christ teachings and principles are always anti-family. And anti-family teachings and policies are also anti-Christ. We believe in Christ and we testify of Him. We are baptized into a covenant with Him. We support and sustain His doctrine and His theology: that He came to this earth to provide for us.

I found a talk given by President Spencer W. Kimball in 1980. It was chilling to me. He said: "Many of the social restraints which in the past have helped to reinforce and to shore up the family are dissolving and disappearing. The time will come when only those who believe deeply and actively in the family will be able to preserve their families in the midst of the gathering evil around us.

" . . . There are those who would define the family in such a nontraditional way that they would define it out of existence. . . .

"We of all people, brothers and sisters, should not be taken in by the specious arguments that the family unit is somehow tied to a particular phase of development a mortal society is going through. We are free to resist those moves which downplay the significance of the family and which play up the significance of selfish individualism. We know the family to be eternal. We know that when things go wrong in the family, things go wrong in every other institution in society."[11]

We are in those times when we are the ones who must preserve our families amid the gathering evil around us. How do we do that? How do Latter-day Saint women do that? We do that by keeping our focus clearly on the blessings of eternal life. It is our responsibility to help ourselves and our families and our loved ones prepare for the blessings of eternal life. The Lord said, "This is my work and my glory—to bring to pass the immortality and eternal life of man" (Moses 1:39). For this purpose the worlds were created and we were created. We need to keep our focus on that.

We know that we are involved in God's work every day, and that changes everything. It changes the way we think. It changes our decisions. It changes the way we dress. It changes the way we talk. It changes the way we live. We have the responsibility and the challenge from the prophet to believe deeply and actively in the family. We will need to do that in order to preserve our families. That means we have to be intentional about everything we do. Our life is not just happenstance. We know where we are going and what we have to do.

Now, my mother has given me permission to tell another story about her. She came today to hear it, and if it is wrong, Mother, we will correct it in the written text. My mother was an older single and living and loving life. She had golf clubs, a tennis racket, her own car, a bowling ball, and skis. She had a university education and a career, and she was having a great time. She was introduced to my father, who was a young bishop and a widower with three children. She said, "When we met each other, all five of us fell in love with each other at once." And so within a short time, her life changed. She was a woman who knew the plan, believed in it, and had taught and defended it. She had been a school nurse and worked in schools and hospitals. She had had a lot of great experiences. Now all of a sudden she was a mother to three beautiful children.

As she and Daddy were traveling along on their honeymoon, she wanted to talk about how they were going to proceed with this family. What are our goals? What is our family going to be like? How are we going to do things in our family? She started writing the answers and their goals, she said, on a paper sack. It was the only paper she had. As they were talking, they said, "What do we want for our children? Are our children going to be married in the temple? Yes, they are. Okay, if we want our children to be married in the temple, what kinds of things do we have to teach them in our home? Well, we will have to have scripture study." So they wrote that down.

"How about family prayer?" Daddy said. "We already have family prayer. That is our habit." "How about going to church?" Going to church every week was on the list. They wrote down things such as manners. "Are we going to teach our children to be polite?" That was a challenge for some of us. They made a goal about who was going to serve a mission. They certainly wanted their sons to serve missions and their daughters to serve missions if they had a desire. They made goals about education, university education, and so on. But Dad said, "Well, I'm not going to pay for it." So Mother said, "Okay, then we'll teach them to work." So they wrote "work" after that.

And they began to develop the culture of their family, which was a Latter-day Saint culture. They were preparing their family to make the covenants and receive the ordinances they needed to prepare them for eternal life, and they knew that there were things their family had to do every day. They wanted children who could contribute and build the kingdom—that is why they wanted their children to get an education. That is why they wanted them to learn things.

They did not know that their family would grow from three to ten children and that teaching table manners to ten children all at once was going to be a process, not an event. They did not know they were going to be in the university business for twenty-five years, helping children find jobs and save money. But they started out with family prayer, family scripture study, family home evening, and preparing children. I am so grateful for parents who were intentional about preparing a family. They created a personalized family plan for our family.

Part of the responsibility that women have—Latter-day Saint women who know—is to bear children. We have been taught through the family proclamation and the prophets that the commandment to multiply and replenish the earth has never been rescinded. President Spencer W. Kimball said a lot of great things about families that were very direct. He said, "It is an act of extreme selfishness for a married couple to refuse to have children when they are able to do so."[12]

Bringing children into the world is the work of creation, as President Dieter F. Uchtdorf said: "If you are a mother, you participate with God in His work of creation—not only by providing physical bodies for your children but also by teaching and nurturing them. If you are not a mother now, the creative talents you develop will prepare you for that day, in this life or the next."[13] He also said, "You are spirit daughters of the most creative Being in the universe. . . . [Creating] is your opportunity in this life and your destiny in the life to come."[14]

I think that there is a special sadness for sisters who desire to bring children into this world and do not have that blessing—because they are not married or were not given that blessing in this life. I remember visiting with my former Laurel adviser, Cleo Shepherd, just before she passed away last year. Cleo was in her eighties, and I have loved her since I was a teenager. She was known for her exceptional friendliness, cheerful attitude, and welcoming nature. In Cleo's long life, she had many experiences, which included being married, but she and her husband were unable to have children. They eventually did adopt five children; one of her daughters passed away as a young mother. By the time Cleo passed away, she had lost her parents, a daughter, and a husband, and now she was suffering from cancer.

She had had such a variety of experiences, and I asked her to tell me about her life. She said, "Oh, it has been a wonderful life. I have had a magnificent life." Then she paused and said, "All except for those ten years when we couldn't have children." That gave me great insight into that special pain. With all the challenges and the losses that Cleo had, that challenge still hurt. Righteous women know, as President Uchtdorf said, that creating is their blessing, now and in the eternities.

Many women in these days do not desire children. They think babies are a lot of trouble. I have even talked to couples who say, "Well, we decided to get a dog instead." I know that a baby does not pay you compliments or ask you how your day is going, but it is one of our blessings to bring spirits into the world.

When the Lord sends children into our family, we have the responsibility to prepare them to receive the ordinances and covenants of baptism and the temple. In the Doctrine and Covenants, section 68, we learn that the Lord commanded parents to teach their children the gospel and prepare them for baptism and for temple covenants.

I am wearing my Young Women medallion today. Why? Because I am helping my family and myself prepare for the blessings of eternal life. I do not want to take my eyes off the temple. I earned the medallion. It taught me much about the temple and preparing to attend the temple. That is what we are teaching our young girls. When they come into the Young Women program, we are not just preparing them to go to camp and have a good time. We are preparing them for the blessings of the temple, which will be theirs if they are worthy.

And so we work on worthiness. We have a huge problem in our families with pornography and the influence that it is having in our families. The powerful feeling that has been coming over me is, "Sisters, fight! Fight, sisters!" You have the responsibility in your homes. Many of our women are being drawn into this behavior also. At our last general conference, President Thomas S. Monson gave "a word of caution to all— both young and old, both male and female."[15] This challenge is our responsibility.

The Church has given us many helps in this fight. We cannot sit and act like victims. This is the work of a determined adversary, and we have to take responsibility for defending our homes. We must teach our families everywhere—in family home evenings, in prayer and scripture study, and at mealtimes. We must create opportunities to teach in formal and less formal settings.

Years ago when we were driving our children back and forth to piano lessons, someone said, "Don't you get tired of driving your children to piano lessons?" I said, "Are you kidding? What a great opportunity I have. My children are captive in my car. I have them and we can talk, teach, and ask questions." That was a wonderful opportunity that allowed us to discuss true principles. My children could not run away from me or be busy. Of course, today, many children have cell phones. Mine did not, so we did not have that distraction. But please do your best to create formal and informal opportunities to teach and help your children.

Family home evening is so important. Here is what the First Presidency said about teaching in home evenings. They sent a letter, and we all listened to it as we sat in sacrament meetings and we nodded our heads, but do we believe it? The First Presidency said: "We call upon parents to devote their best efforts to the teaching and rearing of their children in gospel principles that will keep them close to the Church. The home is the basis of a righteous life, and no other instrumentality can take its place or fulfill its essential functions in carrying forward this God-given responsibility."[16]

They sent another letter in which they reminded us that Monday nights are reserved for family home evenings throughout the Church, which means everywhere in the world where the Church is established.[17] Where practical, members may want to encourage community and school leaders to avoid scheduling activities on Monday evenings. Other interruptions to family home evenings should be avoided. I think sometimes we get in the practice of saying, "Well, we are going to use the time we have on Sunday to teach our children." We should use more of our time on Sundays to be with our families and teach them. That was the plan when the consolidated meeting schedule was established. But Monday nights are reserved for family home evenings. And we should be proactive in defending that time. Why wouldn't we want Monday, in addition to Sunday, to teach our families? President Boyd K. Packer said, "The establishment of family home evening . . . is, in a sense, the sounding of an alarm to all parents . . . to prepare themselves and strengthen themselves against the challenges which now face us."[18]

I read something from President Joseph F. Smith that I found very touching. He lost his mother at a young age, and he said this: "No love in all the world can equal the love of a true mother. . . . It was life to me; it was strength; it was encouragement; it was love that begat love or liking in myself. I knew she loved me with all her heart. She loved her children with all her soul. . . . Whenever . . . temptations became most alluring and most tempting to me, the first thought that arose in my soul was this: Remember the love of your mother. Remember how she strove for your welfare. Remember how willing she was to sacrifice her life for your good.

. . . This feeling toward my mother became a defense, a barrier between me and temptation."

He also said: "If you wish your children to be taught in the principles of the gospel, if you wish them to love the truth and understand it, if you wish them to be obedient to and united with you, love them! . . . You can't do it any other way. You can't do it by unkindness; you cannot do it by driving. . . . You can coax them; you can lead them, by holding out inducements to them, and by speaking kindly to them, but you can't drive them; they won't be driven. . . . You can't force your boys, nor your girls into heaven. You may force them to hell, by using harsh words in the efforts to make them good, when you yourselves are not as good as you should be. . . . You can only correct your children by love, in kindness, by love unfeigned, by persuasion, and reason."[19]

Our homes, because we know we are building for eternity, should be homes based on love. The proclamation on the family declares that we have a sacred duty to love our husbands and children. Husbands need to be loved. I love section 25 of the Doctrine and Covenants, in which Emma Smith is told to be a comfort to her husband in a spirit of meekness. That creates a feeling and climate of faith, hope, and charity in a home, which the world does not teach. It is okay for a wife to cook for her husband. I have a niece who was married recently, and her mother said, "It's okay for you to cook for your husband. You should do it. It's a sign of your love for him and of how you want to take care of him and nurture him." The world would not teach you that, but the gospel does. Love at home creates a climate of faith, hope, and charity. We have to work for it and strive for it.

Now, we will need the Spirit of the Lord with us in greater abundance in times to come than we have ever had. We need to be the ones seeking every day to qualify for the Spirit, to recognize the voice of the Spirit, and to follow the voice of the Spirit because other voices will lead us in the wrong ways. We are preparing for the blessings of eternal life. Anytime we are teaching the rising generation in Sunday School, Primary, Young Women, seminary, or institute, we should remember that we are preparing them for the blessings of eternal life.

This is a faith-based work. The family and the work of women—Latter-day Saint women—is a faith-based work, and we have to call upon our faith in the Lord Jesus Christ and His restored gospel and the principles He taught on the earth. We have to follow Him with all our hearts. We have to have faith in who we are and where we came from, and we have to fulfill our responsibilities on this earth and qualify for eternal blessings.

As we are doing this, we are having a mortal experience. Difficult challenges are coming. I love Moses chapter 5, which describes the feelings of Adam and Eve as they were reviewing the blessings of mortality. They could have stayed in the garden—they had a choice. Everything was provided for them there. They wanted the blessings of eternal life, and the only way to have those blessings was to pass through a mortal experience.

Adam said, "Because of my transgression my eyes are opened, and in this life I shall have joy, and again in the flesh I shall see God. And Eve, his wife, heard all these things and was glad, saying: Were it not for our transgression [what she is saying is: were it not for our mortal experience] we never should have had seed." In other words, she would not have had children. All of her children were not perfect, but she was not sorry. She was glad she was a mother. She continued, "[We] never should have known good and evil, and the joy of our redemption [that we can be redeemed and blessed by the Atonement of Christ], and the eternal life which God giveth unto all the obedient. And Adam and Eve blessed the name of God, and they made all these things known unto their sons and their daughters" (Moses 5:10–12).

I testify to you that these are truths of the restored gospel and that we are sons and daughters of Heavenly Parents. Eliza R. Snow, a former general Relief Society president, wrote, "In the heav'ns are parents single? No, the thought makes reason stare!"[20] That is eternal life.

I testify to you of our Savior Jesus Christ, who came to earth to provide us the opportunity to return to God so we could have the blessings of an eternal family. I testify of the Prophet Joseph Smith, the Prophet of the Restoration, who restored these teachings to the earth in their purity and through whom the priesthood was restored to earth so that the saving ordinances and covenants can be ours. What a blessing!

I testify of our living prophet today, President Thomas S. Monson, who continues to be a clear voice declaring these same principles and doctrines. If we follow him, we will be safe and we do not need to worry. We owe everything to the Lord. We are so blessed to be involved in a faith-based work, a work in which we can create families, support families, defend families, teach families, and prepare them for the blessings of eternal life—and love them, love them, love them.

I bear you my testimony of these truths and leave with you my great appreciation, my confidence that the women of the Church will be the defenders of right and truth, and that you will be seen as lights in the world to those who were taught these principles before they were born. They will recognize these truths as you teach them.

NOTES

1. "The Family: A Proclamation to the World," *Ensign*, November 1995, 102.
2. Spencer W. Kimball, "Families Can Be Eternal," *Ensign*, November 1980, 4.
3. "The Family: A Proclamation to the World," 102.
4. Robert D. Hales, "The Family: A Proclamation to the World," in *Clothed with Charity: Talks from the 1996 Women's Conference* (Salt Lake City: Deseret Book, 1997), 134.
5. Ezra Taft Benson, "What I Hope You Will Teach Your Children about the Temple," *Ensign*, August 1985, 9.
6. Dallin H. Oaks, "The Great Plan of Happiness," *Ensign*, November 1993, 73.
7. David A. Bednar, "Marriage Is Essential to His Eternal Plan," *Ensign*, June 2006, 83–84.
8. Boyd K. Packer, "The Shield of Faith," *Ensign*, May 1995, 9.
9. Packer, "The Standard of Truth Has Been Erected," *Ensign*, November 2003, 25.
10. Thomas S. Monson, "Heavenly Homes, Forever Families," *Ensign*, June 2006, 99.
11. Kimball, "Families Can Be Eternal," 4.
12. Kimball, "Fortify Your Homes Against Evil," *Ensign*, May 1979, 6.
13. Dieter F. Uchtdorf, "Happiness, Your Heritage," *Ensign*, November 2008, 119.
14. Ibid., 118–19.
15. Monson, "Until We Meet Again," *Ensign*, May 2009, 113.
16. First Presidency letter, February 11, 1999.
17. See First Presidency letter, October 4, 1999.
18. Packer, *Mine Errand from the Lord* (Salt Lake City: Deseret Book, 2008), 277.

19. Joseph F. Smith, *Gospel Doctrine* (Salt Lake City: Deseret Book, 1978), 314–17.

20. "O My Father," *Hymns of The Church of Jesus Christ of Latter-day Saints* (Salt Lake City: The Church of Jesus Christ of Latter-day Saints, 1985), no. 292.

"WITH ALL THE FEELING OF A TENDER PARENT"
Elder Cecil O Samuelson and Sharon G. Samuelson

Sharon G. Samuelson: We are grateful for the opportunity to reflect on some very important lessons we have learned about parenting and families from the Book of Mormon. The primary role of the Book of Mormon is to be another witness for Jesus Christ and His great atoning mission. Central to our Father in Heaven's great plan of happiness is the Atonement of His only perfect Son, Jesus Christ. And key to the fulfillment of the plan of salvation or plan of happiness is the success of families who are sealed together and can return to the presence of the Father and the Son to experience eternal life. It is not a small wonder then that the Book of Mormon would not only teach and testify of the Savior and His mission, but also give much-needed counsel and direction in the vital matters of family life and the essential duties and roles of parents. As we have thought about this dimension of this "most correct book," we have learned much that we probably did not fully appreciate when we first gained our testimonies of its truthfulness.

Elder Cecil O. Samuelson is the president of Brigham Young University and a member of the First Quorum of the Seventy. He received his MD from the University of Utah, and fulfilled his residency and held a fellowship at Duke University Medical Center. He taught medicine at the University of Utah, where he served as dean of the Medical School, and as vice president of health sciences. At the time of his call to the First Quorum of the Seventy in 1994, he was a senior vice president at Intermountain Health Care. He and his wife, Sharon G. Samuelson, have five children and twelve grandchildren.

Cecil O. Samuelson: In fact, the lessons taught and available to parents and future parents are so replete and pervasive that only someone looking to avoid them would fail to see their relevance to family life. From the beginning verses in First Nephi to the concluding pages of Moroni, we find remarkable and clear evidence of the centrality of the family in Heavenly Father's Plan and also much of practical help and example for those wishing to be successful parents in nurturing their children, grandchildren, and other younger people in the ways of the Lord. I have known since my youth that "all the prophets who . . . prophesied ever since the world began" (Mosiah 13:33) testified in one way or another of the Savior, Jesus Christ. It is only as I have gained some maturity, a few gray hairs, and a growing posterity that I realized that the prophets have also promised "that God should redeem his people" (Mosiah 13:33) and that families have a very significant role in bringing each other, and especially children, to Christ.

Sharon G. Samuelson: Right from the beginning, Nephi, who confessed "having been born of goodly parents" and thus being "highly favored of the Lord" (1 Nephi 1:1), understood how important family was to his father, Lehi. You will remember that Lehi was instructed by the Lord to leave Jerusalem and go into the wilderness because of the danger and wickedness in that great city. Lehi was immediately obedient. Listen to Nephi's description of his father's priorities and responsiveness:

"And it came to pass that [Lehi] departed into the wilderness. And he left his house, and the land of his inheritance, and his gold, and his silver, and his precious things, and took nothing with him, save it were his *family*, and provisions, and tents, and departed into the wilderness" (1 Nephi 2:4; emphasis added).

Nephi understood that his father and mother considered their family to be most "precious" and far above anything else. In fact, Lehi and Sariah allowed themselves to bring only those things essential to sustaining their family and their lives.

Cecil O. Samuelson: The importance of family and the desire Lehi and the Lord shared that Nephi and his siblings should have a righteous posterity led the Lord to instruct Lehi to send his sons back to Jerusalem a second time. Here they were to enlist Ishmael and his family to their cause so that Lehi's "sons should take daughters to wife, that they might raise up seed unto the Lord in the land of promise" (1 Nephi 7:1).

Incidentally, you will recall that the Lord instructed Lehi to have his sons return to Jerusalem the first time to obtain the scriptures. We will say more about that later; however, we should never forget the significance of the effort required of Nephi and his brethren so that they would be privileged not only to have the word of God with them on their journeys but also as a resource to teach their children.

Sharon G. Samuelson: Speaking of the scriptures and particularly the Book of Mormon, I did something that I have never done before in preparation for this presentation. I have read the Book of Mormon many times over the years, but this time I made a serious effort to go through the entire Book of Mormon and record all of the lessons I could find that relate to parenting and family responsibilities. I must tell you that there are so many that we will not be able to be comprehensive in mentioning all of the great examples we found. I recommend that you think about taking this same approach because it works with respect to almost any issue, doctrine, problem, or concern you might be wrestling with or wishing to understand better. Thus, it really makes sense to study the Book of Mormon regularly because it gives such important insights to so many significant issues.

Cecil O. Samuelson: On a personal note, the first application we can remember of finding family answers from the Book of Mormon occurred about thirty-two years ago. As we have mentioned to some before, our children didn't always come into our family when or how we hoped or planned. At the time in question, we had two sons, ages nine and four, who came into our family in the usual way. We understood it was very unlikely that others would be naturally born to us and so we were thrilled when we learned that we would be able to adopt a newborn set of twins (a boy and a girl) from Guatemala. Further, we knew that their lineage was from father Lehi. As we discussed possible names for our new little ones, the excited big brothers wanted to name their new little brother after King Benjamin, one of their heroes from the Book of Mormon. Our son Ben, as he now likes to be called, might well have been named something else without an understanding of King Benjamin's great and wonderful example.

Sharon G. Samuelson: The boys were not as determined about naming Ben's twin sister from the Book of Mormon lexicon, but we all agreed that we very much liked the name Rebecca with its scriptural associations. Interesting to us, upon reflection after these many years, is that our study of the Book of Mormon from the very beginning with our two oldest sons—as imperfect and incomplete as it always has been—was never focused on finding the names for future children or siblings. In fact, for several years before the twins arrived, we were quite sure that there would not be others. In so many ways, this example teaches the principle that the Lord and the scriptures will reveal important answers to vital questions we have not been smart enough or wise enough to recognize or ask. Thus, while targeted study is essential, as we have mentioned, important insights also come by regularly immersing ourselves in the scriptures.

One of my favorite accounts about the complexities of teaching, loving, helping, and holding children accountable while also honoring their individual agency is Nephi's description of Father Lehi as he dealt with Laman and Lemuel. After his vision of the tree of life in the early years following their escape from Jerusalem, you will remember that Lehi saw the future of his family and rejoiced over what he saw for his wife, Sariah, and his sons Sam and Nephi. He was distressed, however, by the evidence that Laman and Lemuel were likely to refuse to partake of the fruit of the tree of life or to hold onto the iron rod, which symbolized safety and the correct path to eternal life. I hope you will think about this entire eighth chapter of First Nephi because many insights and principles are articulated. Let me just recount what Nephi reports his father said to the two rebellious sons:

"And he did exhort them then with all the feeling of a tender parent, that they would hearken to his words, that perhaps the Lord would be merciful to them, and not cast them off; yea, my father did preach unto them.

"And after he had preached unto them, and also prophesied unto them of many things, he bade them to keep the commandments of the Lord; and he did cease speaking unto them" (1 Nephi 8:37–38).

Cecil O. Samuelson: Father Lehi loved all of his children equally and felt strongly about teaching, counseling, and correcting them. He also understood that they had their own agency and would ultimately need to make their own choices, which they did. While he was deeply and profoundly saddened by the poor choices made by some of his sons, his grief over those going in improper directions did not deflect his joy from the good choices made by other family members. Certainly Lehi was not tempted to violate his own covenants or criticize the Lord for the failings of others. Likewise, while he did his best with Laman and Lemuel and the outcome was not what he had hoped, worked, and prayed for, he also did not find fault with himself for the failings of others.

In both the scriptures and in life, it is very rare to find situations where there are not at least some small family disappointments or choices that someone wished might be different. Think of Alma, himself an adult convert, and his son Alma the Younger. Young Alma and the four sons of Mosiah—all five from righteous families who taught their children the gospel and where parents modeled faithful lives—went about seeking to destroy the Church. These young men considered themselves to be non-believers and at least Alma the Younger is described by the scriptures as "a very wicked and an idolatrous man" (Mosiah 27:8). Although the record doesn't give much detail to this particular point, I would suggest that these young men were a source of great embarrassment to their parents and church leaders. I'm also sure that these faithful mothers and fathers developed calloused knees from their continual prayers because the angel of the Lord who appeared to these young men to call them to repentance said, "Behold, the Lord hath heard the prayers of his people, and also the prayers of his servant, Alma, who is thy father; for he has prayed with much faith concerning thee that thou mightest be brought to the knowledge of the truth; therefore, for this purpose have I come to convince thee of the power and authority of God, that the prayers of his servants might be answered according to their faith" (Mosiah 27:14).

Sharon G. Samuelson: Some of you have likewise uttered both vocal and silent prayers for your errant children. Our hope is that we pray for all of our children and families regularly, daily, and even continually. We don't need to wait for them to have problems, difficulties, sins, shortcomings, illnesses, or any other worry. An added dimension is that not only do we need to pray for them, they need to know and understand *that* we pray for them. Why is that important? Let's return to the experience of Alma the Younger and jump forward a generation.

We know that after Alma's dramatic interview with the angel, he and the sons of Mosiah repented and became exemplary young men and missionaries. Likely some of you have had or will have similar wonderful conversion experiences in your own families, although almost all will not have angelic visitations or visions.

After young Alma became a father, he fully understood the vital role of teaching and example. Although he was not proud of his sinful youth, he felt it important to explain to his own sons in some detail—but importantly not fully—the foibles of his younger years. There is a rather complete summary of the significant details in Alma chapter 36, but the point about his father's prayers and teaching during the time of his rebellion is found in verse 17 of that chapter. Here Alma describes the horrible experience of going through the painful, cleansing repentance process after his interview with the angel. Said he, "And it came to pass that as I was thus racked with torment, while I was harrowed up by the memory of my many sins, behold, I remembered also to have heard my father prophesy unto the people concerning the coming of one Jesus Christ, a Son of God, to atone for the sins of the world" (Alma 36:17).

It would seem likely that Alma the Elder probably felt that his teaching, testimonies, and prayers were falling on deaf ears, at least in the case of his son. Perhaps you have felt like this yourself. We must never underestimate the influence our behavior and faith will ultimately have even in the face of apparent rejection or lack of appropriate immediate response.

Cecil O. Samuelson: Another important point for us to glean from the scriptures, and one we must never forget, is that our children are not all alike. In fact, every person is absolutely unique. What influences one may not faze or touch another. What inspires one might discourage another. What tempts one child might repel a sibling, and so forth. That means our praying, our counseling, our correcting, our teaching, and even our encouraging and complimenting must be customized not only to the person but to the time, the circumstances, and the rapidly changing and varying needs of each person.

You will know that Lehi and Sariah dealt with their sons differently according to their needs and circumstances. Coming back to Alma the Younger, we see that he also did the same with his three sons, Helaman, Shiblon, and Corianton. Try reading and studying chapters 36 through 42 in the Book of Alma. The instruction was carefully and uniquely crafted for each son. Apparently, both Helaman and Shiblon were largely exemplary in their devotions.

On the other hand, Corianton was in need of very direct correction and his father left no doubt, I'm sure, about what was bothering him. I'm also quite sure that prior to this interview, Corianton was fully aware of his father's love and expectations for him. These are the words of Alma:

"And now, my son, I have somewhat more to say unto thee than what I said unto thy brother; for behold, have ye not observed the steadiness of thy brother, his faithfulness, and his diligence in keeping the commandments of God? Behold, has he not set a good example for thee?

"For thou didst not give so much heed unto my words as did thy brother, among the people of the Zoramites. Now this is what I have against thee; thou didst go on unto boasting in thy strength and thy wisdom.

"And this is not all, my son. Thou didst do that which was grievous unto me; for thou didst forsake the ministry, and did go over into the land of Siron among the borders of the Lamanites, after the harlot Isabel" (Alma 39:1–3).

Although there is much more to the story, I think you get the picture, and I'm sure Corianton was not confused about his father's disappointment. Nevertheless, even in Alma's tremendous disappointment, he took care to teach his son specifics about his frustrations. The following example is among the many you will identify and find useful as you study the complete account:

"And now, my son, I would to God that ye had not been guilty of so great a crime. I would not dwell upon your crimes, to harrow up your soul, if it were not for your good.

"But behold, ye cannot hide your crimes from God; and except ye repent they will stand as a testimony against you at the last day" (Alma 39:7–8).

Sharon G. Samuelson: Alma continues to give Corianton much more corrective advice but does not end his conversation on the needed, negative tone of the direct call to repentance. He goes on to be very encouraging to this wayward young man by testifying to him of the surety of the coming of Christ and the healing power of the Savior's Atonement. He then also makes absolutely sure that Corianton understands fully what is expected of him. After reminding him of the mission and reality of the Redeemer, he then reminds him of his particular responsibilities in this way, "And now, my son, this was the ministry unto which ye were called, to declare these glad tidings unto this people, to prepare their minds; or rather that salvation might come unto them, that they may prepare the minds of their children to hear the word at the time of his coming" (Alma 39:16).

Again, there was more instructive and helpful counsel, but think of a faithful father's lesson to his somewhat immature son when he tells the young man that his job is to help those he was to teach "prepare the minds of their children to hear the word at the time of [the Savior's] coming." That tells us not only about this specific correction and counsel but also the clear understanding that our teaching needs to be so good and so focused on the ability of those being taught that they in turn can appropriately teach their own children. We will come back to this vital point with another example shortly.

Cecil O. Samuelson: Before we do so, let's focus on the importance of multigenerational teaching. One of the great lies of the adversary is that "when I sin, I'm only hurting myself." If only all young parents could somehow immediately know what all of us who are grandparents fully understand. That is, that we are always teaching and our youngsters invariably pick up attitudes, habits, biases, traits, and perspectives from their parents and other influential adults whether or not such transmission was intended. The old saying, "Do as I say and not as I do," never has had much influence on young minds. Sending children to church in no way resembles taking them with you. So it is with prayer, honesty, payment of tithes, kindness, generosity, and every other virtue as well as with most vices.

Think how short the Book of Mormon would be if the first Alma had heard Abinadi, but while agreeing with what was taught, felt that faithfulness was too risky and therefore remained in conformance with his old friends, the priests of King Noah. Happily, for his posterity and the rest of us, he chose the better part and we have the faithful and remarkable contributions not only of Alma himself, but of his son Alma, his grandsons, and so on for generations. How and what we teach our children and how we model our faith before them matters ever so much more than any of us can really understand or appreciate in the midst of the toil and trials of daily life.

Sharon G. Samuelson: While it is so important to teach each child or young person in ways that best meet his or her individual needs and circumstances, there are also some core concepts and values that need to be taught to everyone. One of our favorite chapters of parenting advice comes from King Benjamin as he educates his three sons on some fundamental principles. This wonderful example is presented in Mosiah, Chapter 1.

King Benjamin's great concluding address to all of his people was preceded by the counsel and teaching he provided for his own sons. As I review these verses, please think of the applications they have for each of us in our own situations with our children, grandchildren, and other young people in our charge:

"And it came to pass that [King Benjamin] had three sons; and he called their names Mosiah, and Helorum, and Helaman. And he caused that they should be taught in all the language of his fathers, that thereby they might become men of understanding; and that they might know concerning the prophecies which had been spoken by the mouths of their fathers, which were delivered them by the hand of the Lord.

"And he also taught them concerning the records which were engraven on the plates of brass, saying: My sons, I would that ye should remember that were it not for these plates, which contain these records and these commandments, we must have suffered in ignorance, even at this present time, not knowing the mysteries of God.

"For it were not possible that our father, Lehi, could have remembered all these things, to have taught them to his children, except it were for the help of these plates; for he having been taught in the language of the Egyptians therefore he could read these engravings, and teach them to his children, that thereby they could teach them to their children, and so fulfilling the commandments of God, even down to this present time.

"I say unto you, my sons, were it not for these things, which have been kept and preserved by the hand of God, that we might read and understand of his mysteries, and have his commandments always before our eyes, that even our fathers would have dwindled in unbelief, and we should have been like unto our brethren, the Lamanites, who know nothing concerning these things, or even do not believe them when they are taught them, because of the traditions of their fathers, which are not correct.

"O my sons, I would that ye should remember that these sayings are true, and also that these records are true. And behold, also the plates of Nephi, which contain the records and the sayings of our fathers from the time they left Jerusalem until now, and they are true; and we can know of their surety because we have them before our eyes.

"And now, my sons, I would that ye should remember to search them diligently, that ye may profit thereby; and I would that ye should keep the commandments of God, that ye may prosper in the land according to the promises which the Lord made unto our fathers.

"And many more things did king Benjamin teach his sons, which are not written in this book" (Mosiah 1:2–8).

Cecil O. Samuelson: Let me summarize for us the important points of the verses just read.

1. The wise father felt that education generally was very important. He made sure that his sons were, in a broad sense, well-taught and would be men of understanding.
2. He made sure that his sons knew of the prophecies made by the prophets.
3. He taught them about the scriptures and from the scriptures.
4. He reminded these boys that without the scriptures, even faithful parents could not remember enough of the sacred doctrines to teach their children adequately.
5. As we mentioned earlier, King Benjamin understood that he had to teach his sons well so that they could in turn teach their children clearly and thoroughly.
6. He bore powerful testimony to his sons that the things he was teaching them from the scriptures were true.
7. He reminded them that knowing the gospel was not enough. They also needed to keep the commandments of God if they wished to achieve the promised blessings.

Sharon G. Samuelson: King Benjamin was a great prophet-leader and a tremendous father who also understood the power of his personal example. Obviously, this is a typical characteristic of many prophets and leaders but it is also characteristic of faithful, unsung, and relatively unknown disciples of the Master—like most successful parents.

Cecil O. Samuelson: One of the most impressive object lessons in the Book of Mormon is the account of the sons of Helaman. Let me mention as an aside my belief that many of the successes and positive traits I see in our own children and grandchildren are the result of the influence of their mother and grandmother. If we had time, I could give you numerous examples of each of the principles King Benjamin taught by precept that my wife Sharon teaches by example. But back to the Book of Mormon and the impressive devotion and courage of the two thousand young men who had been appropriately taught.

You will remember that Ammon, the son of Mosiah and friend of Alma the Younger, went on his many-year mission to the Lamanites and found himself among the people of King Lamoni (see Alma 17–26). After much sacrifice and suffering, multiple miracles led to the conversion of thousands of these good people who previously had never been taught of the Savior who was to come and the saving principles of His gospel. Because these newly minted Christians had accepted the faith, they were persecuted even unto death by the unconverted Lamanites. Through another series of miracles, they were able to escape and were given lands and protection by the then-righteous Nephites. As a sign of their conversion, the adults of this group of new converts covenanted with God that they would never again go into battle or be willing to kill anyone even if it meant sacrificing their own lives (see Alma 27).

Sharon G. Samuelson: In the following two or three decades, wars and confrontations between the Lamanites and Nephites were almost constant. The situation became so dire that the sons of these righteous Lamanite converts, who themselves had never made the covenant not to bear arms, volunteered to join the Nephite armies with Helaman as their leader. They were valiant in their military achievements and were often miraculously spared from death even when the carnage around them on all sides was extreme. Helaman recorded his affection, admiration, and appreciation for this group of young men in a letter to his military commander (see Alma 56–58). The entire account is interesting and deserves careful study, but these words are particularly impressive as we think about how these young warriors were taught by both precept and example:

"And now I say unto you . . . that never had I seen so great courage, nay, not amongst all the Nephites.

"For as I had ever called them my sons (for they were all of them very young) even so they said unto me: Father, behold our God is with us, and he will not suffer that we should fall; then let us go forth; we would not slay our brethren if they would let us alone; therefore let us go, lest they should overpower the army. . . .

"Now they never had fought, yet they did not fear death; and they did think more upon the liberty of their fathers than they did upon their lives; yea, they had been taught by their mothers, that if they did not doubt, God would deliver them.

"And they rehearsed unto me the words of their mothers, saying: We do not doubt our mothers knew it" (Alma 56:45–48).

It is very instructive to understand that these young men, in a time of serious crisis, not only remembered the specifics of what their mothers had taught them, but also knew that their mothers "knew it." We can only imagine the consistent goodness of these wonderful mothers who probably had no previous insight about what their sons would be called upon to do except they knew instinctively that teaching their children properly by both precept and example was necessary.

Nowhere do the scriptures teach that these mothers were perfect or never made a mistake. The Book of Mormon doesn't tell us that these remarkable women and mothers never became frustrated or disappointed or that they dusted the furniture every day. It doesn't tell us that they made sure that every one of their children was enrolled in every music lesson, dance class, sports camp, or were dressed in the latest fashions. What we can learn and must understand is that they were only perfect in the most important things. They taught their sons so very well because they lived their lives completely consistent with what they believed and knew to be true. Children of all ages and times are very astute judges of authenticity and character, and these mothers had both.

Cecil O. Samuelson: As we speak of teaching children, one of the most impressive tutorials is found in Third Nephi when the Savior appeared to the people on this continent "soon after the ascension of Christ into heaven" from Jerusalem (3 Nephi 10:18). His visit among these faithful people is recorded in chapters 11 through 26 of Third Nephi. All of what He taught to the people at that time is an essential curriculum for those of us with responsibilities to teach the rising generation now. Particularly, in addition to facts and doctrine, our testimonies must be included as well.

It is touching to know that Jesus' teaching of the people brought them to tears and they pled with Him not to leave them. He sent them home to ponder on the things He had told them and taught them. He then asked them to return the following day. He healed their sick, He lifted up the depressed and discouraged, and as He did so, they bathed His feet with their tears as they kissed them (see 3 Nephi 17). And then Jesus did this:

"And it came to pass that he commanded that their little children should be brought.

"So they brought their little children and set them down upon the ground round about him, and Jesus stood in the midst; and the multitude gave way till they had all been brought unto him.

"And it came to pass that when they had all been brought, and Jesus stood in the midst, he commanded the multitude that they should kneel down upon the ground" (3 Nephi 17:11–13).

And then He and the entire multitude knelt down and the Savior prayed for them to the Father. Although it was not possible for anyone to record specifically what Jesus said in His prayer, it is recorded that "The eye hath never seen, neither hath the ear heard, before, so great and marvelous things as we saw and heard Jesus speak unto the Father" (3 Nephi 17:16). Likewise, it was impossible to even conceive of the joy they felt when they heard the Redeemer pray to the Father for them. Then, after the prayer was uttered, Jesus did this remarkable thing:

Sharon G. Samuelson:

"And it came to pass that Jesus spake unto them, and bade them arise.

"And they arose from the earth, and he said unto them: Blessed are ye because of your faith. And now behold, my joy is full.

"And when he had said these words, he wept, and the multitude bare record of it, and he took their little children, one by one, and blessed them, and prayed unto the Father for them.

"And when he had done this he wept again;

"And he spake unto the multitude, and said unto them: Behold your little ones.

"And as they looked to behold they cast their eyes towards heaven, and they saw the heavens open, and they saw angels descending out of heaven as it were in the midst of fire; and they came down and encircled those little ones about, and they were encircled about with fire; and the angels did minister unto them.

"And the multitude did see and hear and bear record; and they know that their record is true for they all of them did see and hear, every man for himself; and they were in number about two thousand and five hundred souls; and they did consist of men, women, and children" (3 Nephi 17:19–25).

If Jesus felt this way about children, and we testify that He did and does, then what does this tell us about the responsibilities we have in our relationships with our little ones? Think of what He did and how He did it. Although no task has ever been too big for Him, He took the children "one by one." Even with big families or large classes, every child needs and deserves individual attention. Likewise, the attention they require also must be customized to their needs.

Cecil O. Samuelson: Certainly, the Savior was exemplary in all He did and His focus on the children is no exception. But what of those of us who fall short on occasion or who may struggle with the family challenges we encounter? Since I believe every parent falls into this category at least some of the time, what solace or direction does the Book of Mormon provide for us? I think there are a number of examples, but the one I want to mention briefly is both poignant and relevant.

Sariah, the wife of Lehi and the mother of a family of sons, had, I'm sure, a rather long litany of challenges and frustrations. While little detail is provided except in one example, I have wondered about her feelings and reactions to the developments in her life. We know nothing of her youth, her courtship and marriage, and early family situation in Jerusalem. We do know that she was willing to support her prophet-husband Lehi when he was instructed to leave Jerusalem and essentially all of the comforts and conveniences of their circumstances there. She apparently went willingly into the desolate desert and endured various hardships that we can only vaguely imagine.

There came a time, however, when the aggregated pressures just became too much for her. You will recall that Lehi sent their four sons back to Jerusalem for the brass plates. They were delayed on their return to the family camp in the wilderness and Sariah did not know why, but feared the worst—as mothers often do. She mourned for them and criticized her husband for exposing them to this serious danger.

When the sons finally rejoined their parents and the rest of the family, great joy was expressed and testimony borne by Sariah of Lehi's calling and revelations. In pondering this account found in First Nephi 5, I found several lessons that are both comforting and instructive.

First, Sariah made no pretense of perfection and she let her husband know of her concerns. Likewise, while Lehi confirmed his vision and reasons for sending his sons on their errand, he did not overly react to his wife's frustrations. Second, while they had both been open, honest and candid, they were careful not to violate their fundamental trust of each other and so, when their sons returned, they were able to experience immediately the joyful occasion together. Third, Sariah confessed that she had learned something from this episode and willingly described that it had strengthened her convictions about the correctness of her husband's charge from Heaven. In addition, she also bore her testimony of the Lord's protection for her sons as they were on His errand (see 1 Nephi 5:8). Lastly, both Sariah and Lehi shared their feelings and insights with their sons in ways that these young men could also profit from their parents' experiences. Remember, it was Nephi who recorded the details of this instructive episode.

Sharon G. Samuelson: I also love this account. Of course, there are other great examples of good parenting and parental counsel in the Book of Mormon. We talked about the marvelous examples of Jesus and His teaching and blessing of children, but the sacred text also gives us wonderful insights into how God the Father interacts with His children. We all know that our own children are also His spirit children and therefore we need to do our very best to make sure that we follow His example as closely as we are mortally able to do. Let me mention just one example that ought to influence our teaching and rearing of children perhaps more than it sometimes does.

You will likely remember many of the lessons Alma and Amulek taught as they interacted with—and corrected—Zeezrom. He opposed the message of the prophets and preached against the then-future coming of the Savior. Sometimes, as was the case on this occasion, teaching or counseling intended for one child or person is observed by many (see Alma 12:2). Thus, we must be careful because what we say and do—as well as what we don't do—may make an unintended impact on the larger audience.

After accurately describing the issues related to Zeezrom's conduct and behavior, Alma sensed that a perfect teaching moment had occurred. Alma resisted what might have been a temptation to rush right into telling Zeezrom what he must do. Listen carefully to this explanation as to how God would handle the situation, "Therefore God gave unto them commandments, *after* having made known unto them the plan of redemption" (Alma 12:32; emphasis added). He was careful to explain the "why" before he instructed them on the "what."

Cecil O. Samuelson: We have already discussed King Benjamin's private family teaching. He also was very attentive to these issues as he taught his people generally in his prophetic leadership role. In his famous benedictory address to his flock at the temple, he taught them about their personal duties and then focused on parental responsibilities. Said he,

"And ye will not suffer your children that they go hungry, or naked; neither will ye suffer that they transgress the laws of God, and fight and quarrel one with another, and serve the devil, who is the master of sin, or who is the evil spirit which hath been spoken of by our fathers, he being an enemy to all righteousness.

"But ye will teach them to walk in the ways of truth and soberness; ye will teach them to love one another, and to serve one another" (Mosiah 4:14–15).

Much like our day, in Book of Mormon times some of the children and young people were inspired to live faithful lives because of the teaching of their parents, and others chose a different path in spite of good examples, careful teaching, and other advantages. I find no evidence in the Book of Mormon which suggests that parents who did their very best in teaching and tutoring their children were ever judged by the mistakes and sins of their progeny. Indeed, the Book of Mormon gives us some of the most profound insights to the essentiality of agency in Heavenly

Father's plan. We don't have space to explore this theme extensively, but I recommend a careful study of Lehi's instruction to his son Jacob, found in Second Nephi, chapter two.

Jacob's father emphasized two critical and foundational doctrines. First is the requirement and centrality of the Atonement of the Messiah, and second is the necessity for agency if there is to be the possibility of progression and eternal life. I very much like this summary verse:

"Wherefore, men are free according to the flesh; and all things are given them which are expedient unto man. And they are free to choose liberty and eternal life, through the great Mediator of all men, or to choose captivity and death, according to the captivity and power of the devil; for he seeketh that all men might be miserable like unto himself" (2 Nephi 2:27).

Sharon G. Samuelson: It is interesting to me to wonder if Lehi gave such wonderful instruction to Jacob not only because he was younger than Laman, Lemuel, Nephi, and Sam, but also because Lehi himself had learned more and understood better these important principles in his later years than he had when his oldest children were young. I think my husband, for example, might be an even better grandfather than he was a father.

In that same great chapter we have just been discussing in terms of agency, Lehi also taught Jacob about the fall of Adam and Eve and its necessary role in allowing them to have children and create multigenerational families (see 2 Nephi 2:19–25).

Cecil O. Samuelson: And as we think about multigenerational families and parents teaching their children so well that they can in turn teach *their* children, think about Jacob's own teaching. Perhaps nowhere else in scripture is there an account of the directness demonstrated by Jacob as he chastised and called to repentance wicked Nephite husbands and fathers. I'll not share all that he said, but listen to these words:

"And also it grieveth me that I must use so much boldness of speech concerning you, before your wives and your children, many of whose feelings are exceedingly tender and chaste and delicate before God. . . .

"Wherefore, it burdeneth my soul that I should be constrained, because of the strict commandment which I have received from God, to admonish you according to your crimes, to enlarge the wounds of those who are already wounded, instead of consoling and healing their wounds; and those who have not been wounded, instead of feasting upon the pleasing word of God have daggers placed to pierce their souls and wound their delicate minds" (Jacob 2:7, 9).

This isn't all that he said about their immoral conduct, but it is clear that he was appropriately influenced by his father, Lehi, and his older brother Nephi, both of whom had by then died. What we do, and don't do, as parents and teachers will have a great influence long after we have exited the stage ourselves.

Sharon G. Samuelson: While we haven't exhausted all that we have learned, we appreciate what we have been able to think about and share. It is clear that the Holy Ghost will help us find answers and solutions in and through the Book of Mormon about families, children, and parenting. I leave you my testimony that the Book of Mormon is true and its truth becomes even more apparent in terms of our needs and concerns when we devote the time and effort, in the proper spirit, to seek out its counsel and examples.

Cecil O. Samuelson: I add my testimony to that of Sharon and express my gratitude to belong to a Church that not only values families and children, but is also so helpful in teaching us about their special and essential role in the plan of our Heavenly Father for each of us. Because it is true that families are forever, it is more important than we can currently even imagine that we do all we can to love our children, to teach them all that we can as they learn the essential truths of exaltation, and make sure that they are sealed to us and we to them in all the generations that come before and after our own.

God does live and He really is our Father. Jesus Christ is our Savior and Redeemer and our prophet-leaders of this dispensation are their authorized agents and servants. The Book of Mormon is true and testifies of Jesus and of families.

CHANGING WEAKNESSES INTO STRENGTHS

Brad Wilcox

When my wife asked me about my topic for Women's Conference, I accidently mixed up my words as I responded, "I've been asked to speak on changing strengths into weaknesses."

"Well," she exclaimed, "that's a unique twist. All I can say is that they certainly got the right guy for the job!"

As qualified as I am to address that particular topic, it's probably best if I switch the words back around and focus on changing our weaknesses into strengths. As members of the Church we are usually keenly aware of our weaknesses and may have even learned to see them as blessings as they turn us to the Lord. However, we are less sure about exactly how the Lord will help us change and what He requires of us in that process.

In 2 Nephi 25:23 we read, "For we know that it is by grace that we are saved, after all we can do." This is one of the most widely quoted scriptures in the Church, but yet may also be one of the least understood. Until we fully comprehend it, the scripture can sometimes be a source of discouragement rather than hope.

Brad Wilcox is an associate professor of Teacher Education in the David O. McKay School of Education at Brigham Young University. He holds degrees from BYU and the University of Wyoming, and is the author of, among other titles, The Continuous Atonement *and, with his son Russell,* Keep Texting from Taking Over. *He presided over the Chile Santiago East Mission from 2003–2006. He and his wife, Debi, have four children.*

The meaning of a sentence can change depending on which word is emphasized. For example, if we say, "*That* lady said it" the meaning is different than stating, "That *lady* said it" and "That lady *said* it" carries a different meaning than, "That lady said *it*." In the same way, as we vary the emphasis on the words found in 2 Nephi 25:23, we see the verse in a new light.

AFTER ALL WE CAN DO

For a long time I believed the word *after* in the verse was time related. I believed I had to do all I possibly could and then grace would kick in—as if it were a finishing touch to all I had to first accomplish alone. Then I thought of Paul and Alma the Younger who did nothing first or even at all and yet received great spiritual blessings. I reflected on the many manifestations of grace in my own life which I received long before I did "my part."

Stephen E. Robinson wrote, "I understand the preposition 'after' in 2 Nephi 25:23 to be a preposition of separation rather than a preposition of time. It denotes logical separateness rather than temporal sequence. We are saved by grace 'apart from all we can do,' or 'all we can do notwithstanding,' or even 'regardless of all we can do.' Another acceptable paraphrase of the sense of the verse might read, 'We are still saved by grace, after all is said and done.'"[1]

Robert L. Millet agreed when he wrote, "Nephi seems to be emphasizing that no matter how much we do, it simply will not be enough to guarantee salvation without Christ's intervention. To paraphrase Nephi, *above and beyond* all we can do, it is by the grace of Christ that we are saved."[2]

Christ's power is not an emergency generator which turns on once our supply is exhausted. It is not a booster engine once we run out of steam. Rather, it is our constant energy source. If we think of Christ only making up the difference *after* we do our part, we are failing to keep the promise we make each Sunday to remember Him *always*. Elder Bruce C. Hafen confirmed, "The Savior's gift of grace to us is not necessarily limited in time to 'after' all we can do. We may receive his grace before, during, and after the time when we expend our own efforts."[3]

AFTER ALL WE CAN DO

Can we ever do *all* that is possible? I remember reading the biography of President Spencer W. Kimball when I was quite young.[4] I was amazed by how much this prophet could accomplish in twenty-four hours. He awoke early, went to bed late, and filled each day to the maximum. He typed letters and wrote thank-you notes as he rode in cars. He scheduled interviews between meetings and often left meetings to take plates of food to security guards. Even now, whenever I have an especially busy schedule, I call it a President Kimball day. Then I become discouraged when I can't keep up a similar pace all the time.

Once, after helping to clean up after a ward activity, I arrived home late and exhausted. I collapsed on the family room couch and said, "I'm beat. I don't think I could do one more thing."

My daughter teased, "What? Dad stopping already? Surely there's still time to bake bread for the widows." The sad thing is I actually checked my watch to see if I could squeeze it in!

Because I know that in serving others I am also serving God, I push myself to do my best and give my all. "Could anything less be acceptable to Him?" I questioned for many years. Now I have come to see that actually *any* effort is pleasing to God even if He and I both know it's not my all or my best. It may be far from an acceptable offering, but God accepts it nonetheless because ultimately He is more concerned with the offerer than the offering. Elder Gerald N. Lund wrote, "Remember that one of Satan's strategies, especially with good people, is to whisper in their ears: 'If you are not perfect, you are failing.' This is one of his most effective deceptions. . . . While we should never be completely satisfied until we *are* perfect, we should recognize that God is pleased with every effort we make—no matter how faltering—to better ourselves."[5]

AFTER ALL WE CAN DO

What can any of us do without God? The older we get, the less we have to be reminded of the "greatness of God, and [our] own nothingness" (Mosiah 4:11). Our need for Christ's enabling power becomes more apparent with each passing day. The Book of Mormon makes it clear that we are dependent on the Lord for our every breath and heartbeat (see Mosiah 2:21). With such scriptures in mind, we no longer need to read the words *after all we can do* as a statement. Along with Robert L. Millet, we can rearrange them into a question: "After all, what can we do?"[6]

About a year after the death of her husband, a widow was asked, "When did you feel like Christ stepped in and made your burden bearable?"

She responded, "Was there ever a time when He wasn't shouldering the whole load? There were never two sets of footprints in my sand—only one and it was always His."

Who is bold enough to assume there has ever been a time, however short, when we were not being sustained by Christ? We may not have been aware of His grace, but it was there. To boast otherwise would be like a jockey claiming he could win a race without his horse.

Many of us have heard an analogy in Sunday lessons that goes something like this: There is a man in a hot desert who sees a fountain at the top of a hill. With great effort, he climbs the hill and receives the life-giving water. The teacher then asks, "What saved him? Was it the climb up the hill (his works) or was it the water (grace)?"[7] The answer is they are both essential. While effective in teaching the necessity of both grace and works, the analogy doesn't fairly illustrate the interaction between the two or the extent to which the Savior goes to enable us. The water may be at the top of the hill, but that's not where Christ is. He comes down to the bottom and brings the water to us. That's how we can make the climb—a climb to the top which He still requires because He knows it will strengthen us and be for our best good. Christ is not waiting at the finish line, rather He is finishing our faith (see Hebrews 12:1–2). Grace is not the prize at the end of the climb. It is the enabling power throughout.[8]

After all we can DO

Some people see a long checklist that must be completed before we get to heaven. In reality, each task is simply helping us become the type of people who will want to stay in heaven. Our willingness to plod along here on earth doesn't earn us points in heaven, but helps us become heavenly. We are not called human doings. We are human beings. *Doing* is only a means to *being*.

Scriptures make it clear our works are a significant factor in where we end up. However, not because of what our works earn us, but because of how they shape us. Andrew C. Skinner wrote, "Our condition in eternity will not be determined by what happened *to* us but rather what will happen *in* us as a result of the Savior's atonement."[9] So really, we are not human doings *or* human beings. We are humans becoming.[10]

When Naomi W. Randall wrote the words to "I Am a Child of God,"[11] she wrote, "Teach me all that I must know." President Spencer W. Kimball suggested the lyric be changed to "teach me all that I must do" because knowledge is of little worth unless it is acted upon.[12] Perhaps one day we will all sing, "Teach me all that I must be" because in the final analysis, it is not what we know or even what we've done that matters if by then we have not become the kind of people who can "live with Him someday."[13]

Saints all around the world sing a favorite hymn, "Come, Come Ye Saints" in which the question is asked, "Why should we think to earn a great reward/If we now shun the fight?"[14] Is that really what we are doing—*earning* a great reward? The word *earn* doesn't even appear once in the Doctrine and Covenants. As we face the fight rather than shunning it, God transforms us. The final destination may be "far away in the west," but development is found all along the trail. The "great reward" is not just something we will receive, but what we become through that journey and the grace of Jesus Christ.

As a recent *Ensign* article explained, "Do [we] believe that His grace is necessary to our salvation? Absolutely. Without the grace of Jesus Christ, no one could be saved or receive eternal blessings (see Romans 3:23–24). Through His grace, all will be resurrected and all who believe and follow Him may have eternal life (see John 3:15). Moreover, through His grace, our sacred relationships with spouses and family can continue through eternity (see Matthew 16:19; 1 Corinthians 11:11; D&C 132:19). These eternal blessings are His gifts to us; there is nothing we could do of ourselves alone that would merit or earn them. Nevertheless, the scriptures make it clear that we receive the full blessings of His grace through our faith and obedience to His teachings."[15] What are the "full blessings" of His grace if not fulfilling the measure of our creation by becoming more like God and Jesus?

After all WE can do

After examining all other options, we are left with just one. It is to emphasize the word *we*—not *we* as in you and me, but *we* as in each of us with Jesus. It is this relationship which is the key to understanding 2 Nephi 25:23. It is by grace we (you and I) are saved after all we (Christ and each of us) can do together.

In the Doctrine and Covenants we read a similar scripture: "Let us cheerfully do all things that lie in our power; and then may we stand still . . . to see the salvation of God" (D&C 123:17). Perhaps the words *us, our* and *we* are not referring to you and me, but to Christ and us. C. S. Lewis puts it this way, "We are now trying to understand, and to separate into water-tight compartments, what exactly God does and what man does when God and man are working together."[16]

One of Jesus' names, Emmanuel, means "God with us" (Matthew 1:23). Is there a better definition of grace than this? In the greatest of all companionships, each partner has a part, but they are not stacked on top of each other as if we must meet some minimum height requirement demanded by justice. It is not about height, but growth. We don't reach heaven by seeing Jesus' grace supplementing our works or our works supplementing His grace (see 2 Nephi 31:19; Moroni 6:4). Heaven is not reached by supplementing, but by covenanting; not by defining a ratio, but by building a relationship; not by negotiating, but by cooperating and uniting. Instead of seeing two *parts*, we might do well to see two *hearts* working in conjunction and being conformed to the same image (see Romans 8:29; Galatians 4:19).

I once spoke with a college student who sought a better understanding of the Atonement. "I know," she said, "I have to do my part and then Christ does the rest, but the problem is that I can't even do my part." She then went on to list the many things she should be doing, but wasn't. She also spoke of the anger and jealousy she shouldn't be feeling, but was. Continuing, she said, "I know Christ can fill the gap between my best efforts and perfection, but who fills the gap between the way I am and my best efforts?"

I pulled out a paper and drew two dots on it—one at the bottom and the other at the top. "Here is God," I said, labeling the top dot. "And here we are," I said, indicating the bottom dot. "How much of this distance does Jesus fill and how much is our part?" She started to mark a line at the halfway point, then thought better and marked a line much lower. I said, "Wrong."

"Is the line higher?" she asked.

"No," I responded. "Truth is there is no line. Christ has already filled the whole distance."

"Right! Like I don't have to do anything?"

"Oh no. You have plenty to do, but it is not to fill this gap. Jesus filled the gap that stands between us and God. It is done. We are all going to go back to God's presence. Now the question is how long we hope to stay there. *That* is what is determined by our obedience to Jesus."

Christ asks us to show faith in Him, repent, make and keep covenants, receive the Holy Ghost, and endure to the end. By complying we are not paying the demands of justice—not even the smallest part. Instead we are appreciating what Jesus did and using it to live the life of a disciple and follow a pattern set by Christ Himself—what Joseph Smith called "the life of the righteous."[17] Justice requires either perfection or a punishment when perfection is not achieved. Jesus, who paid justice (see 2 Nephi 2:7), can now forgive what justice never could. By releasing us from the requirements of justice, He is now able to make a whole new arrangement with us (see 3 Nephi 9:20–22; 28:35).

"So what's the difference?" the young woman asked. "Whether our efforts are required by justice or by Jesus, they are still required."

"True, but they are required for different purposes, and that makes all the difference. Fulfilling Christ's requirements is like paying a mortgage instead of rent, investing instead of paying off debts, really getting some-place instead of walking on a treadmill, ultimate perfection instead of forever coming up short."

"But I already told you, I can't be perfect."

"You don't have to be, because justice is no longer in charge. Jesus is, and He only asks that you be willing to be perfected."

CHRIST'S GENEROUS TERMS

Christ's arrangement with us is similar to a mother providing music lessons for her child. Mom, who pays the piano teacher, can require her child to practice. By so doing she is not attempting to recover the costs of the lessons, but to help the child take full advantage of this opportunity to live on a higher level. Her joy is not found in getting her investment back, but in seeing it used. If the child in his immaturity sees Mom's expectation to practice as unnecessary or overly burdensome, it is because he doesn't yet share her perspective. When Christ's expectations feel the same to us, perhaps it is because, as C. S. Lewis put it, "we have not yet had the slightest notion of the tremendous thing He means to make of us."[18] We are helped in this line-upon-line discovery when we focus less on *what* Jesus asks and more on *why* He asks it.

Elder Bruce C. Hafen wrote, "The great Mediator asks for our repentance *not* because we must 'repay' him in exchange for his paying our debt to justice, but because repentance initiates a developmental process that, with the Savior's help, leads us along the path to a saintly character."[19]

Similarly, Elder Dallin H. Oaks has taught, "The repenting sinner must suffer for his sins, but this suffering has a different purpose than punishment or payment. Its purpose is *change*."[20]

When it comes to changing weaknesses into strengths we are all totally dependent on the Lord. Without the faith and repentance required by Christ there would be no Redemption because there would be no *desire* for improvement. Without the covenants and the gift of the Holy Ghost there would be no *means* for improvement. And without the endurance required by Christ there would be no *internalization* of the improvement over time. Just as Jesus obeyed the will of the Father, we must now obey the will of Jesus. Christ's requirements are not so we can make something out of the Atonement, but so that—on His generous terms—the Atonement can make something out of us.

NOTES

1. Stephen E. Robinson, *Believing Christ* (Salt Lake City: Deseret Book, 1992), 91–92.

2. Robert L. Millet, *Grace Works* (Salt Lake City: Deseret Book, 2003), 131; emphasis added.

3. Bruce C. Hafen, *The Broken Heart* (Salt Lake City: Deseret Book, 1989), 155–156.

4. See Edward L. Kimball and Andrew E. Kimball, Jr., *Spencer W. Kimball* (Salt Lake City: Bookcraft, 1977), 351–52, 359–60.

5. Gerald N. Lund, "Are We Expected to Achieve Perfection in This Life?" *A Sure Foundation: Answers to Difficult Gospel Questions* (Salt Lake City: Deseret Book, 1988), 207; emphasis in original.

6. Millet, *Grace Works*, 135.

7. See Glenn L. Pearson, *Know Your Religion* (Salt Lake City: Bookcraft, 1961), 92–93.

8. See Bible Dictionary, s.v. "Grace," 697.

9. Andrew C. Skinner, *The Garden Tomb* (Salt Lake City: Deseret Book, 2005), 56; emphasis in original.

10. See David A. Bednar, "Becoming a Missionary," *Ensign*, November 2005, 44–47, and Dallin H. Oaks, "The Challenge to Become," *Ensign*, November 2000, 32–34.

11. Naomi W. Randall, "I Am a Child of God," *Hymns of The Church of Jesus Christ of Latter-day Saints* (Salt Lake City: The Church of Jesus Christ of Latter-day Saints, 1985), no. 301.

12. See Karen Lynn Davidson, *Our Latter-day Hymns: The Stories and the Messages*, revised and enlarged edition (Salt Lake City: Deseret Book, 2009), 331–32.

13. See Susan Easton Black, *Finding Christ Through the Book of Mormon* (Salt Lake City: Deseret Book, 1987), 49–50.

14. William Clayton, "Come, Come, Ye Saints," *Hymns*, no. 30.

15. "We Believe," *Ensign*, March 2008, 55–56.

16. C. S. Lewis, *Mere Christianity* (San Francisco: HarperCollins, 1980), 149.

17. Joseph Smith, *History of the Church*, 2:229.

18. Lewis, *Mere Christianity*, 205.

19. Hafen, *The Broken Heart*, 149.

20. Dallin H. Oaks, *The Lord's Way* (Salt Lake City: Deseret Book, 1991), 223; emphasis in original.

FACING CHALLENGES

Lord, Increase Our Faith

Camille Fronk Olson

My view of the audience from the pulpit is one of my favorite scenes of Women's Conference: thousands of happy women sitting close together, excited to learn, while producing periodic glimpses of flashing crochet hooks. It reminds me of the Del Parson painting of Christ with Mary and Martha.[1] Mary is sitting at the feet of the Savior as she listens with rapt attention, rarely blinking her eyes. Martha is just as attentive, but is vigorously stirring the contents of her mixing bowl at the same time. Whether it is crocheting or taking copious notes, some of us have minds that become more alert and attentive when our hands are moving. Others of us learn best by sitting still and concentrating on the words that are more felt than heard.

Many men don't understand Women's Conference. Watching a multitude of women get together for two days without anyone trying to be the Alpha Female is a mystery to them. They do not understand that we learn well in groups, when opportunities are given to share our own insights after formal presentations have concluded. In reality, some of the best

Camille Fronk Olson is an associate professor of Ancient Scripture at Brigham Young University. She previously taught seminary and institute in the Salt Lake area, and was dean of students at LDS Business College from 1987–1991. She is the author or co-author of several books, including Women of the Old Testament *and* Too Much to Carry Alone. *She serves as a young single adult institute teacher in her home stake. She and her husband, Paul F. Olson, have two children and three grandchildren.*

ideas for application of gospel principles will be discussed in informal gatherings tonight. After some of those late-night sessions, I have frequently heard men muse, "What can women possibly talk about for so long?" These two days allow us a brief separation from our daily duties at home and work, which gives us a different perspective for creating increased understanding and love in our lives.

THE PROBLEM: UNIVERSAL FEAR

This year may be especially important for clarifying priorities and developing spiritual strength. We know that this mortal life was intended to give us trials, but in the past year, the depth of our cumulative woes have come in tsunami-like fashion. Although this is not the only talk on spiritual strength in challenging times that you have heard this year, my prayer is that the perspective I have elected to consider will complement the inspired counsel we received during general conference and from our ward and stake leaders to rekindle our hope for tomorrow.

Many and diverse problems are hitting close to home—for some of us they come as a daily barrage with barely time to catch our breath. What appeared to be secure jobs are dissipating. Retirement plans are changing because a lifetime of savings has waned. Neighbors or coworkers are persecuting God-fearing people because of their reverence for the family. Debilitating accidents or illnesses are leaving expensive medications and often reduced health insurance in their wake. Children are electing to follow the permissive paths of the world. Divorce is creating another single parent with all the responsibilities of childcare, wage earning, housekeeping, and bill paying. An increasingly tight budget is being stretched to pay the mortgage on a home now worth a fraction of the original loan value. War is snatching the lives of loved ones; selfishness is turning love cold in a marriage; and in later years, healthy spouses are becoming full-time caregivers for their beloved incapacitated partners. We are being emotionally, financially, and spiritually stretched more than we thought possible. In short, one by one, our sources of secular security are being taken away with no immediate bailout in sight.

Ours is not the only period of the world where entire populations have experienced challenging times in nearly every aspect of life. Certainly the people of the Book of Mormon knew about turbulent times, of economic privations, of rebellious children, of the casualties of war, and persecution against the Saints. Moses and the Old Testament Israelites could tell us something about not having a home and surviving on a rather simple diet while pandemic diseases regularly decimated their numbers. And what about the trials of the early Saints in Nauvoo, or those who received assignments to establish a homeland in the desolate west?

Even the twelve men whom Jesus selected to be His original Apostles recognized that daily companionship with the Savior did not insulate them from hardships and fear of the future. At one point, they pleaded with the Master, "Lord, Increase our faith" (Luke 17:5). Although expressed in a variety of ways, the Apostles' plea echoes our own yearning in these days of uncertainty. "Dear God," we pray, "please increase our faith."

Receiving an increase in faith, however, will conversely require the decrease of fear for the future, self-deprecation over past mistakes for which we have already repented, and personal justifications that block spiritual promptings to change. Elder Neal A. Maxwell described such fears that barricade our faith-filled petitions to God: "With little faith, for example, we may actually acknowledge God's past blessings but still fear that He will not deliver us in the present situation. Or we may trust that God will finally deliver us but fear He will do so only after a severe trial which we desperately do not want! . . . Inwardly and anxiously we may worry, too, that an omniscient and loving God sees more stretch in us than we feel we have. Hence when God is actually lifting us up, we may feel He is letting us down."[2]

THE POWER OF FAITH IN CHRIST

No wonder then, that Jesus first wanted His disciples to appreciate the power of even a little faith before they could understand how it is increased. Likening beginning faith to one of the tiniest seeds, Jesus began His response to the Apostles' request: "If ye had faith as a grain of mustard seed, ye might say unto this sycamine [mulberry] tree, Be thou plucked up by the root, and be thou planted in the sea; and it should obey you" (Luke 17:6).

In other words, nothing is impossible—no trial, no loss, no burden—if we have faith in Jesus Christ. Most frequently in scripture, the term "faith" combines belief in the Savior with the profound need and desire to act, to do, and to be stretched beyond our comfort zone. Through multiple scriptural teachings and examples, we learn that living by faith occurs when we are so absolutely sure of what God has promised that we cannot be constrained from doing all that He asks, even when no evidence of how the promise can be fulfilled is visible (see JST Hebrews 11:1).

For instance, take the stirring roll call of the faithful reported in Hebrews 11. I will here cite only two of the verses. First, "by faith Noah, being warned of God of things not seen as yet . . . prepared an ark to the saving of his house" (Hebrews 11:7). To appreciate Noah's faith, I first wonder at young Nephi's faith when the Lord instructed him to build a boat while his family waited by the ocean's edge to travel to the promised land. I marvel further that Laman and Lemuel actually had sufficient trust to get into the boat that their little brother made. Yet how much faith must Noah have had to build a boat when there was no water around? His assurance of what God had promised was so great that he boldly set out to build a large ark, hardly a project that could be hidden from the neighbors. His actions could not be separated from his faith in the Lord even though he saw no evidence of a storm in the forecast, let alone a destructive flood.

A second example, "by faith the harlot Rahab perished not with them that believed not, when she had received the spies with peace" (Hebrews 11:31). A Canaanite woman, a harlot, living among her idolatrous kinsmen, received so much faith in the Israelites' God that she could not be held back from doing something to help the Lord's cause. With only a mustard-seed of faith, Rahab put her own life on the line to protect the two Hebrew spies who came into Jericho, even when she had no evidence of God's promises of protection and spiritual progression. Like Noah, she acted because of her reverence for the only true God, without any expectation of reward.

Many more are named in Hebrews 11, but the common denominator that fueled their stunning increase in faith was challenge. The chapter concludes, "God having provided some better things for them through their sufferings, for without sufferings they could not be made perfect" (JST Hebrews 11:40).

In our day, the present difficulties can become catalysts to increase our faith in the Savior. Given that God created the earth to teach us to live by faith in His Son, our current situations become potential laboratories for testing, refining, and increasing our faith. Please do not misunderstand me. I am not saying that God willed the current financial crisis or incited the wars and turmoil in the world in order to build up our faith reserves. God is never the author of greed and evil.

Neither am I saying that suffering will automatically develop greater faith in us. Remember that after the more than twenty years of war between the Nephites and Lamanites, "many had become hardened, because of the exceedingly great length of the war; and many were softened because of their afflictions, insomuch that they did humble themselves before God, even in the depth of humility" (Alma 62:41). It isn't our environment or the severity of the trial that changes us, but how we respond to the uncertainties. Do we lose hope and fear to act or do we turn to the Lord in faith, ready to go wherever and do whatever He bids us?

Through the Atonement of Jesus Christ, beauty will come from ashes and compensatory blessings will emerge from the filthiest recesses if we come to Him in sincerity and humility. As the Apostle Paul later observed, "Now no chastening for the present seemeth to be joyous, but grievous: nevertheless afterward it yieldeth the peaceable fruit of righteousness unto them which are exercised thereby" (Hebrews 12:11). Or as the Psalmist sang, "Weeping may endure for a night, but joy cometh in the morning" (Psalm 30:5).

THE PARABLE OF THE UNPROFITABLE SERVANT

After giving the Twelve a better appreciation for the tremendous power inherent in having faith in Him, Jesus next responded to their request for an increase in faith by relating to them the parable of the unprofitable servant. This is one of the lesser known and cited parables, perhaps because its connection to a plea for increased faith appears obscure or even unrelated. The Apostles asked Jesus to increase their faith, and in turn Christ told them this parable:

> But which of you, having a servant plowing or feeding cattle, will say unto him by and by, when he is come from the field, Go and sit down to meat?
>
> And will not rather say unto him, Make ready wherewith I may sup, and gird thyself, and serve me, till I have eaten and drunken; and afterward thou shalt eat and drink?
>
> Doth he thank that servant because he did the things that were commanded him? I [think] not.
>
> So likewise ye, when ye shall have done all those things which are commanded you, say, We are unprofitable servants: we have done that which was our duty to do. (Luke 17:7–10)

The Savior is clearly the Master in the parable. He tells us that we are the servant, or more accurately "the slave," as the Greek language renders it. Important doctrines are alluded to in the parable that teach us how faith is strengthened during challenging times. But first, we could benefit from a better understanding of what it meant to be a slave in the Roman Empire at the time of Jesus' mortal ministry.

The term "slavery" calls up horrendous images of abuse and dishonesty that transpired in America's past and inexplicably still occurs in parts of the world today. Slavery in the first century, however, should not be confused with the practice of keeping slaves in this country's history. Slaves in New Testament times were neither recognized by race, nor a lack of education, nor even necessarily by being at the bottom of the socio-economic triangle. Many slaves even owned property.

Because of the *Pax Romana* (Roman peace), slaves in the Roman Empire were less likely to be prisoners of war or victims of kidnappers during the time of Christ. More frequently, slaves in the first century were born to slaves, or forced into slavery to pay their debts, or volunteered to become slaves. Why would anyone choose to be a slave? To improve one's standing in society. Because a slave's individual social standing, honor, and economic opportunity were dependent on the status of his or her owner, chances for improved social standing and careers enticed many individuals to sell themselves into slavery for a time. Not only did slavery offer job security when employment opportunities were thin, but slaves could inherit an improved lifestyle. Frequently, freed slaves became Roman citizens.[3]

Knowing that first-century slaves received the potential for added freedom and opportunities in life makes it easier for us to appreciate why Christ would liken us to slaves in his parable. It also helps to remember that He who is the only completely just and merciful Master is also our Owner. He is also the greatest Exemplar of servitude. Steeped in debt beyond our capacity to repay because of our sins, mistakes, and shortcomings, Jesus Christ bought us with a price; He ransomed us by giving His perfect blood. When we entered into the covenant of baptism, we demonstrated to Him and to ourselves that we needed a Redeemer and desired to make His work our work. In short, we chose to become His servants, or slaves, to go where He calls us to go, to say what He directs us to say, to become what He alone enables us to become. No wonder that the Apostle Paul, a Roman citizen and freeman from birth, used this imagery to describe his willing decision to turn his life over to the Master; he rejoiced at his good fortune to have become a slave for the Savior (see 1 Corinthians 7:22; 9:19).

In the parable, we are not only the Lord's servants, but we acknowledge that we are His "unprofitable servants." Jesus asked His disciples whether the servant who has been working all day in the fields in the parable should expect to be richly rewarded and finally served by the Master in return. Anticipating that his listeners would see the fallacy of such an expectation, Jesus explained that the servant would instead hasten to prepare and serve dinner to the Master before preparing something to eat for himself. Likening his disciples to the servant, the Savior concluded, "Likewise ye, when ye shall have done all those things which are commanded you, say, We are unprofitable servants: we have done that which was our duty to do" (Luke 17:10).

We don't much like being called unprofitable, which is another reason we probably prefer to ignore this parable. In this great era of entitlement, when consulting companies are reportedly hired for the sole purpose of stroking the egos of new employees, when workers expect bonuses for merely showing up to work, and when students anticipate "A" grades because they worked hard in class, the Savior's parable is hard to swallow.

On those days when our confidence is shattered, or when we choose to assume a martyr-like attitude of accepting responsibility for all the problems around us, or when we think that we can never hear enough praise to make us feel acceptable, the lesson that our Savior is teaching in this parable is not particularly welcomed. It can sound like the Lord is asking us to add even more work to our already impossible daily demands. So why not just throw in the towel now? Instead of reminding us of our "nothingness" without Christ, we may prefer to find a scripture which reads, "thou art fine just the way thou art, my daughter, and hast worked hard enough, kick back now and rest, for I will do thy work for thee." But, of course, no such scripture exists.

Through the parable of the unprofitable servant, Jesus seems to be telling us something better. As in Jesus' parable, King Benjamin called his people unprofitable servants, even when he previously described them as "diligent . . . in keeping the commandments" (Mosiah 1:11). In his sermon, this beloved Nephite monarch testified that everything that we are and have we owe "to that God who has created you, and has kept and preserved you, and has caused that ye should rejoice" (Mosiah 2:20). All that God asks of us is to follow Him, and when we do, He immediately blesses us all the more, increasing our debt to Him. King Benjamin concluded, "therefore, of what have ye to boast?" (Mosiah 2:24). Aaron, a great Nephite missionary, taught King Lamoni's father that "since man had fallen he could not merit anything of himself; but the sufferings and death of Christ atone for their sins, through faith and repentance" (Alma 22:14). The closer we come to the Savior, the easier it is to admit that we are nothing without the grace and power of Jesus Christ.

Before jumping to conclusions that our Master's goal is to make us miserable with increased drudgery and heavier burdens, let's look at the parable from a different angle. What if the parable's message is not about how long we work in the Lord's service, or how hard we work for Him, or even what we are specifically assigned to do in our service? What if the Master is teaching us to learn *why* we work and *why* we serve? What if the message is what we learn and become along the way?

The epistle of the Apostle Paul to Philemon in the New Testament tells of a slave named Onesimus, who ran away from his master Philemon. Onesimus' name means "profitable." One wonders whether it was a popular name given to those born to slaves. Well—Onesimus was not profitable when he deserted his duty in Colossae but ended up in Rome where he met the imprisoned Paul. There Onesimus was converted to Jesus Christ and returned to Philemon with a letter from Paul requesting that Philemon forgive his repentant slave. In a delightful play on words, Paul becomes a type of Christ who justified Onesimus because the slave was penitent, albeit still a work in process. The Apostle Paul wrote to Philemon that "in time past [Onesimus] was to thee unprofitable, but now [is] profitable to thee and to me" (Philemon 1:11). Through his faith in the healing power of Christ, Onesimus was declared profitable, worthy, or righteous. Through the grace of Jesus Christ, he became worthy of God's blessing.

Ammon, a Nephite missionary to the wicked Lamanites, embraced the blessing of being about the Lord's work without expectation of praise along the way. Captured by the Lamanites and taken as a prisoner to their king, the young missionary was given an offer to marry the king's daughter. Instead, Ammon requested to be the king's servant. He volunteered to be a slave for Christ. After hearing the incredible report of Ammon's labors during his first day at work in the king's field—gathering scattered sheep and fighting off those who attempted to steal them—King Lamoni inquired as to the whereabouts of this faithful servant, only to learn that Ammon was already preparing the king's horses and chariots as he had been previously directed. Upon hearing this, King Lamoni exclaimed, "Surely there has not been any servant among all my servants that has been so faithful as this man; for even he doth remember all my commandments to execute them" (Alma 18:10).

Is that what the Savior was teaching His disciples when they asked Him for an increase of faith? Was He telling them through the parable that as indentured servants, their faith would increase as they lost themselves in the work, found joy and satisfaction from helping others, and did not seek for recognition? In a day when we may hear more criticism and mocking than praise for our work, the Master is reassuring us that He knows our heart and that He is with us. Jesus is telling us to carry on with a perfect brightness of hope despite the storms that surround us. Mother Teresa became an icon of faith because she wholeheartedly espoused this philosophy. The following advice comes from a poem she thought important enough to post on the wall of her orphanage: "People are illogical, unreasonable, and self-centered. Love them anyway. If you do good, people will accuse you of selfish ulterior motives. Do good anyway. If you are successful, you will win false friends and true enemies. Succeed anyway. The good you do today will be forgotten tomorrow. Do good anyway. Honesty and frankness make you vulnerable. Be honest and frank anyway. The biggest men and women with the biggest ideas can be shot down by the smallest men and women with the smallest minds. Think big anyway. People favor underdogs but follow only top dogs. Fight for a few underdogs anyway. What you spend years building may be destroyed overnight. Build anyway. People really need help but may attack you if you do help them. Help people anyway. Give the world the best you have and you'll get kicked in the teeth. Give the world the best you have anyway."[4]

In his analysis of the parable of the unprofitable servant, Elder John K. Carmack of the Seventy observed a similar conclusion, "Perhaps the Savior was teaching us [in the parable] that if we are serious about desiring greater faith, nothing short of maintaining a constant eternal perspective will do. If we place *any* condition on our willingness to serve the Lord with all our hearts, we diminish our faith. . . . We will continue with pure intent and total commitment the rest of our lives."[5]

My guess is that understanding this principle will not change a lot of what we do or how much we do each day, but it can make a dramatic difference in our attitude and enjoyment of life. Most important, our faith in Christ will increase to sustain us in our challenges. Please consider with me, therefore, three of the many lessons we can learn by serving the Lord without expectation of reward.

We Are Rendered Profitable or Worthy

First, we can learn how we become profitable or "worthy" through our participation in God's work. In modern English, the word "worthy" means having merit and deserving praise.[6] No wonder that many of us feel a tinge of discomfort when, during an interview for a temple recommend, our priesthood leader asks, "Are you worthy to enter the temple?" Those are humbling times, when the Spirit bears witness that we are still a work in process and do not merit praise. An obsolete use of the word "worthy" is actually more helpful here—previously, the word was a transitive verb, meaning "to be rendered worthy," and even "to be exalted."[7]

Through the process of justification, Christ imputes His righteousness to us as servants in His vineyard. Only with our Master Jesus Christ are we worthy. He declares us worthy or profitable, even when we still have shortcomings. As the Apostle Paul taught, "While we were yet sinners, Christ died for us" (Romans 5:8). Through His grace, the Savior gives us His goodness to support us in our desires to become like Him. In other words, to say that "I am worthy" means that I have been rendered worthy through the Atonement of Jesus Christ and therefore have the ultimate hope of exaltation.

I find it instructive that the Savior directed us to call ourselves "unprofitable" in the parable. He does not call us that. Through Joseph Smith, the Lord taught, "Remember the worth of souls is great in the sight of God" (D&C 18:10). In God's eyes, we have worth. The very next verse clarifies how the unprofitable is called worthy: "For, behold, the Lord your Redeemer suffered death in the flesh; wherefore he suffered the pain of all men, that all men might repent and come unto him . . . on conditions of repentance" (D&C 18:11–12). Only through the mercy, merits, and grace of Jesus Christ, are we made profitable. Because of the Atonement, we have worth.

Even when we are "yet sinners," when we exercise faith in Jesus Christ, we may still have the Holy Spirit with us. For example, when I am thinking or doing something that is offensive to God, I often feel the Spirit whisper to me to stop acting or thinking that way. Is the Spirit with me at those times because I am righteous? Of course not. He is with me because of the Savior's righteousness.

And when you have those awful feelings after you have lost your temper and yelled at the kids, do you have to go through all the steps of repentance before you are "worthy" to turn to God in prayer, asking Him to help you calm down and find a better way to respond to disobedient children? Of course not. Because of the Savior, even when we are broken, we can pray directly to our Father in Heaven, and we can worthily partake of the Lord's covenant blessings in our sacrament meetings and in the temple. The prayer of an Old Testament prophet named Zenos reiterates this principle: "Thou didst hear me," he prayed, "because of mine afflictions and my sincerity; and it is because of thy Son that thou hast been thus merciful unto me, therefore I will cry unto thee in all mine afflictions, for in thee is my joy; for thou hast turned thy judgments away from me, because of thy Son" (Alma 33:11). Notice that it was not because of Zenos' righteousness, but because of his sincerity and afflictions and because of the reality of the Redeemer that God heard his prayer. Through His mercy and grace, our Savior does a lot more for us every day than He gets credit for.

Like Onesimus, as members of the Church of Jesus Christ, we are called "Saints," not because we are perfect, but because we have made a covenant with Christ to become like Him by relying on His mercy and grace. In only that way can we confidently and honestly answer, "Yes, I am worthy."

We Gain Experience in Relying Wholly on the Lord

The second lesson of applying the principles of the parable of the unprofitable servant is experience in actually relying on the merits of the Savior. Unfortunately, our faith does not increase by merely citing the scriptures that promise strength when our faith is tried. We need personal experiences that stretch our faith. As President Uchtdorf recently admonished us in general conference, "We need to get off the sidelines and practice what we preach."[8] When God takes us to that place where no one can help us but Him, we enter that sacred realm where spiritual growth and unshaken confidence in God is forged.

I know a family who jumped off those sidelines a couple of months ago and are experiencing what it means to walk by faith. To protect their identity, I will here refer to them as the Browns. Dutifully paying rent each month for a home they hoped to be able to purchase in the future, the Browns returned home one day to find a notice on their door declaring the house in foreclosure and giving them ten days to vacate. Unfortunately, this family is not the only one in such straits today; however, the Browns had recently made some dramatic changes in their life that makes their story especially meaningful to our discussion here. For the first time, they had chosen to include faith in Jesus Christ in their lives.

Brother and Sister Brown married and had a baby boy while they were still in high school. They were baptized into The Church of Jesus Christ of Latter-day Saints when they were children, but had never been active. When their son was eleven years old, the Browns moved to another city. One day the missionaries walked past their home and began chatting with the precocious boy who was playing in the yard. He told the missionaries that he wanted to learn about Jesus Christ and asked his parents for permission to receive the missionary lessons. Soon the son was baptized and bringing his parents to church. He bore his testimony nearly every month in his ward. The day he was ordained to the Aaronic Priesthood, shortly after his twelfth birthday, was only days after the Browns received the foreclosure notice on their home.

During the ensuing fast and testimony meeting, Brother Brown stood to bear his testimony, the first time he had ever done so in his life. He related what had happened to him and his family in the short time they had lived in the neighborhood, including finding the gospel of Jesus Christ—and, unfortunately, trusting in the owner of their home. The Browns were actually ahead in their rent payments, having received word from the landlord that the home was financially stable. After learning that the landlord never paid the mortgage on the home all the while he was collecting their rent, Brother Brown observed, "If this had happened a year ago I would have been so angry that I would have turned to drinking and drugs. Now I am thinking that maybe this was supposed to happen. We have loved this ward, but maybe God wants us to go to a different ward where we can strengthen others who are struggling, the way that you have strengthened us."

Like the Browns, during challenging times we are in a position to see the positive side of adversity. It is by getting off the sidelines and experiencing what it means to live by faith that our faith increases. Only then do we begin to see that working in the Savior's vineyard brings lasting fulfillment and joy, no matter what else anyone says.

WE OBTAIN A CLEARER PERSPECTIVE

The third and final way that our faith increases through applying the message of Jesus' parable is that it changes and informs our perspective of the Lord and, subsequently, of ourselves. In the parable, we see Jesus as our Master on whom we are completely dependent. He is therefore not merely an Elder Brother whose purpose in life is to make us happy by looking after our every need. Neither is He simply a great, moral teacher. As C. S. Lewis wrote, "A man who was merely a man and said the sort of things Jesus said would not be a great moral teacher. He would either be a lunatic—on a level with the man who says he is a poached egg—or else he would be the Devil of Hell. You must make your choice. Either this man was, and is, the Son of God: or else a madman or something worse. You can shut Him up for a fool, you can spit at Him and kill Him as a demon; or you can fall at His feet and call Him Lord and God. But let us not come with any patronising nonsense about His being a great human teacher. He has not left that open to us. He did not intend to."[9]

From our new perspective, Jesus Christ is undeniably our Redeemer and our Savior, who alone saves us from becoming "devils, angels to a devil, to be shut out from the presence of our God" forever (2 Nephi 9:9). An informed perspective of our pitiful situation without the Atonement of Christ helps us see the Savior as "the Rock of Heaven, which is broad as eternity" (Moses 7:53), who is the Only One who sustains and supports us throughout the mighty storms of life. Assuredly, when He becomes the foundation for our lives, we "cannot fall" (Helaman 5:12).

Furthermore, the more clearly we see the power and righteousness of our Redeemer, the less fearfully we view our futures. We see more clearly priorities and ways to simplify our lives. The wealth and power of the world fade in importance while the richness of family, friendships, and the companionship of the Spirit of God expands. President Wilford Woodruff observed, "There is a vail between man and eternal things; if that vail was taken away and we were able to see eternal things as they are before the Lord, no man would be tried with regard to gold, silver or this world's goods."[10] With our new perspective, we discover the gift of being content with our assignment in the Lord's vineyard.

I had an experience several years ago that taught me that God is the anchor of my soul and the only constant in a perpetually changing world. It was one of those times in life when everything seemed to be in turmoil. My job description at work changed daily; my new Church calling was for a responsibility that I did not even know existed; and I was confused and frustrated in a dating relationship. At the time, I was working in downtown Salt Lake City and often walked the mile from my home to work, frequently choosing to follow different streets to get there. One morning in early spring, I saw a tree in blossom at the end of the sidewalk. My father had taught me a lot about fruit trees because of the orchard he planted around our family home, so I quickly recognized that the blossoms were popcorn popping on an apricot tree. Walking past the tree that morning brought back wonderful childhood memories when life was simple, and apricots plentiful.

A few weeks passed, without my taking that same route to work. When I finally did go that same way again, I remembered the apricot tree, now visibly full of green leaves. I quickly calculated the stage of growth in the fruit that I should expect to find. I deduced that there should now be lots of small, green fruit visible on the tree. The closer I came, the more I hoped I was right. Sure enough, when I arrived at it, I saw hundreds of little green apricots that filled the tree.

As I continued my walk to work that day, my satisfaction for having predicted the correct stage of development in apricots quickly changed. My eyes were filling with tears. I could not understand my emotions. Why was I crying? I had just seen an apricot tree bearing apricots at the very time that it should have been. Then I got it. Amid all the chaos and feelings of inadequacy, I had just seen an apricot tree, bearing little green apricots, at the very time it should be. That little tree became an answer to an oft-repeated prayer. Through His creations, God seemed to be saying to me that He was still there and that the promises of the Atonement had not changed. God is the same yesterday, today, and forever. I knew that I had received one of the Lord's tender mercies as I arrived at work that day. My job had not changed, but through the enabling power of the Lord, I knew I could accomplish whatever He wanted me to do.

CONCLUSION

As one who learned the lessons of the parable of the unprofitable servant, the Apostle Paul has become one of my heroes. If ever there was one who could have berated himself for his past life, that person would be Paul. Prior to his marvelous conversion to embracing Jesus of Nazareth as his Master and Savior, Paul boasted of his sinless life under the law of

Moses and his zeal in ruthlessly persecuting the followers of Christ. If ever there was one who could have had a reason to say, "I don't deserve to work in the Lord's vineyard," it was Paul. He could have easily found justification for being paralyzed in his faith, feeling like he could never be worthy to receive the grace of Jesus Christ, or hope to ever experience the sustaining and joyful support of the Spirit in his many challenges.

But, in one of the greatest examples of faith in the power of the Atonement of Christ, the Apostle Paul exclaimed, "I count not myself to have apprehended: but this one thing I do, forgetting those things which are behind, and reaching forth unto those things which are before, I press toward the mark for the prize of the high calling of God in Christ Jesus" (Philippians 3:13–14). Rather than looking back and finding all the reasons he shouldn't qualify for the Lord's forgiveness and strength, Paul's faith in his Redeemer turned him with confidence to the future. "We are troubled on every side, yet not distressed," Paul wrote in faith. "We are perplexed, but not in despair; persecuted, but not forsaken; cast down, but not destroyed" (2 Corinthians 4:8–9). Even while imprisoned for preaching the gospel of Jesus Christ, Paul wrote, "I have learned, in whatsoever state I am, therewith to be content" (Philippians 4:11).

My prayer is that our current trying circumstances will propel each of us to greater faith in the Lord. Rather than adding stress and discouragement, I pray that our present trials will lead us to a deeper acceptance of the Savior's righteousness that He imputes to our account to render us worthy; to a bolder courage to step out into the darkness and experience light as only the Lord offers; and to a clearer perspective of His divinity and constant awareness of each of us, His servants. Let us exclaim with assurance with the Apostle Paul, "If God be for us, who can be against us?" (Romans 8:31). May we look forward with confidence and remember President Thomas S. Monson's declaration, "The future is as bright as your faith."[11]

NOTES

1. See http://www.lds.org/hf/art/display/1,16842,4218-1-2-62,00.html; accessed 10 September 2009.
2. Neal A. Maxwell, *Lord, Increase Our Faith* (Salt Lake City: Bookcraft, 1994), 3.

3. See S. Scott Bartchy, "Slavery (Greco-Roman)," in David Noel Freedman, ed., *The Anchor Bible Dictionary*, 6 volumes (New York: Doubleday, 1992), 6:65–73.

4. "The Paradoxical Commandments," Dr. Kent M. Keith, at http://www .paradoxicalcommandments.com/; accessed 10 September 2009. © 1968 Kent M. Keith, renewed 2001. Used by permission.

5. John K. Carmack, "Lord, Increase Our Faith," *Ensign*, March 2002, 56–57; emphasis in original.

6. *Webster's New Universal Unabridged Dictionary* (New York: Simon and Schuster, 1983), s.v. "worthy."

7. Ibid.

8. Dieter F. Uchtdorf, "The Way of the Disciple," *Ensign*, May 2009, 77.

9. C. S. Lewis, *Mere Christianity* (San Francisco: HarperCollins, 1980), 52.

10. Wilford Woodruff, *Journal of Discourses*, 17:71.

11. Thomas S. Monson, "Be of Good Cheer," *Ensign*, May 2009, 92.

TAKE TIME TO BE HOLY

Mary Ellen Edmunds

The summers I was sixteen and seventeen I worked at Zion National Park. I loved this park long before I had much understanding of what the concept of Zion actually meant. Or Babylon either. (I think my brother worked there—or was it the Grand Canyon?)

Once upon a time there was a fair maiden who divided her time and her heart between Zion and Babylon. Don't get any ideas that this was easy for her. She began to notice that it was increasingly difficult to adjust back to Zion after her worldly adventures in Babylon. She started out at around 90 percent for Zion, 10 percent for Babylon. Zion in the lead. But *oh*, there were such tempting, intoxicating, addicting things in Babylon! She crept towards 80/20, and eventually to 70/30. Babylon was gaining. She was spending more of her time and other resources there.

This realization made her feel dizzy for a few minutes.

If we're not building Zion—God's Kingdom—we're supporting Babylon! As President Brigham Young said: "All Latter-day Saints enter the new and everlasting covenant when they enter this Church. They covenant to cease sustaining, upholding and cherishing the kingdom of

Mary Ellen Edmunds is a retired nurse and the former director of training at the Provo Missionary Training Center. She is the author of MEE Speaks *and* MEE Thinks, *and is a popular speaker at the* Time Out for Women *seminars. She has previously served on the Relief Society general board for eleven years, and served four missions for the Church.*

the Devil and the kingdoms of this world. They enter the new and ever-lasting covenant to sustain the Kingdom of God and no other kingdom. They take a vow of the most solemn kind, before the heavens and earth . . . that they will sustain truth and righteousness instead of wickedness and falsehood, and build up the Kingdom of God, instead of the kingdoms of this world."[1]

And Joseph Smith said: "The building up of Zion is a cause that has interested the people of God in every age; it is a theme upon which prophets, priests and kings have dwelt with peculiar delight; they have looked forward with joyful anticipation to the day in which we live; and fired with heavenly and joyful anticipations they have sung and written and prophesied of this our day."[2] He also said, "Show me a man or woman who has the spirit of the Gospel within them, and I will show you a man or woman whose greatest desire is to build up the kingdom of God upon the earth."[3]

The fair maiden found herself looking forward more to Babylon adventures than to her days in the company of Saints and even her family.

Elder Neal A. Maxwell said: "Like the prodigal son, we too can go to 'a far country.' . . . The distance . . . is not to be measured by miles but by how far our hearts and minds are from Jesus! (See Mosiah 5:13)."[4]

Once she heard a choir sing:

> *Prone to wander, Lord, I feel it, Prone to leave the God I love;*
> *Here's my heart, O take and seal it; Seal it for thy courts above.*[5]

And she paused, pondering that, and felt sad. She found that the more she ignored her conscience—the discomfort in her soul—the less she could hear and feel the still small voice. When she was alone and quiet, this bothered her. But out with the crowd, any discomfort got crowded out.

As Elder Richard G. Scott has said, "When things of the world crowd in, all too often the wrong things take highest priority. Then it is easy to forget the fundamental purpose of life."[6]

Thank goodness this fairy tale has a happy ending.

It took time and hard work, but the fair maiden eventually realized that Babylon was counterfeit—and destructive. What she wanted most was Zion: Happiness, peace, safety, a clear conscience, and sweet, real relationships with her family and friends, and with God.

WHAT'S SO BAD ABOUT BABYLON?

I imagine the sign at the edge of a dangerous town: "Welcome to Babylon—stay a while and you'll stay forever!"

Elder Bruce R. McConkie wrote: "Everything connected with [Babylon] was in opposition to all righteousness and had the effect of leading men downward to the destruction of their souls."[7] It has become the symbol of the wickedness and evils of the world.

President Spencer W. Kimball once said: "Unfortunately we live in a world that largely rejects the values of Zion. Babylon has not and never will comprehend Zion. . . . This state of affairs stands in marked contrast to the Zion the Lord seeks to establish through his covenant people."[8]

We are commanded to flee from Babylon. In fact, the Lord will not spare anyone who remains in spiritual Babylon. In an *Ensign* article, Stephen E. Robinson wrote that one of the major characteristics of the great and abominable church described in The Book of Mormon is that it seeks wealth and luxury.[9] "[The] great and spacious building matches the characteristics of the church of the devil; the artificial structure without foundation represents the carnal world, and its values and life-style include mockery of the kingdom of God."[10]

Listen to the warning Nephi gives based on his father Lehi's dream:

"And great was the multitude that did enter into that strange building. . . . They did point the finger of scorn at me and those that were partaking of the fruit also; but *we heeded them not. . . . For as many as heeded them, had fallen away*" (1 Nephi 8:33–34; emphasis added).

Ouch! Sadly—tragically—some who had partaken of the fruit did heed the mocking and the pointing. They acted as if they were ashamed, and they fell away into forbidden paths and were lost.

Do we heed them? Oh, I hope not!

Have we sometimes joined in the scoffing, the mocking, the gossip, the pointing of fingers? Could it even happen that some would scoff at a Relief Society general president for teaching what she was prompted to share?

Or has anyone ever pointed the finger at *you*, telling you you're far too religious, too obedient, too naïve?

Some are mocked because they try to keep the Sabbath day holy, or dress modestly, or avoid certain movies or so many other things. Have you ever felt ashamed of sacred clothing to the point where you had to tuck or pin or even remove it so you could wear something considered fashionable by the dwellers in that spacious building?

Elder Neal A. Maxwell said: "While casual members are not unrighteous, they often avoid appearing to be *too* righteous by seeming less committed than they really are—an ironic form of hypocrisy. . . . In contrast, those sincerely striving for greater consecration neither cast off their commitments nor the holy garment."[11]

It's a dangerous thing to try to divide our loyalties, isn't it? No one can serve two masters. There's only room for one—either God or someone or something else. *We* choose.

Well, what's so bad about just having a summer cottage in Babylon? For one thing, where is Babylon (or Zion) located? Right here, in our hearts. As the fair maiden learned, there was no way she could develop a pure heart or feel peace with that cottage taking up so much space.

What's so bad about Babylon? Everything!

THEN WHAT IS SO GOOD ABOUT ZION?

Zion is a place of holiness and beauty. Zion is the pure in heart in any day, any time, any place. President Spencer W. Kimball taught: "Zion can be built up only among those who are the pure in heart, not a people torn by covetousness or greed. . . . [Zion is] not a people who are pure in appearance, rather a people who are pure in heart."[12]

What does it mean to be pure in heart? In part, it means to be free from that which dilutes, harms, weakens, or pollutes. To be pure is to be real, genuine.[13]

The people of Zion are described as being of one heart and one mind. They dwell in righteousness, and there are no poor among them—imagine that!

Elder D. Todd Christofferson, of the Quorum of the Twelve, said: "Throughout history, the Lord has measured societies and individuals by how well they cared for the poor. He has said: 'For the earth is full, and there is enough and to spare; yea, I prepared all things, and have given unto the children of men to be agents unto themselves. Therefore, if any man shall take of the abundance which I have made, and impart not his portion, according to the law of my gospel, unto the poor and the needy, he shall, with the wicked, lift up his eyes in hell, being in torment' (D&C 104:17–18; see also D&C 56:16–17). . . . . We control the disposition of our means and resources, but we account to God for [our] stewardship over earthly things."[14]

There are so many ways to be poor. Are we doing all we can to reach out to those in need, those who are poor?

From the Doctrine and Covenants, section 56, verse 16, "Wo unto you rich men, that will not give your substance to the poor, for your riches will canker your souls; and this shall be your lamentation in the day of visitation, and of judgment, and of indignation: The harvest is past, the summer is ended, and my soul is not saved!" The beautiful words of the hymn "Because I Have Been Given Much"[15] teach us what God wants us to learn about sharing with those in need.

Zion is a place of holiness and beauty, and the Lord Himself is the founder and sustainer of Zion.

Elder Bruce R. McConkie taught: "Zion is people. . . . Zion is those out of whose souls dross and evil have been burned as though by fire . . . so as to stand pure and clean before the Lord. Zion is those who keep the commandments of God."[16]

What's so good about Zion? Everything!

HOW IS BABYLON DIFFERENT FROM ZION?

Babylon is the antithesis of the city of Zion, the city of God. It's the exact opposite of all that is good, pure, and holy. It is as dark as Zion is light.

Babylon embodies the love of money, the bondage of perpetual debt and never having enough, of conspicuous consumption, sin, entitlements, the demand for instant gratification—and any addiction. I think those in Babylon seldom if ever have a feeling of contentment or tranquil happiness. Wouldn't we hate missing that?

As Elder Christofferson has said: "We might ask ourselves, living as many of us do in societies that worship possessions and pleasures, whether we are remaining aloof from covetousness and the lust to acquire more and more of this world's goods. Materialism is just one more manifestation of the idolatry and pride that characterize Babylon. Perhaps we can learn to be content with what is sufficient for our needs."[17]

Babylon is bondage, and even with all its present popularity, it is temporary; it *will* fall. Zion is true freedom and is eternal. The Lord calls us to come to Zion:

> Israel, Israel, God is calling, Calling thee from lands of woe.
> Babylon the great is falling; God shall all her tow'rs o'erthrow. . . .
> Come to Zion, come to Zion, And within her walls rejoice. . . .
> Come to Zion, come to Zion, For your coming Lord is nigh.[18]

WHAT DO WE MEAN BY "BEING IN THE WORLD"?

This is where we were sent to spend our mortality—this is our home now. It's part of our education; where important lessons will be learned, where we'll gain experience and make critical choices. We separate ourselves from worldly influences, but not from the world we live in. We can't let our light so shine if we isolate ourselves from our fellow travelers. We can make positive contributions to our family, to the community, and to our neighbors by the way we live, the way we treat others. We can create Zion in our hearts and homes. We can make the world a better place. "And blessed are they who shall seek to bring forth my Zion at that day, for they shall have the gift and the power of the Holy Ghost; and if they endure unto the end they shall be lifted up at the last day, and shall be saved in the everlasting kingdom of the Lamb" (1 Nephi 13:37).

Elder Quentin L. Cook wrote: "After finishing my education at Stanford Law School, I sought employment at a particular law firm. No members of the Church were associated with the firm, but the firm was made up of lawyers of character and ability. After a morning of interviews, the senior partner and two other partners invited me to lunch. The senior partner inquired if I would like a prelunch alcoholic drink and later if I would like wine. In both cases, I declined. The second time, I informed him that I was an active Latter-day Saint and did not drink alcoholic beverages. I received an offer of employment from the firm. A few months later, the senior partner told me the offer of the alcoholic beverages was a test. He noted that my résumé made it clear that I had served an LDS mission. He had determined that he would hire me only if I was true to the teachings of my own church. He considered it a significant matter of character and integrity."[19]

You've heard stories or possibly had experiences like this. Elder Cook's boss was right, wasn't he—it *is* a significant matter of character and integrity that we live what we believe. It was likely *many* such experiences and choices which prepared Elder Cook to become an Apostle.

Our righteousness and our striving to be a little better when we're already pretty good can shine a bright light for others. President Spencer W. Kimball has taught: "Zion is to be in the world and not of the world, not dulled by a sense of carnal security, nor paralyzed by materialism. No, Zion . . . [is] things that *exalt the mind* and *sanctify the heart*."[20]

What Do We Mean by Not Being "of the World"?

The Lord said, "My kingdom is not of this world" (John 18:36), and, "Love not the world, neither the things that are in the world. If any man love the world, the love of the Father is not in him. For all that is in the world, the lust of the flesh, and the lust of the eyes, and the pride of life, is not of the Father, but is of the world. And the world passeth away, and the lust thereof: but he that doeth the will of God abideth for ever" (1 John 2:15–17).

Babylon will fall! It will be destroyed!

Elder David R. Stone of the Seventy wrote, "sensuality, corruption, and decadence, and the worshipping of false gods are to be seen in many cities, great and small, scattered across the globe. . . . Too many of the people of the world have come to resemble the Babylon of old."[21] By the way, I'm not classifying all who are Latter-day Saints as perfect and those who aren't as imperfect—that's just not true. I'm just talking to those of us who know better.

Stephen E. Robinson has also written: "Individual orientation to the Church of the Lamb or to the great and abominable church is not by membership but by loyalty. Just as there are Latter-day Saints who belong to the great and abominable church because of their loyalty to Satan and his life-style, so there are members of other churches who belong to the Lamb because of their loyalty to him and his life-style. Membership is based more on who has your heart than on who has your records."[22]

What Do We Teach Our Children?

What does a parent teach who chooses to spend $2,000 per season on clothing for a pre-toddler? Or $17,000 on a birthday party for a ten-year-old? Are we teaching them that what they *own* and what they *wear* and how much *stuff* they have is more important than who they *are*?

Children who have been given too much, who have been overindulged, grow up to be adults who have difficulty coping with life's disappointments. As one family therapist has said: "We are training our children to become workaholics . . . in order to compete in the global economy. And parenting has become a competitive sport, with the trophies going to the busiest."[23]

What do we teach our children when we hold on to the "summer cottage in Babylon"[24] in spite of all we say about the importance of Zion?

Do you remember the story Elder Robert D. Hales shared in his April 2009 general conference message about living providently? He said: "Our wedding anniversary was approaching, and I wanted to buy Mary a fancy coat to show my love and appreciation. . . . When I asked what she thought of the coat I had in mind, she replied with words that . . . penetrated my heart and mind. 'Where would I wear it?' . . . Then she taught me an unforgettable lesson. She looked me in the eyes and sweetly asked, 'Are you buying this for me or for you?' In other words, she was asking, 'Is the purpose of this gift to show your love for me or to show me that you are a good provider or to prove something to the world?' I pondered her question and realized I was thinking less about her and our family and more about me."[25]

Have we made the mistake of starting our children on the road of striving to have more and be better than everyone else? Are we convincing them that they can and should have anything they want right now? Are they missing the critical lesson of saving, of waiting—and of realizing that there are some things they just cannot have or cannot do?

Elder Hales told of another lesson from his wife when he wanted to buy her a beautiful dress. She simply said *"We can't afford it."* He said: "Those words went straight to my heart. I have learned that the three most loving words are 'I love you,' and the four most caring words for those we love are 'We can't afford it.'"[26]

What do children learn if they don't realize this—that there are some things you just cannot afford? What do they learn if they never have to work for anything—not for clothing, shoes, makeup, piano lessons; not for a cell phone, or the use of a car—what do they learn? Do they learn there is something for nothing? That's a pretty dangerous lesson.

President Gordon B. Hinckley wrote in the *Liahona:* "We live in a season when fierce men do terrible and despicable things. We live in a season of war. We live in a season of arrogance. We live in a season of wickedness, pornography, immorality. All of the sins of Sodom and Gomorrah haunt our society. Our young people have never faced a greater challenge. We have never seen more clearly the lecherous face of evil."[27]

I think Babylon is intent on pulling families apart. This is cause for extreme concern. The family is meant to be eternal, but Babylon isn't. Babylon is the city of the world; Zion is the city of God. Where do *you* want to live? Where do *you* want to raise your family?

The way we spend our time and our money is an indication of the kind of life and world we want. Where do you want to be when Jesus comes again?—for He surely will come!

Maybe we need a filter around our home, our Zion in the midst of Babylon. Work together to make your home a place of goodness, a place of holiness, a place of peace, a place of refuge and protection, a *Zion.*

Has your home been dedicated? Is this something that would make a difference for you? (It certainly has for me.) Just so you know, the summer home in Babylon can never be dedicated—that alone should make us want to get rid of it.

So what *do* we teach our children? Hopefully we teach them truth. We help our children learn to make wise choices. We help them feel and recognize the Spirit.

Trust your common sense. Be an example! Live a simple life, a compassionate life, be kind, be patient, take care of other people. Be useful, delay gratification, don't be greedy. Be grateful and content.

How Do I Evaluate How I'm Doing?

A poet said: "The world is too much with us."[28] Is that too close to the truth in my life or yours? Is my heart set too much on the things of this world, and not enough on the things of Zion? Are peace, safety, and holiness being squeezed out? It's so noisy in Babylon!

Are there too many things about which we've said "Oh, that's no big deal." But does this attitude include things which *are* a big deal? Are there things in my life or yours which make us uncomfortable? Am I too easily caught up—trapped—in the noise, the rush, the glamour, the enticements of the world, of Babylon? Is my total allegiance to the Kingdom of God? Or just part of it? Just sometimes? Am I too easily distracted? Pulled away from spiritual nourishment?

Elder Richard G. Scott taught us: "Satan has a powerful tool to use against good people. It is distraction. He would have good people fill life with 'good things' so there is no room for the essential ones. Have you unconsciously been caught in that trap?"[29] Elder Neal A. Maxwell said: "Many individuals preoccupied by the cares of the world are not neces-sarily in *transgression*. But they certainly are in *diversion* and thus waste 'the days of [their] probation' (2 Ne. 9:27). . . . Some proudly live 'without God in the world' (Alma 41:11)."[30] Do I live without God too much of the time? Am I making too many compromises . . . Doing too much rationalizing?

Elder Maxwell also reminded us that "the tugs and pulls of the world are powerful. Worldly lifestyles are cleverly reinforced by the rationaliza-tion, 'Everybody is doing it.'"[31]

Do I lack gratitude? What is it that's difficult for *me* to let go of in the world, in Babylon?

Has Zion sometimes become a tiny three-hour island on Sunday, sur-rounded by the rest of the week in Babylon? Elder Maxwell again: "God's plan is not the plan of pleasure; it is the 'plan of happiness.'"[32]

There used to be a Distant Early Warning system in the far north to detect incoming Soviet bombers during the Cold War. It was called the D-E-W Line. Maybe the Holy Ghost can help us have a "D-E-W Line" (a Sheri Dew line?) to warn us of incoming danger of any kind. "Incoming! Incoming!"

Sooner or later (hopefully not *too* late) we will discover that every single thing the Lord has asked of us has been designed to bless us—to protect us—to make us good, to make us happy, to make us holy.

Brigham Young taught the Saints: "We have the promise, if we seek first the kingdom of God and its righteousness, that all necessary things will be added to us. We should not be distrustful, but seek first to know how to please our Father and God—seek to know how to save ourselves from the errors that are in the world, from darkness and unbelief, from the vain and delusive spirits that go abroad among the children of men to deceive, and learn how to save and preserve ourselves upon the earth to preach the Gospel, build up the kingdom, and establish the Zion of our God. Then there is not the least danger, and there should not be the least doubt but what *everything necessary* for the comfort, convenience, happiness, and salvation of the people will be added to them."[33]

Let's examine our hearts, our habits, our choices. What is it we love most? What would we give up in order to come closer to God, to know Him?

As Elder Maxwell taught, "*Personal* righteousness, worship, prayer, and scripture study are so crucial in order to '[put] off the natural man' (Mosiah 3:19)."[34]

One strong impression that came to me was to keep the Sabbath day holy. I'm convinced this can provide for us an oasis—a rest, a break, from all that we're bombarded with through the week. And oh, the temple—if there was ever a place which shows the difference between Babylon and Zion, this holy place, this refuge, this House of God, is that place! Even if you just go sit in the foyer for a while and "leave the world outside"!

TAKE TIME TO BE HOLY

Elder D. Todd Christofferson wrote: "To come to Zion, it is not enough for you or me to be *somewhat less wicked* than others. We are to become not only *good* but *holy* men and women."[35]

Take time to be holy, to free yourself from the world and the strong and alluring influences which are all around you. Doctrine and Covenants 25:10 says, "And verily I say unto thee that thou shalt lay aside the things of this world, and seek for the things of a better."

Thanks to you for seeking the things of a better world. Thank you for your goodness, your holiness—for the difference you make and the lights you shine in a world that is increasingly dark and frightening. We can only become holy through the Atonement—through coming unto Christ.

"Ye shall be holy: for I the Lord your God am holy" (Leviticus 19:2). I love the Protestant hymn "Take Time to Be Holy," written in 1882:

> Take time to be holy, speak oft with thy Lord;
> Abide in Him always, and feed on His Word.
> Make friends of God's children, help those who are weak,
> Forgetting in nothing His blessing to seek.
>
> Take time to be holy, the world rushes on;
> Spend much time in secret, with Jesus alone.
> By looking to Jesus, like Him thou shalt be;
> Thy friends in thy conduct His likeness shall see.
>
> Take time to be holy, let Him be thy Guide;
> And run not before Him, whatever betide.
> In joy or in sorrow, still follow the Lord,
> And, looking to Jesus, still trust in His Word.
>
> Take time to be holy, be calm in thy soul,
> Each thought and each motive beneath His control.
> Thus led by His Spirit to fountains of love,
> Thou soon shalt be fitted for service above.[36]

Take time for personal spiritual refreshment and renewal. Will it be Zion, or will it be Babylon? Think of the implications of our exercise of agency as we are daily pulled between Zion and Babylon, and choose Zion!

Our center, our spirits, seek the safety, peace, and blessings of Zion. We can live as a Zion person, family, and people if we really want to. God will help us if this is truly the desire of our hearts.

Take time to be holy.

Take time to find peace.

Slow down.

Come home.

NOTES

1. Brigham Young, *Brigham Young* [manual]. In Teachings of Presidents of the Church series (Salt Lake City: The Church of Jesus Christ of Latter-day Saints, 1997), 62–63.
2. Joseph Smith, *Joseph Smith* [manual]. In Teachings of Presidents of the Church series (Salt Lake City: The Church of Jesus Christ of Latter-day Saints, 2007), 186.
3. In John W. Taylor, Conference Report, October 1903, 45.
4. Neal A. Maxwell, "The Tugs and Pulls of the World," *Ensign*, November 2000, 36.
5. "Come, Thou Fount of Every Blessing," *Hymns: The Church of Jesus Christ of Latter-day Saints* (Salt Lake City: The Church of Jesus Christ of Latter-day Saints, 1948), no. 70.
6. Richard G. Scott, "First Things First," *Ensign*, May 2001, 7.
7. Bruce R. McConkie, *Mormon Doctrine*, 2d ed. (Salt Lake City: Bookcraft, 1966), 69.
8. Spencer W. Kimball, "Becoming the Pure in Heart," *Ensign*, May 1978, 81.
9. Stephen E. Robinson, "Warring Against the Saints of God," *Ensign*, January 1988, 35.
10. Ibid., 37.
11. Maxwell, "'Settle This in Your Hearts,'" *Ensign*, November 1992, 66; emphasis added.
12. Kimball, "Becoming the Pure in Heart," 81.
13. See *Webster's Collegiate Dictionary, 11th Edition* (Springfield, Mass.: Merriam-Webster, Inc., 2005), s.v. "pure."
14. D. Todd Christofferson, "Come to Zion," *Ensign*, November 2008, 39.
15. "Because I Have Been Given Much," *Hymns of The Church of Jesus Christ of Latter-day Saints* (Salt Lake City: The Church of Jesus Christ of Latter-day Saints, 1985), no. 219.
16. McConkie, *The Millenial Messiah* (Salt Lake City: Deseret Book, 1982), 286.
17. Christofferson, "Come to Zion," 39.
18. "Israel, Israel, God Is Calling," *Hymns* [1985], no. 7.
19. Quentin L. Cook, "Lessons from the Old Testament: In the World but Not of the World," *Ensign*, February 2006, 54.
20. Kimball, "Becoming the Pure in Heart," 81; emphasis added.
21. David R. Stone, "Zion in the Midst of Babylon," *Ensign*, May 2006, 90.
22. Robinson, "Warring Against the Saints of God," 37.
23. Dr. William J. Doherty, "Let's Take Back Our Time"; available at: http://www.uuworld.org/2004/05/feature.2.html; accessed August 13, 2009.

24. Christofferson, "Come to Zion," 39.
25. Robert D. Hales, "Becoming Provident Providers Temporally and Spiritually," *Ensign*, May 2009, 8–9.
26. Hales, "Becoming Provident Providers Temporally and Spiritually," 8; emphasis in original.
27. Gordon B. Hinckley, "Living in the Fulness of Times," *Ensign*, November 2001, 6.
28. William Wordsworth, *The Collected Poems of William Wordsworth* (Hertfordshire: Wordsworth Editions Unlimited, 1995), 307.
29. Scott, "First Things First," 7.
30. Maxwell, "The Tugs and Pulls of the World," 36–37; emphasis in original.
31. Ibid., 35.
32. Ibid.
33. Brigham Young, *Journal of Discourses*, 26 vols. (London: Latter-day Saints Depot, 1954–86), 7:132; emphasis added.
34. Maxwell, "The Tugs and Pulls of the World," 36; emphasis in original.
35. Christofferson, "Come to Zion," 39; emphasis added.
36. William D. Longstaff (words) and George C. Stebbins (music), "Take Time to Be Holy," *The Methodist Hymnal* (Nashville, Tenn.: Methodist Publishing House, 1939), no. 455.

The Lord Looketh on the Heart

Pamela H. Hansen

Recently I overheard a woman talking on her cell phone. I heard her say to the person on the other end, "I'll tell you how my day is going. I had to stop and get a doughnut. That's how my day is going." Wouldn't it be nice if we could eat all the doughnuts or BYU mint brownies we wanted and they wouldn't affect our outward appearance or our hearts?

In 1 Samuel we learn that "the Lord seeth not as man seeth; for man looketh on the outward appearance, but the Lord looketh on the heart" (1 Samuel 16:7).

Have you ever considered just how important the heart is? The heart is the organ that is formed first and stops working last.

Our family learned just how important the heart is when we had a twin daughter who was diagnosed with a heart defect before she and her sister were born. We were faced with a wrenching reality of mortality—that her imperfect little physical body would not live long on the earth. Twelve years and three more children later, a sweet little stillborn son came into our family. Had he lived, this summer he would perhaps be looking forward to his baptism. Never did I imagine I would bury two

Pamela H. Hansen is a wellness coach and the author of Running with Angels *and* Finding the Angel Within. *She is a member of the Women's Advisory Board at Utah Valley Regional Medical Center and a marathon runner. She serves as a Young Women secretary. She and her husband, Mark, have seven children.*

children. And never did I imagine how sharing my story would help others to open up about the incredible adversity they, too, face in this life, and the comforting truth that we are surrounded by angels.

I love what Joseph Smith said, "If you live up to your privileges, the angels cannot be restrained from being your associates."[1]

I certainly felt the influence of my little angels when I lost one hundred pounds and ran my first marathon. And as I continue to strive to keep the weight off, I realize that while I may be a slow learner, I am learning! I am amazed at the remarkable creation that is a physical body. President Hinckley called it God's "crowning creation."[2]

But Elder Russell M. Nelson teaches us that as "remarkable as [our physical bodies are]," a body's "prime purpose is even of greater importance—to serve as tenement for [our] spirit[s]." He says, "Not an age in life passes without temptation, trial, or torment experienced through your physical body. But as you prayerfully develop self-mastery, desires of the flesh may be subdued. . . . [and] you may have the strength to submit to your Heavenly Father, as did Jesus, who said, 'Not my will, but thine, be done (Luke 22:42).'"[3]

However, as Sister Susan W. Tanner explains, Satan "has filled the world with lies and deceptions about the body . . . He tempts many to defile this great gift of the body through unchastity, immodesty, self-indulgence, and addictions. He seduces some to despise their bodies; others he tempts to worship their bodies. In either case, he entices the world to regard the body merely as an object."[4]

There are three questions we can ask ourselves as we change our focus from the outward appearance to the heart. They are:

- What is Heavenly Father trying to teach us?
- How much time and effort do we put forth in learning those lessons?
- What does it mean to truly understand we are children of God?

Often, the sweet simple messages our Father in Heaven is trying to teach us are drowned out by the blaring noise of the world. Unfortunately we cannot escape the world. We are bombarded every day with messages of how the world thinks we should look.

For instance, how many of you looked in the mirror this morning and felt as if you saw a beautiful reflection?

Recently a worldwide survey was taken and the statistics were reported by Dr. Nicole Hawkins, who counsels at the Center for Change in Utah County. When asked the question, "Do you feel beautiful?" what percentage of women throughout the world do you think would describe themselves as "beautiful"? According to the survey, only two percent of women in the world would describe themselves as "beautiful."

"The average model is 5'10" and weighs 110 pounds, whereas the average woman is 5'4" and weighs 144 pounds." It's nice to know that I am above average in some areas! "Only four percent of women genetically have the 'ideal' body currently presented in the media." Which means 96 percent—the rest of us—do not match up to the models and actresses presented in the media.[5]

Even if we don't compare ourselves to media images, we often find that we compare ourselves to the woman down the street, or the sister at church, who seems to have it all. We may see a snapshot view of her life and think that is how it is all the time, and we can't measure up. We compare our worst faults to others' best traits.

One of the greatest messages our Heavenly Father is trying to teach us has been given to us through Elder Jeffrey R. Holland. He counseled us, "Please be more accepting of yourselves, including your body shape and style, with a little less longing to look like someone else. We are all different. Some are tall, and some are short. Some are round, and some are thin. And almost everyone at some time or other wants to be something they are not! But as one adviser to teenage girls said: 'You can't live your life worrying that the world is staring at you. When you let people's opinions make you self-conscious you give away your power. . . . The key to feeling [confident] is to always listen to your inner self—[the *real* you.]' . . . Every young woman is a child of destiny and every adult woman a powerful force for good."[6]

What if we focused more on the stories our bodies could tell, rather than our initial observations? I recently read a column by Ann Cannon in the *Deseret News*. She talked about how her "body tells the story of a happy life." She relates how many women creatively work on scrapbooks. She realizes that her body *is* her scrapbook. She describes it as "my semi-permanent record of where I've been and what I did there." She describes the scar on her little finger from the oilcan in her grandpa's garage and the dead tooth she has because she never could resist jumping on a bed when her parents weren't looking. She goes on to describe "the non-specific 'souvenirs' of wear and tear: wrinkles, frown lines, laugh lines, crow's-feet, stiff feet, age spots, dry skin, crinkly neck." She says, "Frankly, I'm not sure I love how they look on me. But at least I'm happy (mostly) with the stories they tell."[7]

Often I find myself telling the Lord about those stories my body tells. Although I find myself complaining about various aches and pains and asking Him to fix this and take away that, what I hear Him gently answering me is not only to hang in there, but to keep moving forward, putting one foot in front of the other, and to not forget that He is more concerned about my heart. How often do we pause and see in ourselves as well as others the image that the Lord sees?

In considering the second question, "How much time and effort do we spend trying to learn lessons the Lord would have us understand?" we should think about how preoccupied we get with other distractions.

I was speaking once to a large group of people. As is usually the case when someone begins to speak, the pre-talk chatter in the room quieted down. One woman in the very back, however, continued to talk to her neighbors. She was trying to use a quiet voice but it was still quite distracting. She wouldn't quit talking. Once in a while she would stop and turn forward, but then she'd turn back and start chatting away. I became preoccupied with what this woman must be talking about with her neighbors. What could be that important that she was willing to be so rude to the speaker?

She came up afterward with some of the people she had been sitting by. I assumed she had not heard a word I had said. When she got to me she said, "I loved your talk. I would like you to meet my friends from Germany. I was translating everything you said."

Occasionally we find ourselves preoccupied by the judgments we make about how things appear. We may look in the mirror and think, "Oh, I wish I would have listened to my mother and put moisturizer on my face all these years!" We may look at our hips in the mirror and think, "I wish I wouldn't have spent so much time eating last night!" But do we ever say to ourselves, "I sure wish I wouldn't have exercised this morning!" or "I sure wish I wouldn't have spent so much time praying last night!"?

We can spend our time becoming preoccupied with self, with a fixation on the physical. This can be spiritually destructive, and accounts for much of the unhappiness in women, both young and not so young, in the world.

Elder Holland instructed us, "If adults are preoccupied with appearance—tucking and nipping and implanting and remodeling everything that can be remodeled—those pressures and anxieties will certainly seep through to children." If we are "obsessing over being a size 2, [we] won't be very surprised when [our] daughter or Mia Maid in [our] class does the same and makes herself physically ill trying to accomplish it."[8]

He goes on to give us some wise counsel: "We should all be as fit as we can be—that's good Word of Wisdom doctrine. That means eating right and exercising and helping our bodies function at their optimum strength. We could probably all do better in that regard. But I speak here of optimum health; there is no universal optimum size."[9]

Let us, sisters, not spend more time counting calories than counting our blessings. Kristen Oaks, wife of Elder Dallin H. Oaks, said, "Some may have a tendency to spend more time counting calories and working on their external appearance than counting their blessings and cleansing 'the inward vessel' (Alma 60:23)."[10]

It is important to take some time each day to rejuvenate ourselves physically as well as spiritually. On the days I set aside time to take a walk or lift some weights, I feel so much more ready to tackle the day. On the days I set aside time to read the scriptures, pray, or attend the temple, I am much more fit spiritually to handle daily challenges. My son just turned fifteen and got his learner's driving permit. I will definitely be spending more time on my knees!

Finally, we can ask ourselves the third question:

"What does it mean to truly understand that we are children of God?"

Several years ago, when my husband was working long hours and my extended family lived many hours away, I had three small children with one on the way. One day, when the house was a mess, the laundry was piled high, and it was too cold and too much effort to bundle up and go outside, there seemed to be sticky faces and dirty little fingers everywhere I turned. I wanted to just sit down and cry. I loved these children dearly. It seemed some days, though, that my house would never be clean again, that the days of finding time to shower, fix my hair, and put on my makeup without some sweet little interruption were gone for good, and I wondered if there would ever be a time again when I was not tired from lack of sleep.

I was searching through a drawer full of clutter and found some stickers that said "I am a child of God." I gathered my small children around me and put a sticker on each of them. I think we even sang "I Am a Child of God" together. What a difference it made! They kept the stickers on the rest of the day. They helped to serve as a reminder to me just whose those children were. I found that I had to give one daughter quite a few stickers before the day ended, and I even saved a few to stick on my husband after that long day! I certainly should have used a few stickers on myself, as it is important to understand that I am His child, too.

At Women's Conference in 1999, Truman Madsen said, "The Lord gives us glimpses of ourselves. And in self-examination we are most blessed when we see ourselves as we are seen by him and know ourselves as we are known by him; then, knowledge of the Savior and self-knowledge increase together. In this world, we do not really grasp who we are until we know whose we are."[11]

I'd like to tell you about my niece, Geraldine. She is the only daughter in a family of seven children. She recently turned twenty-six. She graduated a few years ago from BYU with a degree in statistics. She has been married now for six years to a wonderful man. She is the mother of two adorable girls, ages five and two. She has always wanted more children.

A year and a half ago, she was diagnosed with an aggressive brain cancer. It appears that there will be many earthly opportunities taken away from this sweet young woman. Her current situation, which includes her present abilities as wife, mother, and homemaker, has been greatly affected by her illness.

She has been working on her life history. As I have spent time visiting with her, I have felt of her tremendous spirit. She is such a sweet young woman who has already touched many hearts. I thank her for graciously allowing me to share excerpts from her journal:

"We define our earthly selves in different ways. Our definitions may include our looks, hair, and body shape; our ability to think and speak; our intelligence; our roles as women, including being a wife, mother, or future mother; our security and confidence; and our plans for the future. Cancer has stripped me of the attributes that I saw as my identity, but it has left the core identity that can never be touched: I am a child of God.

"Almost every measure of my identity has or will be affected. The only thing I feel certain of is that I am a child of God. That can't change, no matter what happens to my body, my mind, and my circumstances.

"I prayed to feel acceptance and love from God. It came. Then in prayer, I asked every question that I worried about. I got clear answers about everything. The answers weren't 'You're going to live, and have a great body, and all your trials are going to go away, and you'll have all your dreams come true.' Each answer was, 'Trust in me and I'll provide' and 'I love you and I love your family' and 'That's not really important right now, just wait,' and finally, 'Look for ways to serve.'

"I've had people tell me that they can't imagine a worse trial—terminal cancer, two to four years to live, two children, ages one and four, and just twenty-five years old. Crazy hair from surgeries and treatments, pain, endless doctor appointments and visits, not being able to have any more children . . . but I *know* God is aware of me. I can't describe the peace I feel, every day. Nothing matters beyond being happy today because I am a child of God."[12]

As Alma asked his people, so we can ask ourselves: "I say unto you, can you look up, having the image of God engraven upon your countenances?" (Alma 5:19). For no matter what sort of physical image looks back at you in the mirror, I testify that in the strength of the Lord, you can find joy as you seek to see yourself as He sees you.

NOTES

1. Joseph Smith, *History of the Church*, 4:605.
2. Gordon B. Hinckley, "Words of the Prophet: The Body Is Sacred," *New Era*, November 2006, 2.
3. Russell M. Nelson, "Self-Mastery," *Ensign*, November 1985, 30, 32.
4. Susan W. Tanner, "The Sanctity of the Body," *Ensign*, November 2005, 13.
5. See Nicole Hawkins, Ph.D., "Battling Our Bodies: Understanding and Overcoming Negative Body Images," http://www.centerforchange.com/articles/124; accessed October 13, 2009.
6. Jeffrey R. Holland, "To Young Women," *Ensign*, November 2005, 29; emphasis in original.

7. Ann Cannon, "Body tells the story of a happy life," *Deseret News*, April 12, 2009, C1.

8. Holland, "To Young Women," 29–30.

9. Ibid., 29.

10. Kristen M. Oaks, *A Single Voice* (Salt Lake City: Deseret Book, 2008), 236.

11. Truman Madsen, "The Savior, the Sacrament, and Self-Worth," in *The Arms of His Love: Talks from the 1999 Women's Conference Sponsored by Brigham Young University and the Relief Society* (Salt Lake City: Deseret Book, 1999), 246.

12. Geraldine Madariaga, personal journal, copy in author's possession.

THE SPIRITUAL LIGHT OF DISCERNMENT

Kristin Warner Belcher

In 2003, I was diagnosed with cancer behind my eye which left me completely blind. This was an absolutely devastating period of my life—both physically and emotionally. I am so grateful to many friends and family who surrounded me and helped me through months of surgeries and recovery.

As I became stronger and healthier, I again interacted with people in public. I was amazed at the things they said to me. Some spoke very loudly or slowly because, of course, if I am blind, then I must not be able to hear or think. I was even asked if I taught my children sign language so that we could communicate. Things like this still occur, and I am glad for a sense of humor, so that I can laugh about it all.

I am frequently asked what the hardest part is about being blind. My answer? Not being able to see! I miss seeing so many things. I miss the color green. I long to see the faces of my children and my husband. I miss seeing the beauty in nature and the changing of the seasons. I wish I could see to avoid the walls which I often run into, and the shoes that are inevitably left on the floor. But most of all, I miss light.

Light is what allows us to see. I no longer have the physical capability

---

Kristin Warner Belcher has a BS in therapeutic recreation from Brigham Young University, and served a mission to Kentucky Louisville. After battling cancer, in 2003 she completely lost her sight. She recently wrote a book about her experiences titled Hard Times and Holy Places. *She and her husband, James, have two children.*

to transfer outside light to my brain, and my days are now very dark. However, I do have the capacity to feel the light of my Savior.

I have learned so much as I have pondered light in my life. We learn in the Doctrine and Covenants that anything that does not edify "is not of God, and is darkness. That which is of God is light" (D&C 50:23–24). If we receive His light and continue in righteousness, we will gain more light, and this light can chase away the darkness.

Light warms, comforts, protects, directs, and leads. Light is truth. Light is one of Christ's names. Another of the Savior's titles is "Father of lights" (D&C 67:9). I love this absolutely beautiful description of the One who provides life and light to the whole world. In James 1:17, we read, "Every good gift and every perfect gift is from above, and cometh down from the Father of lights."

One of the magnificent gifts that we receive is the light of Christ. This allows each of us to distinguish between good and evil, or between light and darkness. If something edifies me and brings me closer to my Savior, then I know it is good and comes from God. If it does not edify, then I know it is darkness and doesn't come from the Father of lights. As we use the light of Christ, we are given more light; however, if we act contrary to it, the light decreases until we become "past feeling" (1 Nephi 17:45) and are no longer able to feel His light.

If we use and develop this spiritual gift, we can be led, protected, warned, and directed. There is another gift available to you and me, which the Father of lights will give us as we seek it. This is the spiritual gift of being quick to observe. Elder David A. Bednar has taught that with this gift, we "look," we "notice," and we "obey."[1]

It is so easy to see faults in others or in the way they do things. However, seeing imperfections and criticizing others is not the same as being quick to observe. When we are blessed with this gift, we notice and hearken to the counsel of our priesthood leaders. We learn from those around us. Each morning, we kneel and petition Heavenly Father to show us how we can be of service, and then act on the revelation we are given. We observe those in need: someone having a hard day, a child who needs encouragement, a job that needs to be done, or a lesson we need to learn. As we develop the gift of being quick to observe, we become prepared to receive another gift: the gift of discernment. Elder Bednar teaches us that "discerning is seeing with spiritual eyes and feeling with the heart—seeing and feeling the falsehood of an idea or the goodness in another person. Discerning is hearing with spiritual ears and feeling with the heart—hearing and feeling the unspoken concern in a statement or the truthfulness of a testimony or doctrine."[2]

Elder Bednar further explains the teachings of Elder George Q. Cannon and Elder Stephen L Richards regarding the gift of discernment, explaining that this gift helps us in four ways: It helps us to see the hidden error and evil in others, and in ourselves, and it helps us discover the concealed good in others and in ourselves.[3]

Isn't this a fabulous blessing? We can be warned of the ill intentions of others and also know of their goodness—which may be difficult to see. However, when we seek for this gift, we must also be ready to see in the mirror placed before us both the good and the error we possess.

So how does this gift actually operate in our everyday lives? Recently, I experienced firsthand the benefits of seeking the gift of discernment. I had a situation in which I was hurt by a family member and hurt him in return. I was so angry and critical of his behavior. I couldn't believe how rude he was to me.

That night, I couldn't sleep. Over and over again, I went through it all in my mind. I criticized him for his treatment of me. I had every right to be angry, didn't I?

However, I knew I didn't want to carry around the anger in my heart. I prayed for help. These principles that I have shared came into my mind and heart. I pled for Father to soften my heart and show me the good in this person. I was then aware of what I needed to change and began to see the situation from this person's perspective. I was led to know how to best handle the problem and I felt the anger and darkness leave.

Elder Oaks was right when he taught, "the primary reason we are commanded to avoid criticism is to preserve our own spiritual well-being, not to protect the person whom we would criticize."[4]

This holds true for our treatment of our children. It is very easy for me to be critical of my sons and become irritated with them. But this is a natural man's way of viewing things. As I choose a higher way, and try to be worthy of the spiritual gift of discernment, I have been helped to be slower to criticize, and have been able to feel and demonstrate more love for my children. Of course, I have a long way to go in developing this gift, but I have felt its effects in my heart and home.

Let's look at how this gift can change our tendency of nay-saying or being negative in our outlook. We can either observe the things going on around us and complain about them as a natural man would, or choose a higher way.

This is demonstrated in 1 Nephi 17 during the journey of Lehi's family through the wilderness. The experience was difficult for everyone, and yet the women, who had born children in the wilderness and had lived on raw meat, "began to bear their journeyings without murmurings" (1 Nephi 17:2). In contrast, Laman and Lemuel complained in their afflictions and wished they had remained in Jerusalem. Death, they thought, would have been better than the suffering they now experienced. Their attitudes are reflected in their words, "we might have been happy" (1 Nephi 17:21).

I would like to think that I would have been in the camp of the non-murmurers, but I have felt feelings similar to those of Laman and Lemuel. After I lost my vision, I didn't think I would ever be able to smile or laugh again. If only I hadn't had to go through the cancer and blindness, I might have been happy. I have experienced much healing, and am now able to be happy, but my earlier feelings were very real.

Perhaps you have thought, "If only I could have gotten married, I might have been happy." Or, "If only I hadn't gotten married, then I might have been happy." "If only my children would have made this or that choice, then I might have been happy." I invite you to evaluate your feelings and see if you might be suffering from the "we might have been happy" syndrome. This type of attitude is damaging and can halt our spiritual progression.

In addition, President Hinckley cautions us to beware of the spirit of negativity that permeates our societies today. His words from 1974 are completely relevant today. He described a time when, as he watched the news and read through several newspapers in Washington D. C., he observed the venom issuing from the reporters and pundits. They used their talent to craft words to bite at, criticize, and tear down President Ford. He said, "surely this is the age and place of the gifted pickle sucker."[5]

Do we ever qualify for the label of a "gifted pickle sucker"? Do our sour, complaining words illustrate our negativity? If so, how can we change our outlook and attitudes?

Again, we can rise above the natural man and seek for the spiritual gift of discernment—the gift to see the good around us, which may be disguised. With this gift, we will, as President Hinckley counseled, be able to "stop seeking out the storms and enjoy more fully the sunlight."[6] We, through the Spirit, will be able to "look a little deeper for the good, [and quiet] our voices of insult and sarcasm."[7] Then we will see the good where there really is good, and true evil which needs to be fought or avoided.

It is important to understand that with the gift of discernment, we are looking for hidden evil or evil influences. When we notice the faults, failings, or weaknesses of others, we need not confuse this with receiving spiritual warnings. Instead, we will pray to see the hidden good in those around us, and to learn the evil that may be within ourselves. We will not pass along disparaging comments about others, even if what we know is true.

Speaking about gossip, the Prophet Joseph Smith stated, "If the sisters [love] the Lord, let them feed the sheep, and not destroy them . . . Sisters of the society, shall there be strife among you? I will not have it. You must repent, and get the love of God. Away with self-righteousness."[8]

Self-righteous gossip will be eliminated from our lives as we strive to develop this spiritual gift. We will want to walk peaceably with others and before God. We will chase away darkness and walk in light.

I love the account of the people in Fourth Nephi who had no self-righteousness and "no contentions and disputations among them" (4 Nephi 1:2) because of the love of God in their hearts. There were no Lamanites or Nephites "nor any manner of -ites" (4 Nephi 1:17). There were no divisions or distinctions among the people, but they were all followers of Christ.

In our day—in our communities, in our homes—do we create -ites among ourselves? We may have the "neighbors who don't take care of their yard-ites," "members who take too long bearing their testimony-ites," "children who don't make their bed or clean their room-ites," or the "ones with all the money-ites." Creating -ites is another damaging way of being critical and finding fault with each other. However, we can rise above such tendencies and live a higher way.

I know that as we receive light from the Father of lights, and pray for and develop the spiritual gift of being quick to observe and the gift of discernment, we will be as the people in Fourth Nephi. Our hearts will be filled with the love of God. We will be less critical, less negative, and seek only to build up those around us. We will qualify for this beautiful promise from the Prophet Joseph Smith, "If you will put away from your midst all evil speaking, backbiting, and ungenerous thoughts and feelings: humble yourselves, and cultivate every principle of virtue and love, then will the blessings of Jehovah rest upon you, and you will yet see good and glorious days; peace will be within your gates, and prosperity in your borders."[9]

NOTES

1. David A. Bednar, "Quick to Observe," *Ensign*, December 2006, 32.
2. Ibid., 36.
3. Ibid., 35–36.
4. Dallin H. Oaks, "Criticism," *Ensign*, February 1987, 68.
5. Gordon B. Hinckley, "Let Not Your Heart Be Troubled," *Speeches of the Year 1974* (Provo: Brigham Young University Press, 1975), 266.
6. Ibid.
7. Ibid.
8. Joseph Smith, *History of the Church*, 5:24.
9. Ibid., 4:226.

Thou Shalt Be Made Strong

Vicki F. Matsumori

About five years ago while vacationing in Florence, Italy with my husband, Jim, I rolled my foot on a cobblestone, resulting in a broken right ankle. Miraculously, and with the help of a priesthood blessing, I managed to walk with very little pain for the next four days until we arrived home.

Actually, this ankle weakness isn't something new. Over the years I have on numerous occasions twisted my ankle resulting in falls that left me with skinned knees and scraped elbows. That is probably not an unusual look for a nine-year-old girl. However, I tumbled down stairs in my high school; I tripped up stairs trying to get to my college classes on time. Even the painted lines used to designate parking stalls give me an occasional problem.

So, since breaking my right ankle five years ago, I have diligently done toe raises and ankle circles. Not only have I written the alphabet with my foot, I've composed full-length essays by wiggling my sneakers around. And I've done all of this with the intent of strengthening this physical weakness.

Vicki F. Matsumori is the second counselor in the Primary general presidency. She earned her bachelor's degree in journalism and English with a teaching certificate from the University of Utah. She has taught junior high school English and was an adjunct instructor at Salt Lake Community College. She has served as a member of the Primary General Board, a member of a stake Relief Society board, a ward Primary president, Relief Society president, Young Women president, and Young Women adviser. She and her husband, James, have three children and one grandchild.

What has been the result of all this hard work? Recently the Draper Temple was dedicated. Jim and I were invited to attend one of the dedicatory services in the temple. As instructed, we arrived an hour early and the first thing we were asked to do was cover our shoes with white booties so we wouldn't get the temple carpet dirty. It was just at the entrance to the temple that I did a face plant. And yes, I sprained my ankle—this time it was my left ankle, and I also skinned my right knee.

Just imagine what I looked like, sitting in the temple with a throbbing left ankle and something wet oozing from my right knee, slowly working its way down my shin. I wondered how I was ever going to make it to the celestial kingdom if I couldn't even show up to the celestial room without dirt on my skirt and holes in my panty hose. The analogies to my life were glaring. Despite my best efforts at strengthening and overcoming a lifelong weakness, it seemed there had been no progress.

Thankfully I received comfort in the form of a talk by Sister Cheryl C. Lant, the Primary general president. Her message at the temple dedication was that we did not need to be perfect to attend the temple. We only needed to be worthy. That was my answer. Although not perfect, I have diligently tried to overcome my failings. And that was sufficient. Perhaps what I can best share with you is what I have learned about overcoming weaknesses "in the strength of the Lord."

Everyone Has Weaknesses

Weaknesses are just part of our mortal experience. At the fall of Adam, man was introduced into a world filled with frailties, problems, temptations, and trials. He became a "natural man" (see Mosiah 3:19) with tendencies to be greedy, short-tempered, judgmental, and disorganized. Other shortcomings included failings in athletic, musical, speaking, or writing abilities. And there were physical limitations, financial circumstances, or family situations which also proved challenging.

What I have learned over the years is that everyone deals with limitations in strength, power, and knowledge. Even great prophets have felt the weight of being imperfect. Just three years after receiving the First Vision, Joseph Smith reflected on the persecutions he had encountered and said, "I often felt condemned for my weakness and imperfections" (JS–H 1:29).

Nephi cried out, "O wretched man that I am! Yea, my heart sorroweth because of my flesh; my soul grieveth because of mine iniquities. I am encompassed about, because of the temptations and the sins which do so easily beset me" (2 Nephi 4:17–18).

Moroni, who was responsible for keeping the Nephite records, expressed concern about his weakness in writing. He told the Lord, "thou hast made us mighty in word by faith, but thou hast not made us mighty in writing. . . . And thou hast made us that we could write but little, because of the awkwardness of our hands. . . . Thou hast also made our words powerful and great, even that we cannot write them; wherefore, when we write we behold our weakness, and stumble because of the placing of our words" (Ether 12:23–25).

It is from Moroni's experience that we learn about the purpose of weaknesses in our lives and what we can do to overcome them. The Lord said, "And if men come unto me I will show unto them their weakness. I give unto men weakness that they may be humble; and my grace is sufficient for all men that humble themselves before me; for if they humble themselves before me, and have faith in me, then will I make weak things become strong unto them" (Ether 12:27).

WHAT IS MY WEAKNESS?

It may seem strange to have to ask the Lord to show us our shortcomings. Sometimes we feel that our failings are all too evident to those around us. But the Lord tells us that if we come to Him, He will show us our weakness. Perhaps it is necessary to go to the Lord because it is not always easy to discern our real weakness.

For example, was my fall several weeks ago really caused by weak ankles? Or was it caused by my love of cute, but very impractical shoes? Oh, no! That just can't be. Or, if I want to be painfully honest, was the reason I was wearing cute, but impractical high-heeled shoes to a temple dedication due to the weakness of pride? Perhaps I was merely proof that "pride cometh before the fall."

Elder Neal A. Maxwell once observed, "It is not an easy thing . . . to be shown one's weaknesses. . . . Nevertheless, this is part of coming unto Christ, and it is a vital, if painful, part of God's plan of happiness."[1]

With the Lord's help, we can know our weaknesses. We can recognize those traits which are inherent because of our mortality, and we can become aware of those challenges custom-designed for us individually. What is important is that once we have identified our weakness, we work to either overcome it or to change it into a strength.

WHY HAVE I BEEN GIVEN MY SPECIFIC WEAKNESS?

Not surprisingly, our initial reaction to identifying our weakness may be a "why me" attitude. We may think it's unfair that others do not have to struggle with a short temper or with shyness. We may want to know what we have done to warrant coming from a broken home, or living with a physical impairment. However, those weaknesses are ours for a purpose. You might recall that the Lord stated that "I give unto men weakness that they may be humble" (Ether 12:27).

I love a story Sheri Dew tells that illustrates how our circumstances can make us humble. A mother of eight children was briefly frazzled one afternoon as she worked with her young children. She called her husband for comfort at that difficult moment. With humor in her voice she said to her husband, "Remind me, why *did* we have eight children?" To this he replied, "Because the Lord knew we could have handled seven just fine."[2]

Being humble makes us aware of our dependence on God. The Apostle Paul had what he called "a thorn in the flesh." He wrote, "For this thing I besought the Lord thrice, that it might depart from me" (2 Corinthians 12:7–8). We may have similarly called upon the Lord repeatedly to help remove a thorn from our own flesh. However, that thorn was a reminder to Paul and our thorns are a reminder to us of our complete dependence upon the Lord.

The Lord taught the children of Israel this principle. In Judges we read that under the direction of Gideon, the Israelites gathered an army of 32,000 men to fight against the Midianites. The Lord told Gideon that that was too many men and to have those who were frightened return to their homes. 22,000 men departed, leaving an army of 10,000. This was still too many. The Lord told Gideon to take the men down to some water to drink. The men would have to drink by either putting their heads to the water or by cupping their hands and bringing the water to their mouths. Only 300 men drank by cupping their hands. The Lord wanted them. So with an army of 300 men—not 32,000—the Israelites went out to fight and defeat the Midianites (see Judges 7).

Why did the Lord send the Israelites into battle with such a distinct disadvantage? Because with a large army, the tendency for the Israelites would have been to take credit for their triumph. But with only 300 soldiers, it was very clear that the victory had come because of the Lord's help, and not because of their own ability. They had won "in the strength of the Lord."

Without challenges we too may want to take credit for our successes. Instead, when we are aware of our weakness, we realize that we are completely dependent on the Lord for help. Occasionally, we may want to excuse our shortcomings by blaming others for them or by telling others, "That's just the way I am."

However, President Spencer W. Kimball counseled, "One's parents may have failed; our own backgrounds may have been frustrating, but as sons and daughters of a living God we have within ourselves the power to rise above our circumstances, to change our lives. Man can change human nature. Man must transform his life . . . We can overcome. We must control and master ourselves."[3]

WHAT CAN I DO TO CHANGE?

I love the quote that President Heber J. Grant popularized: "That which we persist in doing becomes easier for us to do; not that the nature of the thing itself is changed, but that our power to do is increased."[4]

I believe that to be true. I've even imposed that philosophy on our own children. Like any good mother of a Suzuki-method music student, I encouraged our daughter, Kathryn, to repeatedly practice the hardest parts of her violin solos first. And we could tell that as her ability to play those difficult sections increased, the rest of the piece became easier for her to play.

The world has many other theories on how to improve oneself. You can buy self-help books, view self-improvement courses online, or check into self-control clinics. Yet clearly something more is needed. Whether it is weak ankles—my euphemism for "pride"—recurring addictions, or anger management, the world's solutions are not sufficient.

It is only through coming to Christ with faith and humility that we truly can change. His grace is sufficient to help us make such a transformation. The Bible Dictionary defines grace as an "enabling power."[5] That enabling power can change us.

Elder Bruce C. Hafen wrote, "The Savior desires to save us from our inadequacies as well as our sins. Inadequacy is not the same as being sinful—we have far more control over the choice to sin than we may have over our innate capacity . . . A sense of falling short or falling down is not only natural but essential to the mortal experience. Still, after all we can do, the Atonement can fill that which is empty, straighten our bent parts, and make strong that which is weak."[6]

You'll remember Paul's feelings about the thorn he carried. As far as we know, that thorn was never removed. However, Paul wrote: "I can do all things through Christ which strengtheneth me" (Philippians 4:13). It is the Atonement of Jesus Christ that allows each of us to remove our thorn or to help us turn that thorn into a source of strength. In either situation, it is with the help of the Lord we are able to move forward with our lives with renewed commitment.

Several months ago I met a beautiful young sister at the MTC. Sister Slaeman was born in Iraq and then relocated with her family to a refugee camp where she lived for nine years. It was in this camp that her family met the missionaries. They were baptized several years later. But that is not the end of her story.

The Atonement has allowed her to move forward. She writes, "I was in one of the most dysfunctional families: lots of abuse and more. Six months after we were baptized, my family went inactive and they did not allow me to go to church. Two years later I moved out and made the choice to go back to church. I can't explain how hard it was. I cried myself to sleep every night for months . . . I stayed in bed for days sometimes . . . I viewed myself as nobody. [But] I had a testimony that the Atonement could fix that.

"Changing my life around was not easy . . . but the light of the Atonement of Jesus Christ gave me comfort and hope that I was here for a reason. Through faith and praying daily, I came to a greater knowledge of the Atonement and the healing power of it started working in my life more and more.

"I know I would not be going to Romania to serve, if it was not for my Savior. It would be impossible for someone like me to be a missionary without my Savior, Jesus Christ."[7]

Today Sister Slaeman is a missionary in Romania. She serves with little family support but with the best support system of all—an understanding and knowledge of the Atonement of Jesus Christ. The Lord said: "These commandments are of me, and were given unto my servants in their weakness, after the manner of their language, that they might come to understanding. . . . And inasmuch as they were humble they might be made strong, and blessed from on high, and receive knowledge from time to time" (D&C 1:24, 28).

How Can I Turn My Weakness into a Strength?

Just as the Lord promised, we too can "be made strong, and blessed from on high, and receive knowledge from time to time." With His help, we can turn our weaknesses into strengths.

I love a story circulating via e-mail that illustrates this. It tells of a ten-year-old boy who decided to study judo despite the fact that he had lost his left arm in a car accident. The boy's lessons with an old Japanese judo master went very well. Yet this ten-year-old couldn't understand why after three months of training the master had only taught him one move.

The boy finally asked, "Sensei, shouldn't I be learning more moves?"

The sensei patiently explained, "This is the only move you know, but it is the only move you'll ever need to know."

Not understanding, but trusting his teacher, the boy continued to practice the one move. Several months later the boy entered his first tournament. Surprisingly, he easily won his first two matches. The third match was more difficult, but using his one move, the boy won the match.

Now the boy was in the finals. This time his opponent was bigger, stronger, and more experienced. At first the boy seemed to be over-matched. The referee called a time-out. Fearing for the young boy's safety, he wanted to stop the match. But the sensei intervened and said, "Let the boy continue."

Soon after the match resumed, the opponent made a mistake. He dropped his guard. Instantly the boy used his move to win the match and the tournament. He was the champion.

On the way home, the boy summoned enough courage to ask what he really wanted to know, "Sensei, how did I win the tournament with only one move?"

The sensei replied, "You won for two reasons. First, you've mastered one of the most difficult throws in all of judo. And second, the only known defense for that move is for your opponent to grab your left arm."

THE LIFELONG PROCESS

We too only need to master one move—and that is to develop faith so we can rely upon our Savior Jesus Christ and His Atonement. However, learning to master that move is a lifelong pursuit. It takes time, and sometimes we may wonder if we really are making progress (like with my weak ankles). Why is that the case?

C. S. Lewis gave us insight. He said: "When a man turns to Christ and seems to be getting on pretty well (in the sense that some of his bad habits are now corrected) he often feels that it would now be natural if things went fairly smoothly. When troubles come along—illnesses, money troubles, new kinds of temptation—he is disappointed. These things, he feels, might have been necessary to rouse him and make him repent in his bad old days; but why now?"[8]

That's the question I think we all ask: Why now? Why are there still challenges even when we have worked to overcome them? I love the answer Lewis gives:

"Because God is forcing him on, or up, to a higher level: putting him into situations where he will have to be very much braver, or more patient, or more loving, than he ever dreamed of being before. It seems to us all unnecessary: but that is because we have not yet had the slightest notion of the tremendous thing He means to make of us."[9]

That is why our trials and weaknesses continue even when we have made efforts to overcome them. It is why the Lord wants us to be humble, to have faith in Him, to depend on Him and to understand how to use the Atonement in our lives. We are His children. We have a divine inheritance and "we have not yet the slightest notion of the tremendous thing He means to make of us."

The 1968 Summer Olympics, held in Mexico City, produced a little-known story with a message for all of us about our efforts to never give up. I identify with it because the story involves an injured knee.

John Stephen Akhwari, representing Tanzania, was one of the favorites to win the marathon, but halfway through the race he fell. He had a gash in his calf and an injured knee. Rather than quitting, Akhwari continued to run. More than an hour after the 73 other marathon runners had crossed the finish line and the medals had been awarded, word was passed to the press box and then down to the few thousand spectators who had remained in the stadium. The final runner was approaching. It was John Stephen Akhwari.

With "his leg bloody and bandaged," and wincing with every step, Akhwari hobbled on. Those who were in attendance stood and cheered for this racer who limped around the track to finish dead last. The reporters later asked him why he had continued to run when he was obviously in pain and had absolutely no chance of winning. He simply answered, "My country did not send me to Mexico City to start the race. They sent me to finish."[10]

We too have been sent to finish a race. We have been sent to earth not with the expectation of being the first, the best, the brightest, the prettiest, or the strongest. We have been sent to earth with the intent that we would strive to overcome our challenges and imperfections with humility and faith, thus enabling us to ultimately return to the presence of our Father in Heaven.

When we finish that race, having done our best and with the help of the Atonement, we are promised, "Because thou hast seen thy weakness thou shalt be made strong, even unto the sitting down in the place which I have prepared in the mansions of my Father" (Ether 12:37).

NOTES

1. Neal A. Maxwell, "Hope through the Atonement of Jesus Christ," *Ensign*, November 1998, 63.

2. Sheri Dew, *God Wants a Powerful People* (Salt Lake City: Deseret Book, 2007), 89; emphasis in original.

3. Spencer W. Kimball, *Faith Precedes the Miracle* (Salt Lake City: Deseret Book, 1976), 176.

4. In Heber J. Grant, *Gospel Standards: Selections from the Sermons and Writings of Heber J. Grant,* ed. G. Homer Durham (Salt Lake City: Deseret Book, 1941), 354.

5. Bible Dictionary, s.v. "Grace," 697.

6. Bruce C. Hafen, *The Broken Heart* (Salt Lake City: Deseret Book, 1989), 19–20.

7. Personal correspondence in the author's possession.

8. C. S. Lewis, *Mere Christianity* (San Francisco: HarperCollins, 1980), 204–5.

9. Ibid.

10. See http://en.beijing2008.cn/education/stories/n214077658.shtml; accessed October 13, 2009.

"I Can Do All Things through Christ Which Strengtheneth Me"

Cheryl C. Lant

I have been asked to speak on the scripture found in Philippians 4:13, "I can do all things through Christ which strengtheneth me." More specifically, the title of this session is "Facing Challenges in the Strength of the Lord."

When I received my assignment, I couldn't help but contemplate the many challenges that are present in our everyday lives—all of our everyday lives. By this I mean every day, and every woman. I thought of women whose families are struggling economically, struggling just to keep their jobs, their homes, their security. I thought of the sweet woman who weeps every day because her husband is not living up to the priesthood which he holds and is breaking eternal covenants as he views pornography and is unfaithful. I thought of the mother who struggles to find ways to help her wayward son or rebellious daughter. I thought of the single mom who has to do it all. I thought of the young mother who has so many children she doesn't know what to do, and the young wife who grieves because there

---

Cheryl C. Lant is the general president of the Primary. She studied early childhood development at Brigham Young University and has spent most of her adult life teaching children, both as the mother of nine and as an educator. She is the cofounder and co-owner with her husband of Learning Dynamics Academic Preschool and the cofounder and developer of Frontline Phonics, a beginning reading program. She has served as a member of the Primary General Board, a stake and ward Primary president, a counselor in a stake Relief Society presidency, a ward Young Women president, and as a Primary teacher. She and her husband, John, have nine children.

are no children at all. I thought of the woman who has never married and who is searching for her purpose. I thought of women who care for their aging and ailing parents. I thought of women who have been abandoned and women who have lost faith and turned to sin in their own lives. I thought of those who have lost hope. I thought of women whose husbands and sons are away serving in the military. I thought of women who are ill themselves or who care for loved ones in poor health. I thought of the young widow, the older widow, those who are weary, those who are lonely. I thought of those who are grieving. I thought of those who have heavy responsibility and stress in their lives, and, on the other hand, those who long for something productive and meaningful to do. I thought of women who lack confidence or, even worse, have lost sight of who they are. I thought of women whose faith and endurance are being tested. Then my thoughts went to you, each of you, knowing that while each of our challenges are unique and personal, we all have them, and so I wondered what burdens you brought with you today. I wondered what the Lord would have us learn so that we might access His help and His love.

During this process of preparation, I came to realize more fully how much I have learned through my experiences, and how much I am continually learning as I move through my own unique learning opportunities. Now, I call my challenges "learning opportunities" because I think that challenges and struggles are part of Heavenly Father's plan. We must struggle in order to grow. We must sorrow in order to rejoice. We must be sent seeking in order to find. Now, you may be thinking, "Wait, I didn't sign up for this!" But actually you did, and so did I. In some ways, knowing this can help us, because knowing that having challenges is part of the plan means we do not need to see ourselves as alone or somehow targeted to suffer. We can accept this as a pattern of life that is part of life and that will bring us eternal life if we will let it. We can know that the very challenges that we seek to overcome are the means by which we can attain great blessings.

I want to share with you one of my most recent challenges. It was a situation that I never would have chosen to experience, but through which I have learned much about the special help that comes from Heavenly Father through the Atonement of Jesus Christ.

Just nine months ago, in July 2008, my husband and I received a phone call just as we returned home from a morning walk. It was our daughter-in-law telling us that her husband, our youngest son, had been in an accident on his way to work and had been taken to the hospital, and asking us to meet her there. We jumped into the car and took the freeway. On the way we kept reassuring ourselves that everything would be all right—praying silently that it would be so.

As we exited the freeway, we found ourselves right in the middle of the accident scene. There were about eight emergency vehicles and a TV news crew there, and we began to realize the gravity of the situation. Minutes later, as we walked into the emergency room, we were greeted with the words that no parents ever want to hear. The accident had been fatal. Our son had been on his motorcycle and had been hit by a semitrailer truck. He had died on impact. He left behind a wonderful wife and three beautiful daughters. It was a tragic accident for our family, for the driver of the truck, and for his family.

But it also began a beautiful experience for us. We immediately felt the enveloping love of the Lord, even as we processed the information we had just received. And even though we have had moments of intense grief, and of seeking the help of our Heavenly Father, we have also learned a great deal about how His help comes, and have even felt a great gratitude for this opportunity to experience a new dimension of the Atonement.

Now, I have chosen to share this today, not because I want to dwell on any of our specific challenges, but because I want to talk about what we learn as we go through them. We are going to focus on what we can do about our challenges and how the influence of the Holy Ghost can help us access the blessings of the Atonement of Jesus Christ.

We may each face our challenges a little differently. This is because we are different from one another. We are different in talents and gifts, different in weaknesses, different in personality, different in circumstance and opportunity. And yet, as I look into your faces, I know that even more important than our differences are our similarities. We are alike in many ways. Each of us is a daughter of a loving Father in Heaven. Each of us has the gospel of Jesus Christ, and the great blessing of the Atonement. Each of us has agency to choose for ourselves. Each of us has a great longing to live well, become better than we are, experience joy, and find peace in our lives. For this reason, we are going to talk about some of the principles of the gospel that are common to us all. These are principles that can strengthen us and help us find what we are seeking, even through the trials of this earthly life.

The first and foundational principle we need to understand is faith in the Lord Jesus Christ, and more specifically, faith in His Atonement. In our heads we understand that Christ atoned for our sins and died that we might live. We believe in repentance and the Resurrection. Jesus Christ has made the Atonement. It is already done. He has experienced all that we are experiencing—every pain, every worry, every sorrow, every illness, every disappointment, every regret for sin. He has paid the ultimate price for all of it, for all of us. He loves us beyond our understanding. These are the things we know, but we must have faith in them and take them deep into our hearts, in order to really understand and to be able to allow the Atonement to take effect in our lives. I say allow, because it is up to us to accept the Atonement's great blessings. We allow the Atonement as we have faith in it. We allow the Atonement as we give our challenges and problems to the Lord, and trust that He can take them. He can remove them from us if it is His will. Or if it is not, through the Holy Ghost He can strengthen us, and help us work through them. He can help us endure. He can help us find solutions. He can calm our spirit and comfort our troubled heart. He can do it all.

You will remember the story of Nephi and Laman and Lemuel found in 1 Nephi. After they had obtained the brass plates from Laban, they were sent back to Jerusalem to get Ishmael and his household. I'm sure this was somewhat of a challenge for Nephi and his brethren, although it was a rather pleasant one, considering that Ishmael had a household full of daughters. These young men were able, with the help of the Lord, to persuade Ishmael to leave his home and everything he had to travel in the wilderness with them. But they were not far into the journey when Laman and Lemuel and some of Ishmael's children once again began to murmur and complain. They wanted to return to Jerusalem. I believe what Nephi said to them has a message for us today:

"Yea, and how is it that ye have forgotten that the Lord is able to do all things according to his will, for the children of men, if it so be that they exercise faith in him? Wherefore, let us be faithful to him" (1 Nephi 7:12).

In this case the challenge facing Nephi and his family was not taken away. They still had to leave everything and travel into the wilderness, under great hardship, but the Lord blessed them. Eventually they reached the promised land and we have their wonderful record as a second witness of Jesus Christ. But this account also gives a witness "that the Lord is able to do all things according to his will." This tells me that if it is for my best good, the Lord can take the challenge away, but it must be according to His will—and it is all dependent upon our faith. We have to allow the Atonement and accept His will for our lives. Doing this brings great peace.

So the question arises, "How do we do this?—How do we allow the Atonement to work in our lives?" It begins by having the desire to let Jesus into our lives—a desire to let Him help us carry our burdens. It begins with a humble heart. Have you ever felt like your heart was broken? Have you ever felt it right here in your chest? It is very painful, and yet, in the words of a friend of mine, a broken heart is an open heart. Visualize that with me. A broken heart is an open heart. An open heart is ready to be healed and can let the influence of the Holy Ghost and the healing power of the Atonement inside. It is a humble heart. A humble heart is a believing heart. And what does it mean to have a believing heart? It means that, aside from knowing that the Savior made the Atonement, each of us must believe that He did it for *me* and that it will work for *me*.

That is a problem for some of us. Perhaps we feel we have done things that have somehow worked us outside the circle of His atoning reach. Or perhaps we have misinterpreted the idea that "after all we can do" (2 Nephi 25:23), the Lord will make up the difference, meaning that we are on our own until after we have done "all we can do." Maybe we just don't think we are worth it, or that our problems are too small for Him to worry about. Or maybe we feel angry that we have problems at all. Maybe we are worn down and are weary of the fight. Whatever the reason for our not allowing the Atonement to help us, the bottom line is that if we do not, we pay the price. For the person who does not accept the healing powers of His Atonement, it is as if it did not happen at all.

I bear my witness to you that the Atonement of Jesus Christ is real. He paid for our sins. He died for us so that we might live. He suffered the pain of every sin, of every sorrow, of every illness, and, as Elder Holland taught us in April 2009 general conference, the pain of spiritual death, in order to know how he could succor us in our need.[1] He did this because He loves us absolutely and completely with a perfect love. He never will turn His back on us. He will bless us and help us along every step of every challenge we have to face. All of this He will do, He is waiting to do, if we will just allow Him to do it.

If you do not know these things for yourselves, seek to know. Seek to have the witness of the Holy Ghost. Seek to have the Holy Ghost with you at all times because it is through the Holy Ghost that Christ blesses you. Seek to have faith sufficient to access the blessings you so desire. I know that you can know. As we are told in Doctrine & Covenants 4:7, "Ask, and ye shall receive; knock, and it shall be opened unto you."

Perhaps one of the questions you have is "How do I ask? How do I knock so that I might have that kind of faith?" The answers are rather basic. In fact, I am sure they are on your "to do" list already. They are things like pray, read the scriptures, go to the temple, and fast. They are probably part of your daily routine right now. So why are you feeling that your faith is inadequate or that you cannot find the peace you desire? Perhaps the answer lies in how we do these things. Do we do them just because we are supposed to do them? Do we do them so that we can check them off our list? Or are we really seeking the Lord?

When we pray do we express the feelings of the man who brought his son to the Savior that he might heal him? When he asked Jesus to heal his son, Jesus said:

"If thou canst believe, all things are possible to him that believeth. And straightway the father of the child cried out, and said with tears, Lord, I believe; help thou mine unbelief" (Mark 9:23–24).

Those last words, "help thou mine unbelief" are so important. Here was a man really seeking. He wanted to believe. He prayed that his belief would be magnified in order to receive the desired blessing. He depended on the Lord for it all, for the process of getting there, and for the blessing. Do we pray like that, praying to our Heavenly Father in the name of His Son for the strength to be faithful enough to receive the blessing we want? Do we pray with great desire, and then listen with a quiet and willing heart? Do we get up from our knees and move forward with a will to do what the Holy Ghost directs?

When we read the scriptures, do we just read, or do we seek the Holy

Ghost to help us as we ponder and pray and apply the principles to our own lives with a desire and determination to do better, and be better? Do we seek answers from the Lord through the scriptures, knowing that they are His voice to us? Do we routinely pray for a witness of the doctrines we learn in the scriptures?

When we go to the temple and when we fast, do we do it in a spirit of worship and with a deep desire to draw closer to the Lord and learn of Him? Do we allow ourselves to receive answers to our questions and prayers while we do these things? Do we allow the sweet Spirit in the temple to wrap around us and fill us with comfort and peace?

I ask these questions of you, but I also have to ask them of myself—continually—in order to feel the Atonement working in my life. It seems that I have to start over every time a challenge arises. It seems to be a continual cycle. I try to keep my self spiritually prepared for life's trials, but then along comes a new challenge. My "mother's heart" wants to fix it, to make it better. I struggle along, worry a lot, and generally feel miserable. When I finally really go to my Heavenly Father and seek the blessing of Christ's Atonement and let Him lift the burden from me, there is always sweet relief.

This happened just as I was preparing this talk. I became aware of some real difficulties in one of our families. For a day and a half I struggled with that knowledge, not knowing what I should do, what I could do. It affected me in many ways. Finally, I awoke in the middle of the night, fretting. The thought came into my mind, "You need to do yourself what you are teaching these sisters to do in your talk." That was it. I knew that these principles are true—I needed to act on them myself. So I got up and spent some time in prayer, pouring my heart out to my Heavenly Father, telling Him that I trusted Him to take this challenge and handle it His way, and telling Him that I was willing to be an instrument in His hands if He would help me to know what I should do to help. When I returned to bed, I felt the comfort of the Holy Ghost. I felt relief, I felt peace, I felt ideas flowing into my mind about what I needed to do. Now, the challenge has not gone away, and it will not for some time. But I know that Heavenly Father loves me and my family and He is blessing us to work through this situation and will continue to do so as long as we look to

Him. This is possible because of the Atonement of His Son, Jesus Christ. Blessings come from the Father, through the Son, by the Holy Ghost.

Our family had this same experience at the passing of our son. Our hearts were broken, but even though it was hard and we struggled, we endeavored to look, individually and collectively, to our Heavenly Father in prayer, in the scriptures, in the temple. Through the Holy Ghost we felt His love and His direction in our lives. We have worked to move forward, keeping the commandments so that we might be reunited as a family one day. We have continued to serve others, thereby serving the Lord. And all of this that we might be counted worthy to partake of all of the blessings of the Atonement of Jesus Christ—blessings of comfort, blessings of accept-ance, blessings of commitment, blessings of hope, blessings of increased faith, blessings of increased unity and love in our family, blessings of grat-itude, blessings of peace. And these blessings have come and continue to come.

So, when challenges come, as surely they must—where do we look? We have to make a choice. Do we allow ourselves to look down, filled with worry, discouragement, anger, and despair? Do we look inward, thinking only of ourselves and how hard life is? Or do we look up to the Father for help? Do we look to Him with trust and confidence that He will not give us more to deal with than we can handle? (At least it will not be more than we can handle if we have His help.)

Then do we look forward and get up and get moving? There is great power in movement and it takes faith to move forward and do. This means being strictly obedient to all of our Father's commandments, really trying every day to make the gospel part of our lives, knowing that we can never justify a lack of faithful obedience just because things are hard. Then, as we look up and look forward, do we gain the strength to look out to others and serve, knowing that if we can relieve the stress and pain in someone else's life, we are qualifying ourselves for blessings as well? Remember that in the scriptures Jesus taught,

"He that findeth his life shall lose it: and he that loseth his life for my sake shall find it" (Matthew 10:39).

These are some of the things that we can do to allow the Atonement of Jesus Christ to bless our lives. As we do, we become stronger and stronger; and each time we have a new challenge to face, we can do it with greater faith and confidence in Jesus Christ. We no longer need to run to and fro wringing our hands wondering what to do. That takes far too much time and energy—energy that could be used to access relief from the Lord. We can believe His words as recorded in Doctrine & Covenants 101:16, "Therefore, let your hearts be comforted . . . for all flesh is in mine hands; be still and know that I am God."

We can also learn from Joseph Smith's experience in Liberty Jail, where he had suffered severe persecution. He struggled desperately, even asking God, "O God, where art thou? And where is the pavilion that covereth thy hiding place?" (D&C 121:1).

Joseph felt that God had somehow forgotten him and all of the saints as well, for their suffering was so great. He received this reassurance, "My son, peace be unto thy soul; thine adversity and thine afflictions shall be but a small moment; And then, if thou endure it well, God shall exalt thee on high; thou shalt triumph over all thy foes" (D&C 121:7–8).

Because of this assurance, Joseph was able to teach us, "Let us cheerfully do all things that lie in our power; and then may we stand still, with the utmost assurance, to see the salvation of God, and for his arm to be revealed" (D&C 123:17).

We cannot always avoid or change the challenges in our lives. But we can look up to the Lord and allow His Atonement to bless and cleanse our lives, bringing us peace and reassurance even amid the trials. We can receive personal revelation to give us direction and hope. We can look forward and cheerfully do all that we can do to bring about a positive resolution to our problems, trusting that through the Holy Ghost He will help us and that His Atonement will make up the difference in the end. And we can look outward to serve and lift others around us, finding relief as we forget ourselves. In this way, we not only become stronger but we can strengthen and protect our families that they also may feel the blessings of the Atonement.

Life will always have its challenges, but we can be led to find answers. As we face our challenges by allowing the Atonement to bless our lives, we can be refined by the fire of the very adversity we sometimes wish to avoid. We can become more faithful and hopeful. We can feel peace within ourselves and with the Lord. We can be filled with gratitude for all of God's blessings, even those that come at great cost. We can recognize that we are all in His hands and that He will lead us back to His presence, where no more will we feel pain or despair. In this, we can truly come to know the sweetness of the Atonement of Jesus Christ.

NOTE

1. See Jeffrey R. Holland, "None Were with Him," *Ensign*, May 2009, 86–88.

GOSPEL LIVING

"I Love to See the Temple"

Elaine S. Dalton

It is a privilege to share with you my feelings about the most sacred and holy place on earth—the temple. Like each of you, I love the temple! I feel humble because I know who you are. You are part of this noble generation of women who have been reserved to lead and change the world through your lives of covenant. You are elect women. Contrary to what the world would have you believe, you are not ordinary. You are not common. You are daughters of God with nobility in your spiritual DNA, and purpose in your earthly mission. The Doctrine and Covenants describes you when it says, "Even before [you] were born, [you] . . . received [your] first lessons in the world of spirits and were prepared to come forth in the due time of the Lord . . . to take part in laying the foundations of the great latter-day work, including the building of the temples and the performance of ordinances therein" (D&C 138:56, 53–54).

Elaine S. Dalton is the general president of the Young Women. She received a BA in English from Brigham Young University. She has served as both the first and second counselor in the Young Women General presidency, and on the Young Women General Board. Sister Dalton has served in all the auxiliaries of the Church on both the ward and stake levels. Sister Dalton enjoys running, hiking with her family, and dancing with her granddaughters. She loves to read, especially the scriptures, and she loves the Lord. Her favorite scripture and life's motto is found in Proverbs 3:5–6: "Trust in the Lord with all thine heart; and lean not unto thine own understanding. In all thy ways acknowledge him, and he shall direct thy paths." She and her husband, Stephen, have six children and thirteen grandchildren.

When I was a young girl, my grandfather used to tell me about the temple. He said that the day would come when temples would literally dot the earth. I could hardly imagine what that meant. Today we are eye-witnesses to these events and temples do dot the earth. Brigham Young said, "To accomplish this work there will have to be not only one temple, but thousands of them, and thousands and tens of thousands of men and women will go into those temples and officiate for people who have lived as far back as the Lord shall reveal."[1] Have you ever wondered what you did or who you were in the premortal realms to deserve this honor, privilege, and sacred trust to be on the earth now—living in this, the dispensation of the fulness of times?

When our children were young, my husband was away from home serving in the bishopric, and gas was cheap, I used to load the children into our little brown Pinto and take them for what we fondly referred to as "night rides." I was desperate! It was my attempt to settle the children and make them sleepy enough to go to bed when we returned home. We would drive into downtown Salt Lake City to the temple and circle Temple Square. As the children looked toward the temple, we would talk about the temple spires, the granite blocks carved by pioneers, and the angel Moroni. I would tell the children about the day that their father and I were married in the temple. They never tired of this ritual or this story even though it was always the same. In fact, they would correct me if I forgot a detail of the story.

As we drove toward home, I would ask the children, "Where are you going to get married?" Our little Emi would reply with her two-year-old enthusiasm, "The nemple, the nemple!" How eternally significant have been the days when each of our six children went to the "nemple" and were married. It seemed just a blink away since those "night rides" of their youth. I now believe those night rides, taken by a young, desperate mother, were a great blessing in our lives, because as we circled the temple, the temple encircled our children. It is the desire of my heart that all young women like Emi will look toward the temple and prepare to enter there someday. That is why our vision for the young women of the Church is all about preparing every young woman to be worthy to make and keep sacred covenants and receive the ordinances of the temple. Everything we do in Young Women, every lesson, every value, every activity, every Personal Progress experience leads to the Lord and His holy house.

Looking toward the temple on those night rides also blessed and strengthened me. I found that the words inscribed on the east side became emblazoned on my heart. "Holiness to the Lord. The House of the Lord." What does "Holiness to the Lord" mean? I believe it means purity, righteousness, and sanctification. In 2 Nephi 9:20, "O how great the holiness of our God! For he knoweth all things, and there is not anything save he knows it," the footnote to "holiness" uses the word "committed" to define the use of the word "holiness." When we are holy before the Lord, we are pure and worthy and like Him. We are *committed* to Him through our covenants. We are committed to His plan of happiness, to His ways, to His standards. Our commitments didn't start at the temple; they began in the premortal realms where each one of us made a commitment to our Heavenly Father, and to His Son, and to the plan that was proposed by the Father.

Our pioneer ancestors knew it was all about the temple. That is one of the reasons the Relief Society was organized—so that the women could assist in the work of the temple. They made shirts for the men as they worked to build the Nauvoo Temple. They provided meals. They provided relief so that in their poverty a temple could be built. They knew it wasn't about possessions, but about power and strength derived from eternal covenants and eternal ordinances. They knew that they were on a journey back to their heavenly home. They glimpsed eternity. On the wall of the Nauvoo Temple they inscribed in gold: "The Lord has beheld our sacrifice, come after us."[2] They intended those words for us. They wanted us to make temples and the work therein our priority also. They knew that they were establishing the foundation upon which our exaltation would rest. They understood their identity, they were virtuous and pure, and they had a testimony of the covenants burning deep within their hearts. They were willing to give their all. They knew it wasn't about an earthly home, it was about the temple. They knew the journey they were on. They knew that they would be strengthened because they understood the promises of the endowment and the covenants available through the restoration of the priesthood keys and sealing powers. I am so grateful to those noble saints, our ancestors, for their vision, their faith, their sacrifice, and their example. To them I would say, "We have seen your sacrifice. It is not in vain. We will come after you!"

As temples now dot the earth, their presence is felt. How do we commit ourselves and our lives in such a way that we qualify for the blessings of the temple? What can we do to put aside the things of the world and seek for the things of a better world?

First, we must understand our identity. In the Book of Mormon we are described in this way: "Ye are the children of the prophets; and ye are of the house of Israel; and ye are of the covenant which the Father made with your fathers" (3 Nephi 20:25). Elder Russell M. Nelson of the Quorum of the Twelve said, "Once we know who we are and the royal lineage of which we are a part, our actions and our direction in life will be more appropriate to our inheritance."[3] When we truly know that we are daughters of God and have an understanding of our divine nature, it will be reflected in our countenance, our appearance, our actions, and our priorities.

Alma tells us that we were "called and prepared from the foundation of the world according to the foreknowledge of God, on account of [our] exceeding faith and good works" (Alma 13:3). Not just faith but exceeding faith and good works! We had faith in the Savior, in the Father, and in the plan that was presented, and we are here now to do that which we said we would do then. It is a divine compliment that you and I are on the earth now, in this the dispensation of the fulness of times. Today we have the gospel which has been restored to the earth. We have prophets and priesthood power. We have the Book of Mormon. We have holy temples where we can make covenants that will protect and direct us, as we have experiences that refine us and make us pure to again return to the presence of God and His beloved Son. We have a great work to do.

We are not of the world. We are elect daughters of God who have made and must keep sacred covenants. No wonder scripture admonishes us to "arise and shine forth, that [our] light may be a standard for the nations" (D&C 115:5). No wonder the Lord himself told Emma Smith that she was "an elect lady" (D&C 25:3). No wonder He also told Emma to "walk in the paths of virtue" (D&C 25:2) and to "cleave unto the covenants" (D&C 25:13). His voice to her was His voice to all of His beloved daughters. We are women who have been prepared and reserved to be on the earth now. We are women who have made covenants. Each of us is an "elect lady"; that means we were chosen. Now, the world won't tell us that. The world won't help us understand who we really are and our potential. Only the Spirit will teach us these things. We must cultivate our ability to listen to that Spirit, and to screen out the loud and worldly voices.

We must be virtuous and pure in order to enter into the Lord's holy temple and do the work we have been prepared and reserved to do. In the dedicatory prayer for the Kirtland Temple we read that "no unclean thing shall be permitted to come into thy house to pollute it" (D&C 109:20). Satan knows this and he has launched his attack to disqualify and distract each of us from the work to be done in temples. We, as the Young Women general presidency, continue to call for a return to virtue. Virtue is chastity. Virtue is sexual purity. Virtue is prerequisite to entering into the Lord's holy temples. It is the only way we can qualify for the companionship and guidance of a member of the Godhead—the Holy Ghost. We must firmly set our hearts on those things that matter most. We cannot allow ourselves to become distracted, distraught, or discouraged. Think of the transformation that could occur in the world through the righteous influence of each woman within the sound of my voice.

What would happen if each of us simply determined not to be lured away from those things that matter most? As Nehemiah tried to build a wall around the city of Jerusalem for protection from the enemy, he said, "I am doing a great work, so that I cannot come down" (Nehemiah 6:3). He simply would not be distracted or lured to lower ground. Each season's fashions get just a bit more revealing. Each season's TV and movies get just a bit more risqué, and each season's language gets just a bit more harsh. We can't come down. We must "arise and shine forth" (D&C 115:5). We are women who have made covenants that set us apart from the world in elegant, classy, beautiful ways. We are virtuous. We cherish virtue. We seek those things which are virtuous, praiseworthy, and lovely. As women, wives, and mothers, our righteous influence and actions can and will change the world.

The Lord has made it clear that He desires to have a pure and virtuous people. We as covenant women are uniquely positioned to teach and exemplify virtue and chastity, and we must. If we don't call for a return to virtue, who will? Will you join with me in calling for a return to virtue?

A virtuous woman is refined because she understands her identity.

She does not have to allow the voices of the world to define her. She is worthy to enter the Lord's holy temple. The temple provides the perfect pattern for such refinement. It is no accident that the symbolic color of the new Young Women value of virtue is gold. Gold is pure and soft and it shines because it has been refined. When gold is refined, it is put under intense heat and melted into a liquid state, and then a material called flux is added. Flux causes the impurities to part from the gold. It is a refining process. The interesting thing about flux is that it has to be pure in order for this process to work. There is meaning in this process for our lives. We become refined as we prepare for and go to the temple. It is within these hallowed walls that we may "receive a fulness of the Holy Ghost" (D&C 109:15). Receiving the Holy Ghost purifies and refines us as if with fire.

When we enter the temple, we make a physical parting from the world. Our actions, our dress and our language, not to mention our priorities are different—they are refined. Every ordinance and covenant binds us to the Savior. It is through His example and pure and perfect life that we are strengthened and enabled. It is because of His infinite Atonement that we can repent and become pure and virtuous. *He* is the pure addition we need that will enable us to enter into the Father's presence once again. His Atonement is the basis for every temple ordinance. Every ordinance and covenant we make refines us and binds us to the Savior. In the scriptures the question is asked, "Who can find a virtuous woman?" (Proverbs 31:10). I believe that may well be a latter-day question, and my invitation to you is the same as the prophet Joshua: "Sanctify yourselves: for to morrow the Lord will do wonders among you" (Joshua 3:5).

Our temple covenants set us apart from women of the world. A covenant is a binding agreement between man and God. When we keep our covenants, the Lord has promised us spiritual blessings. As covenant keepers we act, speak, and respond differently. When we keep our covenants we also dress differently. Our covenants not only define us but they refine us. Why did the Lord tell us to "cleave unto [our] covenants"? It is because making and keeping covenants will help us be worthy to hear and receive promptings from the Holy Ghost, and enable us to navigate successfully in an ever darkening world. It is because of the "protecting power of the ordinances and covenants available in the house of the Lord."[4] If we, as women and mothers, want that protection from the adversary, it can be found as we keep our covenants. The dedicatory prayer of the Kirkland Temple petitions the Lord that all who enter the temples may "go forth from this house armed with thy power, and that thy name may be upon them, and thy glory be round about them, and thine angels have charge over them" (D&C 109:22).

These are glorious promises.

The sacrament we partake of each week helps us renew our covenants, and it is there that we covenant to "be willing" to take His name upon us. Elder Bednar taught: "The baptismal covenant clearly contemplates a future event or events and looks forward to the temple. . . . The process of taking upon ourselves the name of Jesus Christ that is commenced in the waters of baptism is continued and enlarged in the house of the Lord. As we stand in the waters of baptism, we look to the temple. As we partake of the sacrament, we look to the temple. We pledge to always remember the Savior and to keep His commandments as preparation to participate in the sacred ordinances of the temple and receive the highest blessings available through the name and by the authority of the Lord Jesus Christ. Thus, in the ordinances of the holy temple we more completely and fully take upon us the name of Jesus Christ."[5]

I resonate with the scripture in Doctrine and Covenants section 109 in which "the testimony of the covenant" (D&C 109:38) is invoked on all who attend the temple worthily. I bear my testimony of these sacred covenants and the power that comes into our lives as a result. I testify that when we attend the temple, the promise of being armed with power and angels having charge over us is real. Elder Bednar confirmed this in his April 2009 conference address.[6]

Satan will not only try to discredit the work we are here to do in temples but also to distract us from that work. We may become too busy, or we may think that since all is not perfect in our homes or relationships, that we should not go. These voices tell us to wait, that surely if a son or daughter is not doing what is right, that we as their mothers are failures and not worthy of temple blessings. These are false and deceiving voices. We simply cannot listen to them when they speak. It is time to "run to the temple!"

President Uchtdorf said, "Now is the time to adjust your lives to be able to have a temple recommend and use it."[7] Living the standards and making and keeping sacred covenants go together. So does purity and virtue and entrance into the Lord's holy house.

In the temple we learn everything we need to know and do to return back into the presence of our Heavenly Father and His Son Jesus Christ. Every ordinance helps us understand the redeeming and enabling power of the Savior's Atonement. Moroni understood this: "Yea, come unto Christ, and be perfected in him" (Moroni 10:32).

At the end of the Book of Mormon, Moroni issued the final ultimate appeal to each of us to be virtuous and pure and to keep our covenants. "Come unto Christ, and lay hold upon every good gift, and touch not the evil gift, nor the unclean thing. . . . Awake, and arise from the dust . . . yea, and put on thy beautiful garments, O daughter of Zion; . . . that the covenants of the Eternal Father which he hath made unto thee . . . may be fulfilled" (Moroni 10:30–31).

My prayer is the same as Moroni's—that we, the daughters of Zion, may "come unto Christ, and be perfected in him" (Moroni 10:32), that "when he shall appear, we shall be like him" (see Moroni 7:48)—"purified, even as [he is] pure" (D&C 35:21). I know that as we understand our identity and place in this matchless plan, our lives of virtue and covenant will bless generations. I testify of Christ. He lives. He loves us, and He wants us to return home. May we each look to the temple and go forward in the strength of the Lord.

NOTES

1. Brigham Young, *Discourses of Brigham Young,* sel. John A. Widtsoe (Salt Lake City: Deseret Book, 1954), 394.
2. Heidi S. Swinton, *Sacred Stone: The Temple at Nauvoo* (American Fork: Covenant Communications, 2002), 136.
3. Russell M. Nelson, "Thanks for the Covenant," in *Brigham Young University 1988–89 Devotional and Fireside Speeches* (Provo: Brigham Young University Press, 1989), 59.
4. David A. Bednar, "Honorably Hold a Name and Standing," *Ensign,* May 2009, 99.
5. Ibid., 98.
6. See ibid., 97–100.
7. Dieter F. Uchtdorf, "The Way of the Disciple," *Ensign,* May 2009, 77.

DOING YOUR BEST VS. BEING THE BEST

Janie Penfield

Who are we? Or maybe a better phrase would be, who do we think we are? Perhaps you are a ballroom dancer, a mother, a secretary, a grandmother, a financial advisor, a genealogist, a sister, an event planner, a fashion designer, a cake decorator, or an athlete. But is that who you are? No. You *are* a daughter of God first and foremost.

Society teaches us to define ourselves by our talents, circumstances, age, etc. Heavenly Father teaches us to define ourselves as daughters of God. As a daughter of God we have been given talents and gifts to expand and grow. We have not been given *all* gifts and *all* talents. Therefore, we will be better at some things than others—and I'll bet we've each noticed this. Just as the accomplished athlete does, we need to embrace our talents and develop our individual attributes (the ones we have been given), eventually reaching the pinnacle of performance—our best—not *the* best, but *our* best.

President Dieter F. Uchtdorf recently said, "Our splendid sisters sometimes undervalue their abilities—they focus on what is lacking or

Janie Penfield is the Associate Athletic Director/Senior Woman Administrator (SWA) at Brigham Young University. She holds a BA in English from Colorado State University and an MBA from BYU. She was a four-year starter on the Colorado State volleyball team and has played professionally in Finland, and was an assistant volleyball coach at Boise State. She serves as a youth Sunday School teacher and enjoys adventure, sewing, and reading.

imperfect rather than what has been accomplished and who they really are."[1] How can we focus on the good in ourselves and in others and appreciate others' gifts?

Let's start this discussion by establishing a common understanding. Elder L. Tom Perry said, "All of us are endowed with abundant talent, beauty, and ability."[2] Whether or not you see it, or believe this applies to you or others—it is true and it does. For if it is our purpose on earth "to bring to pass our own immortality and eternal life," we must find a way to focus and appreciate the good in ourselves and in others. I'd like to suggest four essentials for accomplishing this feat and continually being able to do it. They are:

1. Pray,
2. Keep our expectations within reach,
3. Focus on the good, and
4. Allow time for personal growth.

PRAY

Pray for strength, pray for insight, pray for faith, pray for generosity in judgment, whatever we do, most of all we must call on the Lord. This is the first essential because it is an essential element in all efforts to be close to and be like our Heavenly Father and is applicable no matter where you are in the process.

I'd like to remind us why we pray: Zeniff told us, "And God did hear our cries and did answer our prayers; and we did go forth in his might" (Mosiah 9:18). Our Heavenly Father will hear us, answer us, and strengthen us. As we ask for His participation in our lives, He will respond!

President Lorenzo Snow said, "We may think that we cannot live up to the perfect law, that the work of perfecting ourselves is too difficult. This may be true in part, but the fact still remains that it is a command of the Almighty to us and we cannot ignore it. When we experience trying moments, then is the time for us to avail ourselves of that great privilege of calling upon the Lord for strength and understanding, intelligence and *grace by which we can overcome the weakness of the flesh.*"[3] Throughout our time on earth, but especially as we seek to emulate the Savior, we must learn to turn to the Lord for strength, understanding, intelligence, and grace to overcome our weaknesses—it is imperative! This is especially true in trying moments.

Pray: He will strengthen us in numerous ways and He will help us overcome our weaknesses—two very good reasons.

Keep Our Expectations within Reach

First, let's talk about expectations. Sometimes they get out of hand and we expect ourselves to be Martha, Mrs. Brady, CEO, Primary president extraordinaire, Nurse Nancy, without a single flaw. We must keep our goals within our reach. But how do we do that?

As daughters of God, we have been commanded to be perfect. The Savior said, "Be ye therefore perfect, even as your Father which is in heaven is perfect" (Matthew 5:48).

2 Nephi 31:20 says: "Wherefore, ye must press forward with a steadfastness in Christ, having a perfect brightness of hope, and a love of God and of all men. Wherefore, if ye shall press forward, feasting upon the word of Christ, and endure to the end, behold, thus saith the Father: Ye shall have eternal life." Nephi offered a deeper understanding of the commandment Matthew recorded—if we press forward with hope and love, feasting upon the Word, and endure, we'll have eternal life. That sounds more possible than perfection, doesn't it? Nephi doesn't mention perfection—but instead breaks things down, providing a plan that will lead us to perfection if we will but implement the plan.

President Howard W. Hunter gave us even more insight into our challenge to be perfect and keeping our expectations within reach. He said, "Some of us feel we are falling short of our expected ideals. . . . Each of us desires to achieve a measure of greatness in this life. . . . Realizing who we are and what we may become assures us that with God nothing really is impossible. From the time we learn that Jesus wants us for a Sunbeam until we learn more fully the basic principles of the gospel, we are taught to strive for perfection. . . . . The difficulty arises when inflated expectations of the world alter our definition of greatness."[4]

Wait—so President Hunter is saying that the "inflated expectations of the *world* alter our definition of greatness"? I think he's right—that definitely happens to me, more often than I'd like. What is defining greatness for you? The Lord's standard or the world's? Do you expect yourself or others to be the best at everything you attempt, or maybe just at too many things? We need to choose to be satisfied at not being the best at some things, and not being good at all at some things. The Lord does not expect us to be perfect at everything, He expects us to press forward and endure. He knows that we have limitations!

"One of the signs of mature Latter-day Saint life is the ability to see a limitation in ourselves without letting it *cast a shadow* over all the many other good things we do and say."[5] Do we see our limitations as faults or enormous hurdles in our path to perfection? Do we let the limitations bring us down or diminish the great talents we have? Do we let others' limitations lead us to criticism or diminished respect, regardless of their talents? We must eliminate the "shadows" and allow ourselves to be average or bad at some things, while at the same time pressing forward, doing *our* best but not expecting to be *the* best.

The fact that I am not a great dancer doesn't keep me from watching the beautiful ballerinas twirl, spring, and glide and wanting to be on their stage right then and there. I even sometimes leave the ballet with a longing in my heart for the many, many more ballet classes that I should have taken so I could have been a true ballerina. Then I come back to reality and I realize that I'm 6' 1" tall, I am not small-boned, my feet would have a stinking awful time supporting my body *en pointe*, I loved my years of volleyball and collegiate sports, I wouldn't be working where I am, on and on, if I'd pursued ballet instead of volleyball. I think everyone can relate to this story in some way. There's no shadow in having chosen a different righteous path. There is no shadow in being a volleyball player rather than a ballerina—they are both good choices and it is unrealistic of me to expect to be both. As we strive to keep our expectations in reach, we should remember what we would have to give up in order to be *the best* in a field we are not. We should also remember what we have already sacrificed and consecrated to develop the talents we already have.

We can change our hearts, thoughts, and minds and move from focusing on what we don't do well (our limitations) to doing our best, to controlling what we can control and being satisfied with our best efforts when we are on the right path. We need to see our limitations without shadows—for limitations are not bad, they are a reality—everyone has them. They are also opportunities for growth. This applies to how we view ourselves as well as others. Do we let our failures go? Do we allow ourselves and others to make mistakes? We *must*.

As a first-year assistant volleyball coach at Boise State University, I was put in charge of our teams' travel—hotel arrangements, plane tickets, rental cars, everything. For one tournament, we flew to Spokane, Washington to play the University of Idaho. The morning after our match we showed up at the airport to check in and I found that I had booked our return tickets for the previous day. We had no tickets for the current day. I started to panic. I was twenty-three years old, I had spent thousands of dollars incorrectly and might have stranded sixteen people in Washington state, with the additional cost of sixteen last-minute, one-way tickets to boot! As I approached my boss, our head coach, I was anxious. I didn't know how he was going to respond.

He chose to make my failure a learning experience. He calmly told me that since we couldn't change it, we needed to solve the current problem of getting out of Washington and back to Boise. He said we'd talk about the problem when we got back. I couldn't believe it! We bought the plane tickets and flew home to Boise. When we were back in the office on Monday we reviewed the situation, and took note of how it happened so I wouldn't make the same mistake again.

I have made many mistakes and I have practiced this exercise numerous times. When I spill milk, I clean it up and pour another glass or pour something else. We must allow ourselves and others to "spill" on occasion and allow for mistakes. Our Heavenly Father *planned* for us to make mistakes and fall short of perfection, so much so that He provided us with a Savior and Redeemer. It only makes sense that as we grow and work toward perfection, we should allow our best—even though we may make mistakes—to be enough.

Focus on the Good

President Gordon B. Hinckley said, "Be true to yourself and the best you have within you. That best is very good. Shakespeare said, 'To thine ownself be true, /And it must follow, as the night the day, /Thou canst not then be false to any man' (*Hamlet* 1.3.78–80). Many . . . women . . . suffer from lack of self-esteem. . . . Be true to yourselves, and your respect for yourself will increase. Know that yours is a divine birthright. *Cultivate a good opinion of yourself.*"[6]

Here's an example: I'm sure you've heard of Rachael Ray and the Barefoot Contessa, Ina Garten, both of whom have shows on The Food Network. They are both excellent, successful cooks. Rachael Ray is quick, and makes food anyone can make and eat. It's easy, unpretentious food. However, the Barefoot Contessa, Ina Garten, makes elegant, decadent, rich, full-flavored foods, with time-consuming recipes. Although both are talented at creating delicious food, they are not the same. If they were to try to be like each other I am sure they would find the dissatisfaction we often find in ourselves when we try to be like the people around us instead of playing to our own talents and gifts.

President Howard W. Hunter, then a member of the Quorum of the Twelve, said that "Our quest is to seek out the talents the Lord has given us and to develop and multiply them, whether they be five, two, or one. We need not attempt to imitate the talents given to other persons."[7] A key component to our progression and personal growth is satisfaction with the gifts we have been given. We need to be satisfied and work to develop our own gifts.

Elder Richard G. Scott said, "Discover who you really are. . . . look beyond the daily routine of life. . . . discern through the Spirit your divinely given capacities."[8]

How do we do this—when the world screams that we are not enough, when we constantly hear the cries of our friends and other women who are dissatisfied with themselves? It can be a serious challenge. But as we pray for guidance and assistance, it will come to us through the Holy Ghost. We will be blessed with the ability to see ourselves as the Lord sees us and to see the good in ourselves again or for the first time.

Doctrine & Covenants 112:10 says, "Be thou humble; and the Lord thy God shall lead thee by the hand, and give thee answer to thy prayers." We know that if we humble ourselves before the Lord, He will buoy us up. Take the time to be thoughtful. Meditate on your gifts and talents. Study your patriarchal blessing—oftentimes the Lord lays out our talents for us in them. Pray for strength to see the talents of others. The Lord will guide us to the greatness in others if we will look for it. Just as we have to sit back and look for the beauty in the world around us, we also have to sit back and look for the beauty in the people around us and even in the woman in the mirror.

This is my favorite quote from a latter-day prophet: President Ezra Taft Benson said, "Be worthy trustees. . . . Be cheerful in all that you do. Live joyfully. Live happily. Live enthusiastically, knowing that God does not dwell in gloom and melancholy, but in light and love."[9] Are we as President Benson calls on us to be? Are we joyful, happy, worthy trustees?

Another aspect of focusing on the good is to never doubt your abilities or self-deprecate. Pray for the strength you cannot find within you to leave the bad behind you, whether it is sin or doubt. Repent. If you have repented, allow yourself to move on.

The Savior and His eternal Atonement will take away our struggle with focusing on the bad. "Come unto me, all ye that labour and are heavy laden, and I will give you rest. Take my yoke upon you, and learn of me; for I am meek and lowly in heart: and ye shall find rest unto your souls. For my yoke is easy, and my burden is light" (Matthew 11:28–30). Give your burdens to the Savior. Utilize the Atonement and find the light and love where God dwells.

As women, we often struggle with comparisons, tearing ourselves or others down in the process. President Hunter asked, "Why do we allow ourselves to waste such energy and emotion comparing ourselves to others when our real task is to develop what we are and what we have, to be all that we can be. This is especially true in matters of the spirit and salvation."[10]

In addition, President Gordon B. Hinckley said, "Do not nag yourself with a sense of failure. Get on your knees and ask for the blessings of the Lord; then stand on your feet and do what you are asked to do. Then leave the matter in the hands of the Lord. You will discover that you have accomplished something beyond price."[11] We also need to do this for the people we love and interact with. Stop gossiping. Stop focusing on people's faults. Get on your knees and ask for the Lord's help for them and for yourself, then move on.

In Doctrine & Covenants 112:11, the Lord says, "I know thy heart, and have heard thy prayers concerning thy brethren. Be not partial towards them in love above many others, but let thy love be for them as for thyself; and let thy love abound unto all men, and unto all who love my name."

I have an identical twin sister. We are pretty competitive people—we were both Division I volleyball players. We can easily compare ourselves in just about everything because we have the same genetic makeup. We compare our shapes, our sizes, our patience, our craftiness, our grades, and even our dating histories (mine is much more interesting because she got married at twenty-two). But we have developed our competitive tendencies into tactful assistance at helping each other be better.

Weed out jealousy and covetousness—Elder Marvin J. Ashton said, "There is a natural, probably a mortal, tendency to compare ourselves with others. Unfortunately, when we make these comparisons, we tend to compare our weakest attributes with someone else's strongest. For example, a woman who feels unschooled in the gospel may take particular note of a woman in her ward who teaches the Gospel Doctrine class and seems to have every scripture at her fingertips. Obviously these kinds of comparisons are destructive and only reinforce the fear that somehow we don't measure up."[12] Remember President Uchtdorf and Elder Perry's comments—we must not undervalue our abilities, beauty, and talents for they are in us in abundance.

ALLOW TIME FOR PERSONAL GROWTH

The race is *not* to the swiftest; it is to those who endure and finish. There are an infinite number of winners. However, we actually must go through the natural progression of change and continuous improvement toward perfection—having a desire, taking action, actually changing, and then making corrections when we fall short.

Two fantastic quotes support these ideas of progression, personal growth, and direction:

President Howard W. Hunter said, "In this mortal life the direction we are moving is more important than a particular degree of perfection. We all experience cycles of progression and times when we fight against these inevitable challenges of regression. Great blessings from the Lord attend our efforts to progress. And progression is certainly more effective if it is a process, a long-term commitment, rather than just a series of iso-lated and irregular events."[13] I love that President Hunter focuses on the process and how this progression is a long-term commitment in personal growth.

Elder Marvin J. Ashton states: "I am . . . convinced of the fact that the speed with which we head along the straight and narrow path isn't as important as the direction in which we are traveling. That direction, if it is leading toward eternal goals, is the all-important factor."[14]

Alma gives us more insight into process and direction, "Now ye may suppose that this is foolishness in me; but behold I say unto you, that by small and simple things are great things brought to pass; and small means in many instances doth confound the wise" (Alma 37:6).

Why do we expect others to run a perfect race, or to be at a point of the race where we think they should be considering their spiritual or phys-ical progression? It *is* enough that they are on the path. It *is* enough that they are moving toward the finish line. It *is* enough that we are on the strait and narrow.

Look at others through the Lord's eyes. He does not require perfec-tion here on earth in everything. He requires diligence, progress, and cor-rection. We can be perfect in some things and we should be—be perfect in paying your tithing, saying kind things, keeping the Word of Wisdom, attending the temple, being virtuous, or in any other way *you* can reach perfection. But where you cannot, do your best:

"Every one of [us] was endowed by [our] Father in Heaven with a tremendous capacity to do good in the world. Train your minds and your hands that you may be equipped to serve well . . . Cultivate the art of being kind, of being thoughtful, of being helpful. Refine within you the quality of mercy which comes as a part of the divine attributes you have inherited."[15] "Cultivate" and "refine" are time-consuming verbs. They cannot take place in a short period of time. They require patience, dili-gence, and attention, just as our efforts towards perfection must require. As we cultivate and refine ourselves spiritually and physically, we must allow time for progression and personal growth.

I know that each of us will have difficulty at some point, if we have not already, with sorting through the world's expectations and the Lord's when it comes to the Lord's commandment to be perfect. Although we have been blessed with abundant gifts, we cannot expect ourselves or those around us to be perfect. We must pray, keep our expectations within reach, focus on the good, and allow time for personal growth. Instead of undervaluing our own and others' abilities, I challenge each of us to focus on the good in ourselves and others by choosing to do exactly those four things.

One final quote from President Gordon B. Hinckley. He said: "You need never feel that you were born without talents or without opportunities to give them expression. Cultivate whatever talents you have, and they will grow and refine and become an expression of your true self appreciated by others."[16]

NOTES

1. Dieter F. Uchtdorf, "Happiness, Your Heritage," *Ensign*, November 2008, 117.
2. L. Tom Perry, "Staying Power," *Ensign*, July 2003, 42.
3. Lorenzo Snow, "Blessing of the Gospel Only Obtained by Compliance of the Law," *Liahona*, February 1979, 37.
4. Howard W. Hunter, "What Is True Greatness?" *Brigham Young University 1986–87 Devotional and Fireside Speeches* (Provo: Brigham Young University Press, 1987), 111.
5. Hunter, "The Dauntless Spirit of Resolution," *Brigham Young University 1991–92 Devotional and Fireside Speeches* (Provo: Brigham Young University Press, 1992), 40.
6. Gordon B. Hinckley, "Stand True and Faithful," *Ensign*, May 1996, 92.
7. Hunter, *The Teachings of Howard W. Hunter*, ed. Clyde J. Williams (Salt Lake City: Bookcraft, 1997), 70.
8. Richard G. Scott, "Realize Your Full Potential," *Ensign*, November 2003, 41.
9. Ezra Taft Benson, "Your Charge: To Increase in Wisdom and Favor with God and Man," *New Era*, September 1979, 42.
10. Hunter, "The Dauntless Spirit of Resolution," 41.
11. Hinckley, "To the Women of the Church," *Ensign*, November 2003, 114.
12. Marvin J. Ashton, "On Being Worthy," *Ensign*, May 1989, 20.
13. Hunter, "The Dauntless Spirit of Resolution," 41–42.
14. Ashton, "On Being Worthy," 20.
15. Hinckley, "The Light Within You," *Ensign*, May 1995, 99.
16. Ibid.

"BE NOT AFRAID, ONLY BELIEVE"

Margaret S. Lifferth

I hope you know that every child of God born into mortality knows fear. Infants have a natural fear of falling. Most children are afraid of the dark. Teenagers fear rejection or ridicule. And all of us fear inadequacy, weakness, temptation, temporal insecurity, ignorance, sin, rebellion, failure, illness, and death. As women, we then multiply these fears we have for ourselves to include our loved ones. What mother's heart has not also feared all of this for her loved ones as well?

If personal fears were not enough, there are many scriptural warnings about events of the last days—our day. Reading these scriptures, it is easy to be fearful of what will come and of what we are witnessing around us every day.

You know these phrases from scripture. They are as familiar as they are harrowing:

"And in that day shall be heard of wars and rumors of wars, and the whole earth shall be in commotion, and men's hearts shall fail them."

"And the love of men shall wax cold, and iniquity shall abound."

Margaret S. Lifferth is the first counselor in the Primary general presidency. She has served her community on elementary and high school parent-teacher association boards and on the BYU Women's Conference Committee. She has served the Church as a member of the Primary General Board, a counselor in a stake Relief Society presidency, a ward Relief Society president, a ward Young Women president, a counselor in a ward Primary presidency, and a volunteer docent at the Museum of Church History and Art. She and her husband, Dennis, have seven children.

"They shall see an over-flowing scourge; for a desolating sickness shall cover the land."

"There shall be earthquakes also in divers places, and many desolations; yet men will harden their hearts against me, and they will take up the sword, one against another, and they will kill one another."

"And they shall behold blood, and fire, and vapors of smoke. And before the day of the Lord shall come, the sun shall be darkened, and the moon be turned into blood, and the stars fall from heaven" (D&C 45:26, 27, 31, 33, 41–42).

With these warnings ringing in our ears, it is no wonder that from Abraham to Joseph Smith, scriptures also reveal the comforting words of the Lord: "Fear not." You also know these scriptures. They are as familiar as they are comforting:

"Fear not, Abram: I am thy shield" (Genesis 15:1).

"Moses said unto the people, Fear ye not, stand still, and see the salvation of the Lord" (Exodus 14:13).

To Elijah, "Fear not: for they that be with us are more than they that be with them" (2 Kings 6:16).

To the shepherds, "Fear not: for, behold, I bring you good tidings of great joy" (Luke 2:10).

From Paul to Timothy, "For God hath not given us the spirit of fear; but of power, and of love, and of a sound mind" (2 Timothy 1:7).

To His twelve Apostles, "Fear ye not . . . ye are of more value than many sparrows" (Matthew 10:31).

To John Whitmer, "Open your mouth in my cause, not fearing what man can do, for I am with you" (D&C 30:11).

To each of us, Christ says, "Fear not; I am the first and the last: I am he that liveth, and was dead; and, behold, I am alive for evermore . . . and have the keys of hell and of death" (Revelation 1:17–18).

I think the scriptural message is clear: If we are to have peace in our hearts, we must learn how to preserve it in the midst of trouble and trials. And we have been given the key. The answer is revealed in the story of Christ raising the daughter of Jairus as found in Mark. Jesus is teaching amid a great crowd of people when:

"Behold, there cometh one of the rulers of the synagogue, Jairus by name; and when he saw him [Christ], he fell at his feet, and besought him greatly, saying, My little daughter lieth at the point of death: I pray thee, come and lay thy hands on her, that she may be healed; and she shall live. And Jesus went with him; and much people followed him, and thronged him" (Mark 5:22–24).

It is at this point, while they are moving through the crowd, that the woman with an issue of blood touches the hem of Christ's robe and is healed. While this exchange is taking place, another message comes from the house of Jairus:

"Thy daughter is dead: why troublest thou the Master any further? As soon as Jesus heard the word that was spoken, he saith unto the ruler of the synagogue, *Be not afraid, only believe*" (Mark 5:35–36; emphasis added).

Can you imagine the conflicting emotions in the heart of Jairus? Overwhelming sorrow, fear of false hope, and yet, the request to believe in the impossible.

Jesus takes Peter, James, and John, and continues on with Jairus to his home, "and seeth the tumult, and them that wept and wailed greatly. And when he was come in, he saith unto them, Why make ye this ado, and weep? the damsel is not dead, but sleepeth.

"And they laughed him to scorn. But when he had put them all out, he taketh the father and the mother of the damsel, and them that were with him, and entereth in where the damsel was lying.

"And he took the damsel by the hand, and said unto her, . . . Damsel, I say unto thee, arise. And straightway the damsel arose, and walked; for she was of the age of twelve years. And they were astonished with a great astonishment" (Mark 5:38–42).

"Be not afraid, only believe." The key to peace in our hearts is faith in Jesus Christ. Believe in Him. Believe that He knows you and loves you. Believe in His redeeming power. Believe that this is His Church and He will help us do His work. Believe in His promises. Believe that His promises are personal and are meant for you. Believe that because of Him, every fear can be overcome and every trial will sanctify us. Believe that because of His Atonement, every wounded soul and every broken heart will ultimately be healed. Be not afraid, only believe.

We know that faith in Christ calls for action. It calls for obedience and willful desire to follow Him. But the Lord promises us more than just what we can do through our own hard work and commitment. Because of the restoration of The Church of Jesus Christ of Latter-day Saints, we can have access to the very power of God as we face life's fears.

Nephi had a vision of us in these last days. His record in 1 Nephi 14 can give us great hope:

"And it came to pass that I beheld the church of the Lamb of God, and its numbers were few, because of the wickedness and abominations of the whore who sat upon many waters; . . .

"And it came to pass that I beheld that the great mother of abominations did gather together multitudes upon the face of all the earth, among all the nations of the Gentiles, to fight against the Lamb of God. [Are we beginning to see this? Then we can take courage from the next verse:]

"And it came to pass that I, Nephi, beheld the power of the Lamb of God, that it descended upon the saints of the church of the Lamb, and upon the covenant people of the Lord, who were scattered upon all the face of the earth; and they were armed with righteousness and with the power of God in great glory" (1 Nephi 14:12–14).

We learn that there are two great powers in the world: the power of Satan and the power of God. I also learned this principle in a Primary class. I was teaching a class of six-year-olds and the lesson was on the First Vision. The manual suggested using a video clip which I had at home. I watched it and was a little concerned about the depiction of Joseph being overcome by Satan, but decided to show it anyway. At the end of the lesson, the children were to draw a picture of the First Vision to take home and share with their families. I watched as six-year-old Sara took a black crayon and began to fill her page with darkness. I asked her to tell me about her picture. She said it was when Satan came to the Sacred Grove. I looked straight into her blue eyes, and said, "Sarah, do you know that Heavenly Father and Jesus are always more powerful than Satan and they will always protect you?" She hesitated for a minute and then took her black crayon and drew two figures up in the corner of the page. She then picked up a yellow crayon and filled the page with light.

I testify that the power of God *is* always more powerful than that of Satan, and through our faith in Jesus Christ, we can arm ourselves with righteousness and the power of God. The Young Women theme for 2009 asks each one of us to "be thou an example of the believers"

(1 Timothy 4:12). With faith, we can not only "be not afraid," but we can be an example to our families and to the world of a believer. How do we do it?

In vision, Nephi also saw the restoration of The Church of Jesus Christ of Latter-day Saints. Because of the restoration of true doctrine and true authority, we can have great confidence in the power of prayer, the power of the word of God, the power of the priesthood, the power of the Holy Ghost, and the power of covenants and temple blessings. These blessings are not only restored principles but provide very personal ways to enable each of us to "be . . . an example of the believers" as we arm ourselves with the power of God.

We can be an example of the believers as we access the power of prayer. If I were to ask this audience to share their experiences with prayer, there would be many stories of the power of prayer giving us confidence to "fear not."

Joseph Smith learned this lesson many times, but it was after months in Liberty Jail that he poured out his heart in prayer with these questions: "O God, where art thou? And where is the pavilion that covereth thy hiding place? How long shall thy hand be stayed?" (D&C 121:1–2). You remember that the Lord's answer includes the idea that difficult experiences are for our good. I believe that too. But this is the verse I like in the Lord's response: "Thy days are known, and thy years shall not be numbered less; therefore, fear not what man can do, for God shall be with you forever and ever" (D&C 122:9).

I know that the power of prayer to relieve fear is not only scriptural, it is personal. I remember one summer night years ago when our oldest son had taken a date to a concert in Park City, Utah. I had fallen asleep while waiting for him to come home, but I was awakened at about 2:30 A.M. with a phone call. It was from the father of the girl he had invited for the evening, wondering where she was. That is never a happy moment. This happened before there were many cell phones, and so I really had no idea what had caused their delay, but my first thought was that there had been an accident. I remember going out on the front porch of our home and sitting on the steps. It was a warm, beautiful night and I said a prayer, not only for their safety, but that I could feel peaceful if things were all right. My heart was flooded with confidence that all was well. It wasn't long after that my son arrived home. There *had* been an accident on the freeway, and traffic was stopped for some time. He had tried to call from a public phone, but the lines of youth trying to reach their parents were so long that he just headed for home.

I know that not all of our prayers have a happy ending, but my faith is strengthened when I know that my "days [and the days of my loved ones] are known," and that God can be with me "forever and ever." Be not afraid, only believe.

We can be an example of the believers by understanding the power in the word of God. Joseph Smith's first assignment was to bring forth the Book of Mormon. Thanks to him, we also have the Doctrine and Covenants, the Pearl of Great Price and the Joseph Smith Translation of the Bible. Why is our canon of scripture so important in relieving fear, building faith, and accessing the power of God?

You remember Lehi's dream and the rod of iron that symbolized the word of God and the power it had to lead those who held fast to it to the tree of life. After Nephi had seen the same vision, his brothers wanted to know the meaning of the dream. They asked Nephi,

"What meaneth the rod of iron which our father saw, that led to the tree?" (1 Nephi 15:23).

Note the power of God manifest in this answer:

"And I said unto them that it was the word of God; and whoso would hearken unto the word of God, and would hold fast unto it, they would never perish; neither could the temptations and the fiery darts of the adversary overpower them unto blindness, to lead them away to destruction" (1 Nephi 15:24).

I love reading the scriptures. In them, I gain understanding and hear the promises of the Lord to me. I bear testimony that scriptures nourish the soul, build faith and invite the Spirit into the events of the day. Arm yourselves and your families with the power of the word of God that you may "be not afraid, only believe."

Exemplify a believer by accessing the power of the priesthood. It was while translating scripture that Joseph Smith and Oliver Cowdery sought the Lord in prayer to learn more about baptism. Joseph records this:

"While we were thus employed, praying and calling upon the Lord, a messenger from heaven descended in a cloud of light, and having laid his hands upon us, he ordained us, saying: *Upon you my fellow servants, in the name of Messiah, I confer the Priesthood of Aaron"* (JS–H 1:68–69; emphasis in original). I love that phrase, "fellow servants." Later the Melchizedek Priesthood was restored, as was the sealing power.

Priesthood is literally the power of God given to men on earth. Each of us can access this power through covenants, ordinances and priesthood blessings. In late February 2009, I was assigned to speak in the April general conference. I prepared in every way I knew how. The night before I was to speak, I asked my husband for a priesthood blessing. The blessing addressed every one of my fears. Saturday morning came. I was to follow Elder Hales, and knew that when he began the last paragraph of his talk, I was to leave my seat and go to a small chair just a few feet from the podium. My heart was pounding as Elder Hales finished his talk. Then it was my turn. When I stood at the podium, the miracle came. I was calm. I literally feared not and every part of that priesthood blessing was fulfilled. Be not afraid, only believe.

We are an example of the believers as we make and keep covenants that have power to bind us to the Lord. After Joseph Smith and Oliver Cowdery received the Aaronic Priesthood, they were commanded to baptize each other, then having authority to do so.

At a fireside in New York, I asked if any child wanted to come and bear his testimony. A ten-year-old boy named Christian came to the stand and bore a powerful testimony on the principle of baptism. He said he wanted to be baptized because he knew it would make him clean. He remembered the picture of Jesus being baptized and wanted to follow Him. He said that his baptism day was the best day of his life, and he began to cry. Others in the audience were weeping as well. I did not know until later what everyone else knew about Christian. His mother was an inactive member and his father was not a member at all. All were strengthened by a testimony of a child who recognized the power of covenants.

We have power in our covenants as we are obedient to them. Obedience binds the Lord to bless us. President Ezra Taft Benson taught, "When obedience ceases to be an irritant and becomes our quest, then God will endow us with power from on high."[1]

About the time of the restoration of the priesthood and their baptism, Joseph and Oliver received this counsel from the Lord: "Fear not to do good, my sons, for whatsoever ye sow, that shall ye also reap; therefore, if ye sow good ye shall also reap good for your reward. Therefore, fear not, little flock; do good" (D&C 6:33–34).

We exemplify the believers when we access the power of the Holy Ghost. After Joseph Smith and Oliver Cowdery had baptized each other, Joseph records, "Immediately on our coming up out of the water after we had been baptized, we experienced great and glorious blessings from our Heavenly Father. . . . We were filled with the Holy Ghost, and rejoiced in the God of our salvation" (JS–H 1:73).

The Holy Ghost was given to members of the Church on the day the Church was organized. The Holy Ghost comforts, guides, teaches, protects, and testifies. Personal revelation comes through the Holy Ghost.

In a recent testimony meeting, a young sister expressed gratitude for her husband, who several years ago followed a prompting of the Holy Ghost to get out of debt, save, and acquire food storage. She supported him in that effort and they worked hard to prepare themselves financially. When he recently became unemployed, they were grateful to have followed the promptings of the Spirit. Be not afraid, only believe.

We exemplify the believers as we access the power of the blessings of the temple. I am grateful every day for the restoration of the power of temple blessings through the Prophet Joseph Smith.

I recently witnessed the power of the temple in the lives of parents who had great reason to fear. A couple of months ago, my husband received a call requesting that a pair of shoes be taken to Primary Children's Hospital for a sixteen-year-old young man who had been in a serious accident. They needed to be a size 11 and have support at the ankle. We had exactly the shoes that were needed in our garage. We drove up to the hospital and met the parents of this injured young man. He had serious head injuries and was basically on life support. The shoes were to strengthen the muscles in his feet as he lay in the intensive care unit of the hospital.

We visited briefly with the parents that night and discovered that they were far from the support of friends and family. Consequently, we kept in touch. About a week later, we met them in Salt Lake to get a hamburger. That day, the medical team at the hospital had gathered together and advised them that there was little to no chance that their son would recover and they advised taking him off life support. As we visited, they decided that they would like to go to the temple the next day and seek the will of the Lord. However, in recent trips to the temple, the mother had experienced episodes of overwhelming anxiety. Wanting to help, I told her that if she wanted to go to the temple, I would go with her. She said she would let me know.

Later that evening, she called and we set a time to meet at the temple. It was a sweet session. As we left the temple that day, she expressed her joy at feeling calm and comforted the entire session. Her husband commented that for the first time in many days, he felt at peace. They went home for a few days to confer with other family members, then returned to say good-bye to their son, who quickly passed away. The temple had blessed them not only with confidence to take a difficult action, but with perspective on the purpose of our mortal life, and gratitude for the sealing ordinances which bound them together for eternity. They knew their son was going home to a loving Heavenly Father. "Fear not, little children, for you are mine, and I have overcome the world" (D&C 50:41).

All power to overcome fear is centered in the Atonement and power of Jesus Christ. Over and over, He tells us who He is and how He will bless us if we come to Him in faith. He will not only magnify us, but He will magnify our work. In Him, we need not fear. Listen to His words to us: In the Doctrine and Covenants, He says: "Look unto me in every thought; doubt not, fear not. Behold the wounds which pierced my side, and also the prints of the nails in my hands and feet; be faithful, keep my commandments, and ye shall inherit the kingdom of heaven" (D&C 6:36–37).

From Isaiah, He encourages us: "Fear thou not; for I am with thee: be not dismayed; for I am thy God: I will strengthen thee; yea, I will help thee; yea, I will uphold thee with the right hand of my righteousness" (Isaiah 41:10).

The very last verses of Matthew record that the resurrected Christ appeared to his eleven disciples to give them their charge. We read that "when they saw him, they worshipped him: but some doubted" (Matthew 28:17). How could they doubt? Christ was standing before them. I can only think they doubted themselves. The Savior's reply is interesting in that He didn't try to build their own confidence, but He gave them every confidence to rely on Him:

"And Jesus came and spake unto them, saying, All power is given unto me in heaven and in earth. . . . And, lo, I am with you alway, even unto the end of the world" (Matthew 28:18, 20). Be not afraid, only believe.

I hope you noticed how personal these promises are. They are for you. You are the one who need not fear. He has the power to overcome every sin, trial, and sorrow that besets you. You are the one who can access the power of God to strengthen yourself and those around you. Because of the Restoration, you can access this power through prayer, scriptures, the Holy Ghost, priesthood power, temple blessings, and obedience to covenants. Just as He knew Joseph Smith and the daughter of Jarius, He knows you. He knows your name. He knows your circumstances, challenges, and desires. He knows your fears. He knows the temptations that swirl around you from every side. He loves you and wants you to come home to Him. Be not afraid, only believe.

NOTE

1. Ezra Taft Benson, in Donald L. Staheli, "Obedience—Life's Great Challenge," *Ensign*, May 1998, 81.

RECLAIMING THE JOY OF THE SABBATH

Brent L. Top

One of my favorite hymns is "How Gentle God's Commands." I love these words:

> How gentle God's commands!
> How kind his precepts are!
> Come, cast your burdens on the Lord
> And trust his constant care.
> Beneath his watchful eye,
> His Saints securely dwell;
> That hand which bears all nature up
> Shall guard his children well.[1]

Truly, His commands are gentle and His precepts kind. Through God's commandments, we experience His constant care. By His precepts we are protected and blessed, and as the hymn states, "sweet refreshment find."

The Prophet Joseph Smith taught:

Brent L. Top is department chair and a professor of Church History at Brigham Young University. He has served as the associate dean of Religious Education at BYU, and held the Endowed Professorship of Moral Education. He holds a bachelor's, master's, and PhD from that institution. Prior to joining the religion faculty at BYU, he worked as a seminary and institute instructor and administrator for the Church Educational System. He presided over the Peoria Illinois Mission from 2004–2007, and serves as president of the Pleasant Grove Utah East Stake. He and his wife, Wendy, have four children and fifteen grandchildren.

"Everything that God gives us is lawful and right; and it is proper that we should enjoy His gifts and blessings whenever and wherever He is disposed to bestow; but if we should seize upon those [things] without [regard to God's] commandments, [they] would prove cursings and vexations in the end, and we should have to lie down in sorrow and wailings of everlasting regret. But in obedience there is joy and peace unspotted, unalloyed; and as God has designed our happiness . . . He never has—He never will institute an ordinance or give a commandment to His people that is not calculated in its nature to promote that happiness which He has designed, and which will not end in the greatest amount of good and glory to those who become the recipients of his law and ordinances."[2]

We see that concept taught many times in the scriptures. There is one place in particular, however, where we can see the relationship between God's commandments and His "sweet refreshment"—in the ten commandments in Exodus chapter 20. Although often portrayed in negative ways, those commandments, etched in stone by the finger of God, were an utmost expression of God's tender mercies and His loving-kindness. The nine latter commandments are directly related to the first—to have no other gods before (translated also as "in the place of") our Heavenly Father. That is for our benefit, not to satisfy God's vanity, or as an autocratic and arbitrary demand for exclusive devotion. There is no one or nothing else that can preserve and protect like our Father—the Almighty God of Abraham, Isaac, and Jacob. Hence, every other commandment ties us back to Him—to His watchful care, to His infinite love and devotion.

The fourth commandment declares:

"Remember the sabbath day, to keep it holy" (Exodus 20:8). Perhaps the key word is *remember*. We are to remember to keep the Sabbath holy in order to remember God and our relationship with Him. To keep our heartstrings firmly fastened to the Lord, He gave the Sabbath as a regular reminder of our need to be exclusively devoted to God in order to be protected, preserved, and prospered. The Hebrew word for Sabbath is *Shabbat* and it literally means "rest." Interestingly, the scriptures speak of "rest"—specifically "the rest of the Lord" as much, much, more than the kind of physical rest represented by taking a nap on the family room sofa. The "rest of the Lord" is the presence of God—eternal life. Sabbath observance was a sign between covenant Israel and their God and a continual reminder that real, lasting rest—both here and hereafter—is not found in the world and in worldly ways, but only through a deep and abiding relationship with the Almighty. So important was this doctrine that very specific laws and expectations served to remind the ancients of the sanctity of the day. Work was to cease both by master and servant (see Exodus 20:10), and even seemingly small tasks requiring little or no effort were forbidden (see Numbers 15:32–36). The violation of this sacred commandment was death (see Exodus 31:15), the same punishment as for idolatry, because failing to honor the Sabbath was a form of infidelity toward God and a form of worshipping the false gods of the world. The death penalty also served as a symbolic reminder that failure to remember God in all aspects of life constitutes a kind of death—a spiritual death in which one is cut off from the life-giving powers of God. In contrast, obedience and devotion to God, as symbolized by Sabbath observance, means life—the abundant life.

I must admit that as I was growing up, whenever I would hear the phrase "keep the Sabbath day holy," my mind immediately focused on the "thou shalt nots." Like the Pharisees of Jesus' day, I had a long mental list of all of the "can't dos" that that command imposed upon me. Viewing the Sabbath this way caused me to think of the commandment as a form of punishment, much like being grounded. Instead of looking forward to it as a day of spiritual rejuvenation and a reminder of my covenantal relationship with God, I dreaded the day and often found myself counting the minutes until real life could resume.

Even as I grew older and had many responsibilities in the Church, I often felt frustrated on the Sabbath, thinking that the only reason the Sabbath kept me close to God was that I was so busy and in so many meetings that I didn't have time to sin. Even when I was not blatantly breaking the fourth commandment, I still couldn't fully understand why the injunction to "remember the sabbath day, to keep it holy" (Exodus 20:8) was so closely akin to "thou shalt have no other gods before me" (Exodus 20:3). Then several years ago I caught the vision in a remarkable and unusual way. I came to see the Sabbath truly as evidence of God's special blessing of love for His chosen people. I saw strict obedience to that commandment as a sign of one's deep love for God and gratitude for His bounteous blessings. I saw that the Sabbath was not burdensome or to be resented, but rather could be a much anticipated and celebrated respite from not only the labors but the ways of the world. I learned this profound lesson not while attending priesthood meeting, serving as a bishop, or attending high council meetings (even though I could have learned it there if I had been more spiritually attuned). I learned it while witnessing an orthodox Jewish rabbi and his family not merely observe but truly celebrate the Sabbath.

I became acquainted with Rabbi David Rosen while teaching at the BYU Jerusalem Center for Near-Eastern Studies. David taught classes on Judaism at the center, and I came to appreciate him as a friend, colleague, and wonderful human being. Each semester David would bring his family to the center to celebrate a Jewish Sabbath with the students and staff there. We became his "family" for that Shabbat. While it was designed to be a cultural and educational experience for the students, it became a profound, life-changing spiritual experience for me. As we sang traditional Jewish Sabbath songs at the Shabbat meal, I could see the utter joy and delight on Rabbi Rosen's face. He and his family actually enjoyed the Sabbath—they loved being together, singing together, eating together, and worshipping God together. There were no complaints of what they couldn't do, such as drive the car or use the electric stove to prepare their food. There was just pure delight in remembering the Lord their God. Each of the various Sabbath activities, and even some of the food partaken at the meal, was symbolic of spiritual matters—the "rest of the Lord." Truly, their Sabbath was not just something to get over with but was a celebration of remembering God and basking in the light of His goodness and grace.

From them I learned that the fourth commandment actually contains two different dimensions regarding our Sabbath worship. Those dimensions are found in the words "remember" and "keep." The rabbis teach that remembering involves much more than the memory. It is our deep-seated attitude of reverence and worship. It reflects our profound love for God and our gratitude for His bounteous goodness. It is the *why* we honor the Lord's Day. Keeping the Sabbath holy involves our actions—all of the Sabbath activities that reflect our remembrance of God. It is the *what* we do or don't do on that holy day. The Sabbath will never become truly delightful to us if we only focus on the *what* without the *why*—the keeping without the remembering.

I was moved to tears when Rabbi Rosen and his wife, Sharon, took each of their children into their arms as part of their weekly Sabbath observance and gave them Sabbath blessings or *Kiddush*. "God make thee as Ephraim and Manasseh," states the blessing to the sons, and to the daughters, "God make thee as Sarah, Rebekah, Rachel, and Leah." The words that the Rosens spoke to their children also included these blessings that are uttered each Sabbath in the synagogue: "The Lord bless thee, and keep thee: The Lord make his face shine upon thee, and be gracious unto thee: The Lord lift up his countenance upon thee, and give thee peace. And they shall put my name upon the children of Israel; and I will bless them" (Numbers 6:24–27).

Rabbi Rosen explained that the Jews view the Sabbath as a queen coming to visit their homes. It is a joyous event, a covenantal sign "that ye may know that I am the Lord that doth sanctify you" (Exodus 31:13). A spice box is also used to provide a special fragrance in the home. It represents the sweetness of the Sabbath and the refreshment it is to the soul. At the conclusion of the Sabbath, a special candle, or *havdalah,* is lit; the light and then the darkness that comes when the candle is extinguished represents the conclusion of something that is sacred (Shabbat) and the beginning again of the mundane and profane. Hence, the Sabbath sanctifies one from the world and strengthens and prepares one to live in the world.

As I watched Rabbi Rosen and his family observe the Sabbath, I came to realize how I had actually cheated myself out of much joy and strength that could have helped me in meeting the challenges of a new week. I had cheated myself by viewing the command to keep the Sabbath as a burdensome chore requiring a composite list of "don'ts" rather than as a "day of delight." Instead of viewing the arrival of the Sabbath as a queen who is honoring my home with her presence, I had been guilty of viewing it more like a grinch who was intent on stealing my joys and stifling my opportunities. Isaiah perhaps said it best: "If thou turn away thy foot from the sabbath, from doing thy pleasure on my holy day; and call the sabbath a delight, the holy of the Lord, honourable; and shalt honour him, not doing thine own ways, nor finding thine own pleasure, nor speaking thine own words: Then shalt thou delight thyself in the Lord; and I will cause thee to ride upon the high places of the earth, and feed thee with the heritage of Jacob thy father: for the mouth of the Lord hath spoken it" (Isaiah 58:13–14).

It shouldn't have taken living in Israel and observing an orthodox Jewish family's Sabbath to learn this valuable lesson—that the Sabbath is truly a "day of delight"—a day of peace, a day of joy, a day of blessing. I had read and taught that scriptural passage, and many others like it, scores of times. I knew it in my head, but I guess in the hurry and scurry of my hectic, crazy, busy life, I had somehow forgotten (or taken for granted) the Lord's promises.

As the false gods of this world—materialism, recreation, vanity, entertainment, professional ambition, and all the rest—press ever more suffocatingly around us, the Lord's command seems more loving and more merciful than ever. In today's fast-paced, idolatrous society, Sabbath observance can be viewed as an outward manifestation of inward devotion to God. When the Lord's holy day becomes just another day, so our relationship with God becomes just another of the many mundane demands upon us instead of a sanctifying, ennobling relationship.

Sabbath observance is not merely a matter of not doing certain things or doing other things. It involves our attitudes and our innermost desires and feelings—our whole being—and our love, devotion, and appreciation for God. It reminds us that there is no rest, no peace, no salvation in the world or in following after its many false gods. The Sabbath is our constant reminder to "always remember him" and to walk not after the idols and images of the world, but to love God first and foremost in our lives. Elder Mark E. Petersen declared: "Our observance or nonobservance of the Sabbath is an unerring measure of our attitude toward the Lord personally and toward his suffering in Gethsemane, his death on the cross, and his resurrection from the dead. It is a sign of whether we are Christians in very deed, or whether our conversion is so shallow that commemoration of his atoning sacrifice means little or nothing to us."[3]

In our day, the Lord has reminded us of two divine purposes for the Sabbath. In Doctrine and Covenants section 59 verses 9 and 10, He declares: "Thou shalt go to the house of prayer and offer up thy sacraments upon my holy day; for verily this is a day appointed unto you to rest from your labors, and to pay thy devotions unto the Most High." Listen again to those divine purposes: "Pay thy devotions unto the Most High" and "rest from your labors." Do you see the parallel to the Savior's words in the New Testament, "Come unto me, all ye that labour and are heavy laden, and I will give you rest"? (Matthew 11:28). It is the Savior, not just a Sunday afternoon nap, who gives us rest. In fact, for most of us, we are so busy on Sundays there is no rest in a napping, slowing down, taking it easy, temporal sort of way. Well then, what does it mean to "rest" and what does that have to do with paying our devotions and offering up our "oblations," as the revelation describes our Sabbath worship? To me the answer is found in D&C 59:9:

"And that thou mayest more fully keep thyself unspotted from the world, thou shalt go to the house of prayer and offer up thy sacraments upon my holy day" (emphasis added). It is through the sacrament of the Lord's Supper—not just from a quiet, reverential, restful Sunday—that I become "unspotted from the world." There is nothing more tiring than carrying the burden of sin. There is nothing more wearying than the world and worldliness. The Savior's infinite Atonement—remembered with the sacred tokens of bread and water—can wash away wickedness and world-liness and weariness. That is the "rest" the Lord has promised. No won-der those few minutes in sacrament meeting are to be among the most sacred and profound moments of our lives. The sacrament should be, as President Gordon B. Hinckley taught, "the very heart of our sabbath wor-ship. . . . A blessing without peer."[4]

I have found in my own personal life, when I have been struggling and feeling weighed down either emotionally, spiritually, or physically that the partaking of the sacrament was a source of great spiritual strength and that those quiet, reverent moments during its administration served as a spiritual oasis—"a refuge from the storm" (D&C 115:6). Not only do we renew our covenants with the worthy partaking of the emblems of the Lord's supreme sacrifice, but we also receive anew the promise of having the Holy Ghost as our constant companion—our sanctifier, our guide and comforter. What a blessing of His grace that we have an opportunity each week to focus on the Savior and feel of His love—even for just a few min-utes. I wonder if we realize how important, how powerful, how sustaining those moments really are. The spiritual depth of our Sabbath observance is to a large degree determined by our sacrament worship. That is a daunt-ing thought. I know that sacrament worship may be difficult at times—especially for young mothers. I admit that at times I have been guilty of what I call the "Sunday dreads" because of speaking assignments, leader-ship responsibilities, or in days past, the anticipation of another bout of tag-team wrestling with our children during sacrament meeting. Yet, those moments during the administration of the sacrament need to become our "sacred space" where we can exclusively focus on what matters most in time and eternity. Elder Jeffrey R. Holland gave us some suggestions as to how to do just that: "We could remember the Savior's premortal life and all that we know Him to have done as the great Jehovah, creator of heaven and earth and all things that in them are. We could remember that even in the grand council of heaven He loved us and was wonder-fully strong, that we triumphed even there by the power of Christ and our faith in the blood of the Lamb (see Rev. 12:10–11). . . .

"We could remember Christ's miracles and His teachings, His heal-ings and His help. We could remember that He gave sight to the blind and hearing to the deaf and motion to the lame and the maimed and the with-ered. Then, on those days when we feel our progress has halted or our joys and views have grown dim, we can press forward steadfastly in Christ, with unshaken faith in Him and a perfect brightness of hope (see 2 Ne. 31:19–20).

"We could remember that even with such a solemn mission given to Him, the Savior found delight in living; He enjoyed people and told His disciples to be of good cheer. He said we should be as thrilled with the gospel as one who had found a great treasure, a veritable pearl of great price, right on our own doorstep. We could remember that Jesus found special joy and happiness in children and said all of us should be more like them—guileless and pure, quick to laugh and to love and to forgive, slow to remember any offense. . . .

"We could—and should—remember the wonderful things that have come to us in our lives and that 'all things which are good cometh of Christ' (Moro. 7:24). Those of us who are so blessed could remember the courage of those around us who face more difficulty than we, but who remain cheerful, who do the best they can, and trust that the Bright and

Morning Star will rise again for them—as surely He will do (see Rev. 22:16).

"On some days we will have cause to remember the unkind treatment he received, the rejection He experienced, and the injustice—oh, the injustice—He endured. When we, too, then face some of that in life, we can remember that Christ was also 'troubled on every side, [but] not distressed; . . . perplexed, but not in despair; persecuted, but not forsaken; cast down, but not destroyed' (2 Cor. 4:8–9).

"When those difficult times come to us, we can remember that Jesus had to descend below all things before He could ascend above them, and that He suffered pains and afflictions and temptations of every kind that He might be filled with mercy and know how to succor His people in their infirmities (see Alma 7:11–12; D&C 88:6).

"All this we could remember when we are invited by a kneeling young priest to remember Christ always."[5]

I pray that our observance of the Sabbath will be a true reflection of our love and gratitude for the Savior. May we strive to make it truly a day of delight, not a day of dread. May we search our souls more deeply and recommit ourselves by making necessary changes so that our moments of worship during the sacrament can truly be "sacred space" whereby the world is washed away and our burdens are made light. As we do, I promise that we will come to know more personally and profoundly what it means to know the "rest of the Lord."

NOTES

1. *Hymns of The Church of Jesus Christ of Latter-day Saints* (Salt Lake City: The Church of Jesus Christ of Latter-day Saints, 1985), no. 125.
2. Joseph Smith, *Teachings of the Prophet Joseph Smith,* comp. Joseph Fielding Smith (Salt Lake City: Deseret Book, 1976), 256–57.
3. Mark E. Petersen, Conference Report, April 1975, 72.
4. Gordon B. Hinckley, "Priesthood Restoration," *Ensign,* October 1988, 72.
5. Jeffrey R. Holland, *Trusting Jesus* (Salt Lake City: Deseret Book, 2003), 21–24.

MY HOPE CHEST

Elizabeth Tanner

My parents recently gave me a beautiful hope chest. It's made of cherry wood, and it's lined with cedar, as is traditional for hope chests. Cedar is a choice wood because it has a spicy aroma, and it keeps out moths and other cloth-eating bugs. People began using it back in the day to line chests so that their linens and the things they put within it could be preserved. Over the years, my siblings and I have received what we've endearingly called "hope chest items" for Christmas or birthdays: things like linens, china, silverware, things that we can eventually use in a home. So I'm grateful to have a hope chest now to put those things in.

A hope chest traditionally served to have women keep most of what would be their trousseau within it, so that when they did get married they would have a hope chest filled with things to take to their new marriage. I'm so grateful for this hope chest and yet, in a sense, I feel that what it represents has been a little difficult for me to swallow, especially at this stage in my life. It represents hope in a future that could include a family and a husband and a home of my own, and those aren't things that have

Elizabeth Tanner is a nurse and holds a degree in Latin American studies from Brigham Young University and a BS in Nursing from the University of Arizona. She served a mission to Virginia Richmond from 2002–2003. She is the daughter of John S. Tanner, the academic vice president at Brigham Young University, and Susan W. Tanner, the former Young Women general president.

happened for me yet. So, in a sense, having a hope chest almost mocks those prospects that I really desire.

I think that many of us struggle to feel hope in our lives, for various reasons. We may yearn to be married; we may yearn to have children; we may yearn for financial security that we don't have or for physical or emotional health that we may not have. And it's especially difficult to feel hope for ourselves when we look around and we see other people obtaining these blessings while our dreams go unrealized. When we are children, it's easy to have grandiose hopes: I've heard my nieces and nephews talking about the things that they hope for, and I remember that when I was little, I thought I would grow up and star in musicals or be popular in high school and have lots of amazing boys wanting to go out with me. Things like that, they're the kind of grandiose hopes that usually don't necessarily happen just the way you think they will. Experience tends to suck a bit of the hope out of you, because as you grow older and as you experience life in its reality, things don't always work out exactly the way you had planned. And you feel that some of your dreams are deferred.

It's easy to blame ourselves when our hopes aren't realized. I've thought a lot about that as I've struggled. I've felt a sense of despair at times in my life because things hadn't worked out as I'd hoped. I've wondered if it's something that I've done wrong, and I think many of us have had those feelings where we wonder, "Am I living beneath the promises that have been made to me?" I've thought a lot about the story in the New Testament where the disciples come to Jesus and they point to a blind man, and they say, "Who did sin, this man, or his parents, that he was born blind?" (John 9:2). The disciples obviously felt that this blind man was being punished for some reason with blindness. He had a trial that was great. His life hadn't worked out exactly how we would hope that life would. The disciples thought it must mean that he'd done something wrong—either he or his parents must have sinned. I know that I've felt that way at times—and many of us probably have when things haven't worked out as we planned. It's easy to blame ourselves and maybe even blame God and wonder why things are the way they are. But the Savior's response is poignant. He says, "Neither hath this man sinned, nor his parents: but that the works of God should be made manifest in him" (John 9:3).

Part of this life's experience is to go through struggles and to have things not work out as we'd hoped or planned for. Yet, the Savior says that's part of the plan, that the works of God may be manifest in us. It's our responsibility to try to understand as well as we can why our lives are challenging, and then seek to magnify the qualities the Savior would have us magnify so that the works of God can be made manifest in us.

Those who know me know that I can be a little bit dramatic at times. I feel things very intensely, and lately I have taken to quoting the made-for-TV movie *Anne of Green Gables,* whose heroine was also a little bit intense and emotional at times. She says, often, "My life is a perfect grave-yard of buried hopes."[1] I admit that I've repeated that many times, feeling like it sounds so like my life—her life is a perfect graveyard of buried hopes! How many of us have felt that at times? And then she claims to be in the "depths of despair," as I also have claimed at times. Marilla, whom she is living with at the time, says to her, "To despair is to turn your back on God."[2] I never liked it when Marilla said this to Anne in the movie, because I thought, "That's so unsympathetic." But I think that, to a cer-tain extent, that line is true. Despair is essentially a self-pitying, self-centered emotion. Even in the scriptures we're taught by Moroni that despair is a sin (see Moroni 10:22). President Uchtdorf, in his talk "The Infinite Power of Hope," talks about what the feeling of despair can do to us, which I think is the antithesis of hope. He says, "The adversary uses despair to bind hearts and minds in suffocating darkness. Despair drains from us all that is vibrant and joyful and leaves behind the empty rem-nants of what life was meant to be. Despair kills ambitions, advances sick-ness, pollutes the soul, and deadens the heart."[3] Really, despair gives us that graveyard of buried hopes, more than anything else. I've felt those feelings. I've felt when despair has almost bound my heart and sucked the life out of me, and I know that that's not something we want in our lives, and that not only are we *not* supposed to despair but we *are* supposed to hope. The scriptures teach us that. Many times, my dad has said to me that hope isn't just a good thing to feel, but it's actually a commandment. Moroni teaches that without faith, hope, and charity, we cannot enter into the kingdom of God and that without hope we cannot be saved (see Mormon 10:21).

So we know that hope is a commandment, but sometimes knowing something in our minds and being able to put it into practice is a completely different thing. I've found that in my life. For some people it's easier to feel hope; some people are, perhaps, natural-born optimists. And then some of us struggle more to feel that hope because we struggle with anxiety or feelings of fear regarding the future, especially regarding our own lives. Yet we, too, are commanded to have hope. There are some things that we can do that can help us cultivate this important virtue. President Uchtdorf says that "we learn to cultivate hope the same way we learn to walk: one step at a time."[4] In a sense, we can all fashion spiritual hope chests by learning to put into practice certain companion virtues, and also by learning to take a step at a time to cultivate this hope.

I recently watched my little niece Susie learn how to walk, so this quote about cultivating hope one step at a time takes on new meaning. Susie really liked to crawl, and even when she learned how to walk and we'd seen her take a few steps, she always reverted back to her chosen mode of transportation, crawling. This was because when she would take her steps, they were tenuous at first. So she would go back to crawling. But little by little, as she practiced—as we've all seen children do, I'm sure—she decided that walking was actually for her, and she now loves to walk around everywhere. You almost never see her crawl. In some ways this can be a great metaphor for us as we seek to learn how to cultivate hope in our lives one step at a time.

Sometimes despair or discouragement is our chosen mode of transportation because it's a little bit easier, and our steps of hope initially take a lot of effort and may be tenuous. But as we strive to take those steps, we can cultivate hope and we'll be blessed to choose that as our chosen mode of transportation and our chosen way of being.

We have to put forth effort to cultivate hope and to take those steps, but one of the blessings for doing so is that Heavenly Father never leaves us alone. He also has given us the blessing of being able to pray for hope, and in His mercy He will bless us for those efforts that we put forth. He will bless us with the ability to feel the gift of hope in our lives through the Comforter. Moroni taught that the Comforter can fill us with hope (see Moroni 8:26). This hope is a gift of the Spirit, and we can—and we should—pray for it. As we pray for it, Heavenly Father will bless our efforts. I have found that sometimes the best way to cultivate hope is not necessarily by just focusing on having hope, but to focus on specific companion virtues to hope—that's what my dad has called them before. This can increase our hope as we learn to cultivate these companion virtues in our lives. I want to mention four of these virtues that we can hopefully put in our spiritual trousseaus or hope chests.

The first of these is charity, or service. Despair and discouragement are essentially self-centered. They prevent us from being able to look outside of ourselves, to feel charity—the pure love of Christ. To reach out to others is one way that we can lift ourselves as well. Whenever we're feeling frustrated or sad or self-pitying, my mom has always encouraged us to go and do something for other people. Most of the time, that's not what you want to hear, but it does end up being a blessing. She learned this as a little girl: When she was in kindergarten, she was so scared to go to class, she didn't want to leave her mom's side. One day, when she arrived at class, my grandma saw that another little girl was sitting at her desk with her head down crying because she also was scared to be in that kindergarten class. My grandma wisely said to my mom, "Look, Susie, that little girl is so sad to be here. I think you should go over and help her feel better." So my mom dutifully went over and started talking to the little girl, and when she looked up, her mom had left. But it didn't matter because my mom now had a friend. She had somebody that could help her in that time and she was also helping that little girl. That's a simple illustration, but I think that it holds true in our lives. When we're able to reach out to others, then somehow our own burdens seem a little bit lighter.

In a talk entitled "'Brightness of Hope,'" Elder Neal A. Maxwell explained that it's our responsibility to "lift hands which hang hopelessly down."[5] I love this image because, even at times when we feel like ours are the hands that are hanging hopelessly down, we still have that responsibility to reach out to others. We know that our baptismal covenants include what we read about in Mosiah, "to mourn with those that mourn; . . . and comfort those that stand in need of comfort" (Mosiah 18:9). As we do this, Heavenly Father knew that we would be twice-blessed, that the giver is just as blessed as the receiver. So, I think that charity is such an essential virtue to have to help us feel more hope in our lives.

The next virtue is gratitude. I believe that gratitude can help us cultivate hope in our lives because we're able to recognize the hand of the Lord in our lives in the past, which helps us have hope for the future. My mom has given us, on a number of occasions over the years, gratitude journals. (I guess she thought we needed the reminder.) And she has encouraged us to look for the blessings that we have each day. This isn't a new idea in the Church. In 2007, President Eyring counseled in his talk, "O Remember, Remember" that we should remember the blessings we have each day and answer this question at the end of every day: "How have I seen the hand of God reaching out to touch us or our children or our family today?"[6] There is great power in asking ourselves this question because it helps us recognize that God is blessing us. There's great power in writing down our answers, because sometimes when I feel in the depths of despair or I feel discouraged, it's hard for me to count my blessings and it's hard for me to remember that God has blessed me. If it's written down, it's a lot harder to dispute or forget. I recently was going through one of my gratitude journals (which, in many attempts to keep, only lasted for a little while). It was at a time when I was living in Arizona and I was all alone. I moved there to go to school, and it was a time that I remember as being a hard and difficult experience. Yet as I read through this journal, I recognized that Heavenly Father had blessed me—maybe not necessarily in the ways that I was hoping for at the time, but He had blessed me and was aware of me at that time, as He is at all times for each of us. So it's important to cultivate that gratitude to help us to feel hope for the future.

The third virtue that I want to talk about is an eternal perspective and having hope in eternal promises. This is one of the most important things that we can do in our quest to have hope. We need to recognize that Heavenly Father has eternal promises He will bless us with. Sometimes it's a little bit frustrating to me because it seems like the experiences that you read about that the Saints had or that the prophets had were really hard. As I've studied the scriptures—I know their experiences were so trying. In some ways, they don't get better for us, either. Abinadi was burned at the stake; Nephi watched his brothers apostatize and deny the faith; Mormon and Moroni watched as their people were destroyed; there was carnage, both literal and spiritual, all around them. Yet they all still had hope. It wasn't the hope that things would go as they wanted them to go right then, but it was the eternal hope that there was a greater hope and greater promises in store. (My dad's presentation will be about seeing these promises afar off.)

Elder Maxwell distinguishes between this ultimate hope and proximate hope. He said, "Prophets have always had and taught ultimate hope in Christ. . . . Having ultimate hope does not mean we will always be rescued from proximate problems."[7] I've learned from experience that, in fact, we aren't rescued from all of our proximate problems, but we will be rescued from everlasting death. "Meanwhile, ultimate hope makes it possible to use the same three words used centuries ago by three valiant men. They knew God could rescue them from the fiery furnace, if He chose. '*But if not,*' they said, nevertheless, they would still serve him!"[8] Those are powerful words. We may not be rescued from all of our proximate problems in this lifetime, *but if not,* we can still serve God. Not only can we still serve God, but because we have an eternal perspective, we can overcome our daily struggles a little bit better.

I noticed in this past general conference a theme of people talking about trials and struggles. It's because trials are such a universal experience. All of us face despair or deferred dreams at times. President Monson related stories about these in one of his talks titled, "Be of Good Cheer." He told three stories that were in some senses completely depressing if you weren't looking at them with an eternal perspective. One that struck me was of a woman who lived in East Prussia during World War II. Her husband died during the war, and she was told that she needed to move to West Germany. So she took her small children all by herself and made the journey to West Germany, and in the process lost every single one of her children.[9] I thought, "How are we supposed to be of good cheer when we hear stories like this?" But although she hadn't been rescued from her proximate problems, she still recognized, when she was in the depths of despair, a need to pray. And when she prayed she felt her heart comforted because of the ultimate hope she had in the Savior, Jesus Christ.

That is the final virtue—the one that I think is most important that we can cultivate to increase our hope: cultivating a testimony of and a relationship with the Savior, Jesus Christ. When everything seems dark, we can still cultivate a testimony of Jesus, the Savior. As I have studied about hope, this is what it always comes back to: that the Savior is our ultimate source of hope. I love His title, the "Hope of Israel" (Jeremiah 17:13), because He truly can become our hope and He *is* the hope of Israel. Because of what He suffered in life and death and in His Atonement, He is our true source of hope. Moroni writes, "And what is it that ye shall hope for? Behold I say unto you that ye shall have hope through the atonement of Christ and the power of his resurrection, to be raised unto life eternal, and this because of your faith in him according to the promise" (Moroni 7:41). President Uchtdorf says, along those same lines, "No matter how bleak the chapter of our lives may look today, because of the life and sacrifice of Jesus Christ, we may hope and be assured that the ending of the book of our lives will exceed our grandest expectations."[10]

I know that the Savior is our source of hope, and I'm grateful for that. I'm grateful for Elder Holland's insights about the Savior. Many times I've felt that he has such a great understanding of who the Savior is, and how He can be truly our Balm of Gilead. In his November 1999 general conference talk, "'An High Priest of Things to Come,'" he talked about the familiar story of the Savior calming the sea, about how the Savior wasn't just a distant bystander during that storm, but that He was on the boat with the disciples, and He felt the waves crash, and the trial they were experiencing. Because of that He was better able to calm the storm.[11] I love that insight; I love understanding that because the Savior was on the boat with His disciples, He knew exactly the trials that they were passing through. He wasn't judging them. He was truly on their side and understood their feelings perfectly. I know that, because of the Atonement, we can know that the Savior understands our feelings perfectly, and He can give us the true comfort that we need. He is our true source of hope, the Hope of Israel. Elder Holland says that because He was on the boat with those people, "Christ knows better than all others that the trials of life can be very deep and we are not shallow people if we struggle with them."[12] I know that we have a Savior who doesn't think that we're shallow people when we struggle or feel discouraged, and I know ultimately we can feel hope because of His Atonement and Resurrection.

I have some favorite scriptures that talk about the Atonement. One of them is in Hebrews 4:15. It says that "we have not an high priest which cannot be touched with the feeling of our infirmities; but was in all points tempted like as we are, yet without sin." And then along those same lines, Alma 7:11–12 explains that the Savior "shall go forth, suffering pains and afflictions and temptations of every kind . . . and he will take upon him their infirmities, that his bowels may be filled with mercy, according to the flesh, that he may know according to the flesh how to succor his people." I know that we do have an High Priest that is aware of our feelings and our infirmities, and that He can be touched because He suffered the great atoning sacrifice. He understands and knows each of us, and our emotions, personally. He knows them. He is not a distant bystander, but He is there to hold us up during trials.

This understanding can give us hope. Elder Holland described in the April 2009 general conference the lonely road that the Savior had to walk to Calvary, abandoned not just by the crowds that had adored Him, but by His friends and disciples and even family.[13] Most of us have probably felt a little bit of this type of loneliness. Recently, all of my siblings and many of my friends have gotten married and started families, and though I feel very close to all of them, it's been a bit of a difficult transition. I've felt the loneliness associated with not feeling that I fit in around my closest friends and family. I'm so grateful to know that, although I often feel alone, I'm not alone.

One of the things I like to do is stretch my hand out to touch someone else's hand. People who know me know that I'm a very touchy-feely, tactile person. Lots of times when I see someone I will want to just reach out and hold and squeeze their hand. I remember when I was in Arizona living by myself and struggling because I felt so alone, I felt as if much of the time there wasn't somebody to reach back. I am grateful to know that because of the Atonement, we have a Savior who will reach back and grasp our hands in our most difficult times. This can be a great source of hope for us.

He will embrace us in His arms of mercy in our trying times. He is my anchor and my hope. I know that we can choose to have hope, and that as we cultivate the value of hope, and its companion virtues of charity, service, gratitude, and understanding eternal promises—and especially as we cultivate our relationship with the Savior—that we will be blessed. We will have a spiritual trousseau or hope chest that is filled with a dowry of virtues that are worthy of the Bridegroom when He comes again. I'm so grateful for this gospel and for the knowledge that it gives us and the hope that it brings us.

NOTES

1. *Anne of Green Gables*, DVD, directed by Kevin Sullivan (1985; Toronto, Ontario, Canada: Sullivan Entertainment, 2001).
2. Ibid.
3. Dieter F. Uchtdorf, "The Infinite Power of Hope," *Ensign*, November 2008, 22–23.
4. Ibid., 22–23.
5. Neal A. Maxwell, "'Brightness of Hope,'" *Ensign*, November 1994, 36.
6. Henry B. Eyring, "O Remember, Remember," *Ensign*, November 2007, 67.
7. Maxwell, "'Brightness of Hope,'" 35.
8. Ibid.; emphasis added.
9. Thomas S. Monson, "Be of Good Cheer," *Ensign*, May 2009, 91–92.
10. Uchtdorf, "The Infinite Power of Hope," 22–23.
11. See Jeffery R. Holland, "'An High Priest of Good Things to Come,'" *Ensign*, November 1999, 37.
12. Ibid.
13. See Holland, "None Were with Him," *Ensign*, May 2009, 87.

PROMISES AFAR OFF

John S. Tanner

Isn't Elizabeth great? It's such a privilege for me to be able to be on this program with her. We've both been blessed from having been invited to focus on our assigned topic of hope. I want to begin by telling the story of Elizabeth's birth. My experience on that day made me feel a certain kinship with Abraham on his long journey from Haran to Canaan. My title, "Promises Afar Off," comes from the description in Hebrews of Abraham as a pilgrim and wanderer who set an example for believers in every age who likewise must steadfastly cling to promises afar off.

I missed Elizabeth's birth. I've been trying to make up for this to her ever since—and she often reminds me that I neglected her from the beginning. This is the way it happened: When Elizabeth was about to be born, my wife, Susan, and I were living in Berkeley, California, where I was completing six long years of graduate study. I received a job offer at Florida State University. In order for us to have our insurance cover Elizabeth's birth (Susan's fourth cesarean section baby), Susan had to have the baby

---

John S. Tanner is the academic vice president at Brigham Young University. He holds a BA in English from BYU, and a PhD from the University of California, Berkeley. He taught English as an assistant professor at The Florida State University and is a professor of English at BYU. His book, Anxiety in Eden, was named the best work of the year by the Milton Society of America in 1992. He is married to Susan W. Tanner, the former Young Women general president, and they have five children and twelve grandchildren.

in California where we were insured. I couldn't stay around for the big event because I had to meet a teaching schedule out in Florida. We were poor as church mice, so flying back and forth between Florida and California was not an option, nor was paying movers to haul our meager belongings across the country. So we put everything we had in a little five-by-seven trailer. I then loaded our three small children in the car and drove the children to my in-laws in Salt Lake City, leaving Susan in the care of friends to drive her to and from the hospital for the birth.

The day before Elizabeth's birth was scheduled, I left Salt Lake early in the morning and headed across the country on my journey: all alone, just me and the trailer. Sometime after midnight on the day that Elizabeth was to be born, I was driving through the empty places of New Mexico, on a road I had never driven. The map showed a little detour where I could cut from Highway 40 to Interstate 25. I decided to take it. It was about a forty-mile cutoff. I well remember driving that desolate stretch of road. The sky was black. There were no towns or even houses. There were no lights at all. For the whole forty miles, I saw no other cars, nor anybody else on the road traveling in either direction. I wasn't quite sure that the road I was on was the right road because there were no signs. So there I was with this little trailer in the middle of nowhere, by myself, at night, on a back road, and not entirely sure where I was. It all made me more than a little nervous.

In this state, there came into my mind a phrase from the Pearl of Great Price about Abraham, describing his journey through a strange land: "Therefore, eternity was our covering and our rock and our salvation, as we journeyed from Haran . . . to the land of Canaan" (Abraham 2:16). I kept thinking of the phrase, "eternity was our covering and our rock." It seemed to describe perfectly both the way I felt at that moment and the way Susan and I had often felt on our journey over the past six years of graduate schooling. We had frequently felt like pilgrims, on a journey needing Abrahamic faith and hope to pursue a degree in a field where there were very uncertain prospects for ever finding work and while having our children, the fourth one to be born that very day. As I drove through the night, I thought of Abraham, who traveled under the same sky, taking "eternity" for his covering, rock, and salvation. Abraham was our hero of hope and of faith.

In the morning, I stopped for gas in Socorro, New Mexico. *Socorro*, which means "help" in Spanish, seemed appropriately named. In addition to getting gas, I called Susan, the help ever meet for me, and wished her well on the journey she was about to undertake that day. She was about to go on a journey through the valley of death she had entered three times before. She sounded a little apprehensive. It had been a hard pregnancy; indeed, one discouraged by our doctor. As I hung up and drove south through the desert, I discovered that the highway bordered and sometimes crossed an old Spanish trail called Jornada del Muerto—the Journey of the Dead. It all felt a bit ominous. And I prayed again, as I had in the night, for Susan and for me.

Elizabeth was born later that day. There were no cell phones then. All I could do was pray and wait for a time and place to call the hospital. I finally reached Susan from Ozona, Texas. After she told me the time of day Elizabeth was born, I calculated that she must have been born just about as I was driving by the town of Esperanza, Texas. *Esperanza*, of course, means "hope." So Elizabeth is, in multiple ways, a child of hope for Susan and for me. It thus seems fitting to talk about hope with her, and about Abraham, and about living on promises seen afar off.

In Chapter 11 of Hebrews (one of my favorite chapters in scripture), Abraham is described as a hero of faith and of hope. We are reminded that he lived much of his life as a sojourner, a wanderer, a nomad, a pilgrim. Spiritually, he also lived as a pilgrim. He lived all his life on promises— promises of a son, promises of a land, promises of posterity, and promises of a Savior. In verse 13, scripture holds up Abraham as the example of all the prophets and righteous people who died before Jesus was born, thus before they could inherit the promises. It says, "These all died in faith, not having received the promises, but having seen them afar off, and were persuaded of them, and embraced them, and confessed that they were strangers and pilgrims on the earth" (Hebrews 11:13). Abraham is our great exemplar of what it means to be persuaded of and then hold fast to promises seen afar off.

This is a familiar condition for most of us. We live in expectation. We live on promises, faith, and hope. We live in the middle of things. There's a literary term for this. It's called *in medias res*. Anciently, poets were taught to begin epic poems in the middle of things, *in medias res*. They were not to begin the story at the beginning, but to tell it with flashbacks and visions of future history. Our lives are to us just such epic stories. All of us live *in medias res*. Mortality is about being on a journey somewhere in the middle of things between birth and death. Indeed, as Latter-day Saints, we know that mortal existence itself, already at birth, begins in the middle of things. This is the second act of a three-act play, which we call earth life.

It can be really hard—for me, anyway—to live in the middle of things, *in medias res*. It makes each of us a character in the novel or the movie of our own lives. We don't want to be the character caught in the plot; we want to be the reader or viewer. As characters in our own dramas, we can't read or fast-forward to the end. When my wife gets into a suspenseful novel, she likes to skip ahead to the last chapter so that she can see how (or if) things will turn out. Though I tease her about this, I know why she does it. I feel the same way when I'm watching a suspenseful sporting event. When the game is tight, I often yearn for a fast-forward button. I want to know how it will turn out. The suspense can make me want to put my head down and wait to watch the replay. It's hard to be in the middle of things. Our lives are full of plot twists and turns. They're full of the suspense of not knowing exactly how things are going to turn out. But unfortunately, in the book of our own lives, we can't flip to the last chapter; in the movies we star in we can't push a fast-forward button to see how this is going to turn out. The action is always "live." The only way out is through. Yes, we have ultimate promises of how things will turn out if we are faithful. But these promises pertain to things afar off. Meanwhile, we have to live *in medias res*.

Elder Maxwell called this "living in the muddled, mortal middle," which is a phrase I quite like with all of its alliteration. We must muddle through the mortal middle of our lives. As we do so, we have promises that have been given to us, but they are often afar off. Here's what Elder Maxwell said: "You can have clear faith in the ultimate outcomes at the end of the trail but still find vexing the uncertainties in the steps immediately ahead. The Lord knows the end from the beginning and everything in between. You, however, have to function in the muddled, mortal middle."[1] Most, if not all of us, would like to be like Moses rather than like Abraham. We long for mountaintop experiences, like Moses had, where we are taken up to the top of a high mountain and shown all things, from the beginning to the end of the Earth. Instead, we're consigned to tread in Abraham's footsteps on our journey, holding on to eternity as our rock and covering on this journey of faith. Abraham left his homeland "not knowing whither he went," "sojourned in the land of promise, as in a strange country," dwelled the rest of his life as a nomad in tents, and "looked for a city which hath foundations, whose builder and maker is God" (Hebrews 11: 8–10). The city of God eluded him; nonetheless he continued to cling to promises, taking one step at a time and embracing promises—promises afar off.

In our muddled, mortal middle sometimes things don't work out as we had hoped. Loved ones who are sick sometimes don't recover. Some people don't get married. Some couples don't have children. Sometimes we lose our jobs. Sometimes our friends, our children, and even our spouses deeply disappoint us. As Hamlet says, our lives are subject to "the thousand natural shocks that flesh is heir to"[2]—to heartache and hurt. None of us can escape this; all of us have to go through it. There's no way out but through.

So how do we get through the muddled, mortal middle of things? How do we traverse our own wilderness when it is dark and we are alone and eternity is our only covering and rock? We have to do what the Saints of old did. We have to cling to promises, both proximate and afar off, not only with faith but with a brightness of hope.

Faith and hope are kindred virtues, but they're not identical twins. Faith is a noun. Hope is both a noun and a verb. Hope is active. It is the act of the soul reaching out to the future. And it's personal, not just propositional. You can have faith in abstract propositions about the present and past. For example, you can have faith that the Church is true, or that Joseph Smith was a prophet of God. These are crucial beliefs but they don't speak to what I hope for. I can have faith in the proposition that Jesus can save sinners but despair that He will save me. Hope is essentially and intensely personal. It concerns not only the future but more specifically my own future.

Another way to think of the difference between faith and hope is to look at the antonyms. The antonym for *faith* is *doubt*, which can be a bad thing spiritually but is not always sinful; it can be good to doubt. The antonym for *hope* is *despair,* which is a far worse thing and is inherently sinful, not to mention miserable. *Despair* comes from a Latin root meaning to be without hope, or even against hope. At its deepest sense it is a denial of the Atonement. To deny hope is to deny that Christ has power to redeem us from our misery and make things whole again. This is why many theologians have classified despair as a sin—just as did Marilla to Anne of Green Gables, and as did Mormon in writing to Moroni. We should fight despair, as I have often told Elizabeth, because, finally, to despair is to give up on the Atonement. Things can be different not just in principle or for others but for you and me, because God loves you and me and because Jesus has atoned for you and for me and has promised that He will make all things right—not just in some abstract, cosmic way but for each of us individually.

The lack of hope (that is, despair) seems to me to be an even greater challenge in our age than is doubt. Maybe in any age, but especially in our age. A few years ago I told President Packer that I planned to give a talk on hope. He told me the following story of Elder Theodore Tuttle. Elder Tuttle went into a Greek restaurant with his wife, who looked Greek to the proprietor. The owner of the restaurant was quite taken by her. So he made them an offer. He said, "If you can tell me what the greatest thing in the world is, I'll give you your meal for free." The Tuttles talked together and then said, "The greatest thing is love." The owner of the restaurant, who had survived the Holocaust, responded with feeling, "No, the greatest thing is not love. The greatest thing is hope. You can live without love, but you cannot live without hope." Hope is a heavenly virtue without which we are of all people most miserable. To lack hope is to despair, and there is no hell so awful as the hell of despair.

How can we lay hold upon the anchor of hope in a world awash in self-pity and despair? We can take courage from the example of Abraham and Sarah, who clung to promises however far off they seemed. We must tread as ancient prophets tread, and hope in promises afar off without staggering. Abraham and Sarah had to wait for years before God fulfilled His promise to grant them a son. In an even deeper sense, they along with all the faithful who lived in anticipation of the birth of Jesus, "died in faith, not having received the promises, but having seen them afar off" (Hebrews 11:13). We, too, like Abraham and all those who lived before

Jesus' birth, live before Jesus has come again. Living on this side of the Second Coming, we, too, have to have faith and hope in the grand promises of reunion and redemption. As Paul said of Abraham, we too must "stagger not" (see Romans 4:20) at the marvelous promises of joy which await us at the coming of the Son, just as Abraham staggered not at the promise of a son.

Abraham "staggered not" at this and other promises even though some promises were not realized in his lifetime. Think of the promise that God would give him the land of Canaan. Over and over and over, the Lord repeats this promise—this land will be yours and your multitudinous posterity's. Yet, as the Apostle Stephen said, "[The Lord] gave him none inheritance in it, no, not so much as to set his foot on" (Acts 7:5). In fact, when Abraham's wife Sarah died, he didn't even own enough land in Canaan to bury her. He had to buy a little bit of land in the cave of Machpelah. Both Sarah and Abraham died as nomads. Yet over and over again, the Lord had promised them the land.

It was similar with the child of promise for Abraham and Sarah. How many years did they wait on that promised boy, that son of promise? Yet year after year no son was born. The promise remained unfulfilled. They had to cling to promises afar off, and stagger not at the Lord's promises.

Chapter 11 of Hebrews lists a number of other Old Testament prophets who likewise had to hope for promises afar off. In this life, they often suffered. In Hebrews it says that they were stoned, as Jeremiah was stoned; they were sawn asunder (tradition has it that Isaiah was cut asunder, in half); they were tempted, slain with the sword, wandered about in sheepskins and goatskins; they were destitute, afflicted, and tormented. And yet, like Abraham, we read that "these all . . . obtained a good report" although they "received not the promise" (Hebrews 11:39).

This is our challenge, too. It's to embrace promises, including promises afar off—the promise that we'll be resurrected, the promise that we'll be reunited with our loved ones, the promise of peace on Earth, the promise that God shall wipe away all tears. All these are ultimate, millennial promises. We who live this side of the Second Coming must embrace them with faith and hope. We must also hold fast to the personal promises we've received through patriarchal and priesthood blessings and through the private whispering of the Spirit to our hearts. It's difficult to do because so often such promises seem to be like mirages on the horizon, just receding beyond our grasp as we approach them—promises afar off.

So how can we embrace promises afar off? Let me mention just three suggestions in closing. First, we can expand the horizon of our hope. In everyday usage, we often use the word "hope" to refer to desires and expectations: some proximate, some ultimate; some temporal, some trivial. We say, "I hope my team wins"; "I hope that I get a letter today"; "I hope the cake turns out." We hope for this, that, and the other. Such hopes speak to our whims and wishes. Such hopes may be fleeting and they are not sure. It's good to be hopeful about small things. It's good to have hopes, with a lower case "h." But such hopes are not the Hope we have in Christ, which we might refer to with a capital H. Gospel Hope is sure because it concerns ultimate promises. It is sure because these promises are underwritten by the Savior and His Atonement. These are promises written in blood, as it were, in the blood of the Lamb. We need to expand the horizon of our hopes to see and seize such promises. But such promises are sure. We have the sure promise that ultimately, if we live faithfully, we shall triumph over Satan and death—that is, we shall be resurrected and redeemed. We have the sure promise that if we live the gospel, we shall have "peace in this world, and eternal life in the world to come" (D&C 59:23), even amid tribulations. On such rock-solid promises as these you and I can anchor our little boats through life's tempestuous seas. In such promises we can find hope, sure and solid, that nothing can separate us from the love of God. As Paul says, "For I am persuaded, that neither death, nor life, . . . nor powers, nor things present, nor things to come, Nor height, nor depth, nor any other creature, shall be able to separate us from the love of God, which is in Christ Jesus our Lord" (Romans 8:38–39). We can expand the horizon of our hope.

Second, we can steel ourselves to endure the trial within the trial. There is often a secondary trial within the afflictions we are called to endure. I call this "the trial within the trial." Many trials test not only our ability to suffer them, but our ability to cling to promises afar off that they will pass. We must endure many trials in this life. It may be illness; it may be a broken relationship, a wayward child or spouse; it may be poverty; it may be any number of things. In almost every trial, there's another secondary trial, which is often as difficult or more so than the primary trial.

This is the trial within the trial. It is the trial of uncertainty about *when* and *if* our trials will end and the Lord's promises will be fulfilled. It is the trial of enduring God's timetable. One of the most frequent prayers in the scriptures is this, and it is echoed all throughout the scriptures: "How long, O Lord?" Over and over again, prophets cry out from their agony not just "Spare me!" but "How long, O Lord? How long?" We all want to know when our suffering will end. This becomes the trial within the trial. In our impatience to eliminate suspense and uncertainty, we are often like little children on a trip: "When are we going to be there, Mom? Dad, are we almost there yet?" So we cry to our Father in Heaven: "When is this going to end? Am I almost there? I could endure it if I only knew. But I can't endure not knowing." And so the ancient cry: "How long, O Lord? How long?" Our childish plea, "Am I there yet?" often masks an underlying complaint: "Father, are you still there? Don't you remember how long I've been suffering down here? Have you forgotten me?" This was even the cry of our Savior on the cross. "Here am I" we say, but in an accusatory rather than submissive tone. And the Father responds, "Child, here am I. I am still here. Don't you remember? My promises may seem afar off, but they are sure." We can cling to promises afar off when enduring the trial of uncertainty about God's timetable.

Finally, we can embrace hope in Christ through clinging to our covenants. They contain promises which are immovable and sure. In our covenants are deposited sure, secure eternal hopes, which Christ and God are bound to honor. They are hopes that we can count on; they are sure. This life is about clinging to our covenants and the promises securely deposited therein. These bind us to the Father and the Son through eternity as joint-heirs with Christ. God is trying to fit us to be kings and queens. That blessing is sure if we live faithfully to it. We know that because it's written in blood—the blood of Christ. We have been reminded of that each time He appeared to His prophets after his resurrection. He showed them the wounds in His hands and in His side and in His feet. These remind us of the price paid by our great High Priest and Advocate with the Father. The scripture says that we may enter with "boldness" into the holiest of holies in heaven "by the blood of Jesus" (Hebrews 10:19). His flesh becomes a veil through which we may enter into God's presence (see Hebrews 10:20). This promise is sure. It is guaranteed by the Atonement, as is every hope we have in Christ.

In conclusion, I'd just like to share with you two quick images, artistic representations of what I've been trying to teach about clinging to the promises afar off. The first is captured in one of my favorite pictures. It's by Eugène Burnand. A print of this picture was given to me many years ago by Elder Bruce Hafen. The picture depicts Peter and John running to an empty tomb on Easter morning. Peter is an old man, John is a young man. Both men are running toward the tomb and toward the dawn. We don't see the empty tomb. We don't see Christ risen. The artist captures the figures in a moment in history like the one we occupy: they live with the hope that the message they have heard is true, but on this side of actually meeting him again as a resurrected being. They, like we, live in hope of His return, in hope that a dawn is coming which will change everything. The artist captures them before they have had an actual personal experience, hastening toward a tomb the women had promised them was empty. Both figures are leaning forward into the dawn with expectant and hopeful faces. In one we see the face of youth; in the other a face lined with cares—the face of age. But each one, in their own way, rushing toward the future and leaning into the dawn of an Easter day that will change everything. This is a great image for me of hope.

The other image I'd like to share in closing is of a passage in scripture which both Elizabeth and I love. It's the Psalm of Nephi. It contains Nephi's soliloquy, as it were. It gives us a window into his soul, a glimpse into this struggling being who heretofore has always appeared so confident. The psalm gives us a glimpse into the heart of a great man, someone we may have supposed never had to struggle to embrace hope, someone whose faith otherwise never seems to have faltered. But trials can force any of us to wrestle with doubt, discouragement, and even despair. Remember what had happened just before Nephi records this psalm? His father has just died. This psalm is about what this death means for Nephi. It means that he will now have to assume leadership in a family where his brothers want to kill him, a family which his father had just barely held together. Nephi is experiencing the loneliness of leadership. In this condition he wills himself to recall the mercies and the miracles that the Lord has given him up to this point in his journey, and to look forward and embrace again hope and the rock of his Redeemer. A few years ago, I used Nephi's psalm to compose texts for a couple of songs. I wrote one of them to an old folk tune called "A Poor Wayfaring Stranger." It's a piece that Elizabeth has liked. It reminds us that the Lord will not forsake us on our journey home. We can embrace his sure promises, though they seem afar off. The text is included below.

We need to hold fast to our promises, no matter how far off they seem. Our occasional cries like Nephi's "O wretched man that I am" need to be matched by the resonant resolution "Awake, my soul! No longer droop in sin" (2 Nephi 4:17,28). Don't you love this line? Actually, it's in iambic pentameter, a perfect blank verse line.

In our journey through the dark night, alone, in the wilderness, we can have the Savior as our rock. We can cling to Him as Hope of Israel, as did Abraham and Nephi. Let us resolve to cling to the promises given in our covenants, no matter what, even though they seem afar off. These are sure, these are guaranteed by His Atonement.

SOMETIMES MY SOUL

Sometimes my soul, in deep affliction,
    Cries out, "O wretched man am I!"
When I'm encompassed by temptation,
    When flesh is weak and I comply.
Yet still I know in whom I've trusted,
    He's heard my cries by day and night.
He's filled my heart with love consuming,
    He's borne my soul to mountain height.

Then why in sorrow should I linger,
    My strength grow slack and my heart groan?
I'll not give way to grief or anger,
    For God's great mercy have I known.
Awake my soul! And cease from drooping.
    Rejoice, my heart! And praise thy God,
Who is the rock of my salvation.
    I'll strictly walk grasping his rod.

Awake my soul! And cease from drooping.
Rejoice, my heart! And praise thy God.[3]

NOTES

1. Neal A. Maxwell, "These Are Your Days," *Ensign*, October 2004, 29.
2. *Hamlet*, in *William Shakespeare: Complete Works, Second Edition*, ed. Stanley Wells, et al. (Oxford: Clarendon Press, 2005), 3.1.64–65.
3. John S. Tanner, "Sometimes My Soul," © 2009 John S. Tanner. Used by permission.

NOT ONLY GOOD, BUT HOLY

Janet S. Scharman

The notion of helping each other along life's pathway is, I believe, a key element of true discipleship. President Dieter F. Uchtdorf during the April 2009 general conference referred to "discipleship [as] a journey. We need the refining lessons of the journey," he said, "to craft our character and purify our hearts."[1] As I pondered this topic and the journey each of us has undertaken, my thoughts have kept turning to the Apostle Peter of the New Testament—in so many ways, the model disciple of Christ.

Peter is always mentioned first in the lists of the original Twelve and is depicted in the Gospels as spokesman of all the Apostles. He was a fisherman by trade, called and mentored by Christ Himself to become a fisher of men, an Apostle. Foreordained to fulfill this most holy assignment, Christ demonstrated great confidence in him and compassion for him. Peter was with Christ during events that were witnessed by only a few of the Apostles, such as the Transfiguration. It was Peter who, along with James and John, were sent from heaven to confer the keys of the Melchizedek Priesthood upon Joseph Smith and Oliver Cowdery in 1829.

In return, that love was fully reciprocated by Peter, and his devotion to Christ was always apparent, with Peter often publicly expressing his

Janet S. Scharman is the vice president of Student Life at Brigham Young University. A licensed psychologist, she is a clinical professor at BYU. She and her husband, Brent, have a blended family of ten children and twenty-seven grandchildren.

faith in Christ. He gave "up his occupation and placed all worldly goods on the altar for the cause."[2] When at the beginning of the last supper Christ washed the feet of His disciples, Peter initially refused. Christ then said to him, "If I wash thee not, thou hast no part with me." Peter immediately responded, "Lord, not my feet only, but also my hands and my head" (John 13:8–9).

So it seems stunning that on that night when Christ was arrested and His death imminent, Peter—of all those who walked and talked with Christ, who had professed so boldly his love of Christ and his commitment to the work—that Peter would be the one who vehemently denied Christ three times before the cock crowed.

We're really given very little information surrounding those events. What we must assume, however, is that whatever shortcomings Peter exhibited that night, whatever the extenuating circumstances were that prompted such responses from him, Christ's atoning sacrifice made all whole—for Peter then, for a wayward child today, for a troubled friend, for you, for me. Peter, on his journey of discipleship with all its mistakes and corrections, apparently learned the lessons and made the sacrifices that qualified him to be the one called from among all the Apostles to lead the Church on earth in Christ's stead and to assist in the Restoration. There must have been a process then, just as President Uchtdorf has described a process in place today, that allowed him, and allows us on our journey of discipleship to learn the refining lessons that "craft our character and purify our hearts."

My husband, Brent, was a bishop at the Utah State Prison. The boundaries of his ward included both death row and the maximum security section. Even in this setting where the inmates have been convicted of the most serious crimes, his calling as bishop was to inspire in these men the hope that comes with true repentance. I think it would be difficult to find a group of individuals who wanted to believe more than these men that the Atonement of Christ is real and that it applies to them. Brent often shared with the inmates this quote by President Boyd K. Packer: "The gospel teaches us that relief from torment and guilt can be earned through repentance. Save for those few who defect to perdition after having known a fulness, *there is no habit, no addiction, no rebellion, no transgression, no offense exempted from the promise of complete forgiveness.*"[3] If there is hope for those convicted of the "worst of the worst" actions, then there is, without question, hope for each of us and for our loved ones. Citing President Uchtdorf again: "The gospel [of Jesus Christ] is the way of discipleship. As we walk in that way, we can experience confidence and joy—even during times of peril, sorrow, and uncertainty."[4]

President Uchtdorf goes on to say, "There are some who believe that because they have made mistakes, they can no longer fully partake of the blessings of the gospel. How little they understand the purposes of the Lord."[5] The Lord loves us. His work and His glory is to bring us home to His presence. He is not the one standing in the way of our progression. Elder Jeffrey R. Holland recently said: "There is something in us, at least in too many of us, that particularly fails to forgive and forget earlier mistakes in life—either mistakes we ourselves have made or the mistakes of others. . . . Let people repent. Let people grow. Believe that people can change and improve."[6] Disciples of Christ trust that each of us can repent and grow and be worthy of all that God has to offer us.

As I have read the accounts in the Bible of Peter and especially the events surrounding the Crucifixion, I have thought that perhaps there was a purpose in Peter's denials of Christ. At no time prior to that terrible night do we have any indication that he was timid or hesitant in either word or action in following Christ with loyalty and exactness. We recall the account in Matthew 14:28–31 when Christ, after meeting with the multitudes, sends His disciples ahead in a boat while He goes alone to the mountains to pray. A storm comes up while they are in the middle of the sea. Suddenly, they see something in the distance on the water and it is Peter who recognizes the figure to be Christ. It is also Peter who has the courage and trust in his Savior to step onto the water—into the unknown—to move toward Him. Peter seems to unquestioningly know that if his faith is not quite enough and he falters, Christ will be there to snatch him from the depths and bring him to safety.

At the time of the Last Supper, Christ tells His disciples that He will be betrayed that night. The Luke account quotes Peter as immediately saying, "Lord, I am ready to go with thee, both into prison, and to death" (Luke 22:33). Christ's comment to Peter is interesting: "Simon, Simon, behold, Satan hath desired to have you, that he may sift you as wheat. But

I have prayed for thee, that thy faith fail not" (Luke 22:31–32; emphasis added).

After Christ's lone suffering in the Garden of Gethsemane, He awakens Peter and the others, telling them that the time of betrayal is at hand. Suddenly approaching them is a mob armed with swords and staves, led by Judas. Under these circumstances I think most people would be afraid, even to the point of distancing themselves from the target. Yet, it is at this very time that Peter boldly steps forward, grabs a sword and cuts off the ear of a servant of the high priest. Christ's response? He tells Peter to "put up . . . thy sword" (Matthew 26:52), and then Christ heals the man's ear (see Luke 22:50–51).

When Christ tells Peter that he will deny Christ three times before morning, Matthew's account quotes Peter as saying, "Though I should die with thee, yet will I not deny thee" (Matthew 26:35). Listen to Christ's words to Peter, "Verily I say unto thee, That this night, before the cock crow, thou *shalt* deny me thrice" (Matthew 26:34; emphasis added). Is it possible that Christ's words to Peter were *directive* of responses he should give that night rather than *prophetic?* Can we imagine that Christ might have been saying: "Peter, I know you are courageous and willing to defend me, but the events of tonight must happen. Please do not intervene." Or, could he have counseled Peter: "Tonight will be dangerous. I need you to be safe so that you can carry on the work after I am gone." None of us is privileged to know exactly what their private conversations might have been or what specifically was intended. We have only incomplete information based on observations and reported accounts. Might we assume that, regardless of how things appeared or what others may have judged of Peter's actions that night, he did the best that he could under the circumstances?

Let me share a little prison-related story—likely apocryphal. An older man in Idaho had one son, basically a good boy, but who made some terrible mistakes that landed him in prison. The man's wife had died, and he was living alone. His son stayed connected with him by calling collect from prison when he was able to leave his cell. During one conversation, the father sounded particularly down. "It's potato planting time of the year and you always were the one to prepare the soil for planting. I'm old. My back hurts. I have arthritis. I just don't know if I'm going to be able to do it myself this year." Immediately, his son shouted, "Dad, whatever you do, don't dig in the garden. That's where I hid the guns." The next afternoon the father opened the door to a group of men with a search warrant for his garden. They came armed with picks and shovels and spent the afternoon digging up every square inch of the garden. Finding nothing, they finally left. The father related this unusual experience to his son during their next phone call. "Dad," the son said, "There are no guns. Under the circumstances, it was the best I could do. Go plant your potatoes."

Would it make any difference to you if you truly believed that the people around you—even a disobedient child, an annoying neighbor, an unreasonable supervisor—are really doing the best they can under the circumstances, whatever those circumstances might be? I believe that we cannot totally know and grasp what another person's circumstances are—or the particular meaning they give to their situation. I think that's true even for people who are close to us. We can be sincere and want to understand, but we just don't have the capacity to fully look into another's heart or mind. The solution? We try not to judge. Disciples of Christ identify people's strengths and then build on them. Focus on what people have, not on what they haven't. Be willing to let go of things that don't matter in the big scheme of things. We treat people differently when we view them as good and capable, and in turn people respond in remarkable ways when they feel valued.

Susan Boyle, a forty-seven-year-old single woman who lived alone with her cat, Pebbles, in a little village in Scotland, spent much of her life not feeling valued. One of nine children, Susan was born with learning difficulties and often endured bullying from the local "yobs." (I had to look up *yob* in the dictionary, and it means boy—boy spelled backwards.)[7] The yobs called her names, threw snowballs at her and dared each other to knock on her door and then run away. As a teenager, she often kept to herself, spending hours in her bedroom listening to Donnie Osmond songs over and over and over again—which her brother, Gerard, said drove him mad. Over time, Susan began to realize that she not only loved to listen to music, but she loved to sing as well.

Ten years ago Susan spent all her savings to record two songs which she sent to talent competitions in the hope of becoming a professional singer. She was encouraged by her mother who knew she had talent. Each time Susan was rejected, and one prominent reason seemed to be that she didn't have the right "look." When her mother died two years ago, Susan found herself unemployed and all alone, with little promise for her future.

Life dealt some pretty hard blows to Susan, but she never gave up. In spite of not being perfectly packaged by the world's standards, of enduring many failing experiences and personal losses, of often being ridiculed, Susan picked herself up and continued to do what mattered most to her. On April 11, 2009, Susan competed on the television show *Britain's Got Talent*, singing "I Dreamed a Dream" from the musical *Les Miserables*.

In truth, as Susan walked onto the stage to begin her performance, she did not look the part of the typical contest winner. The audience and judges didn't appear to take her seriously as she began to introduce herself; they were clearly skeptical of what her performance would bring. And then Susan opened her mouth and began to sing. Skepticism quickly transformed to awe and then to enthusiastic cheers, applause, and standing ovations. All three judges gave her a rousing "yes" vote—perhaps the biggest "yes" she had ever received in her entire life. Susan's performance that day thrust her into the public eye and towards a career in music— her lifelong dream. Following her dramatic performance, it was said that Susan Boyle became an overnight international sensation. In her case, overnight took thirty-five years.

The Lord's timetable often differs from the ones we set for ourselves, and perhaps patience and trust are among the lessons we are to learn. As we follow our dreams we often meet with challenges and disappointments, but we're also blessed with opportunities and divine help. Some of our dreams will be of a temporal nature based on our talents and interests. Others will have an eternal focus. As we dream, I hope we will have the courage to do those things that will lead us to the true reward—a return to our Heavenly Father's presence. I also hope our journeys, as President Uchtdorf called them, will not be solitary ones. As we persist in achieving our own goals, we will receive added blessings as we reach out to others, invite and encourage them to join us—so that we can all return home together. That is my dream.

NOTES

1. Dieter F. Uchtdorf, "The Way of the Disciple," *Ensign*, May 2009, 76.

2. Spencer W. Kimball, "Peter, My Brother," in *Speeches of the Year* (Provo: Brigham Young University Press, 1971), 1–8.

3. Boyd K. Packer, "The Brilliant Morning of Forgiveness," *Ensign*, November 1995, 19; emphasis added.

4. Uchtdorf, "The Way of the Disciple," 75.

5. Ibid., 77.

6. Jeffrey R. Holland, "Remember Lot's Wife," Brigham Young University Devotional, January 13, 2009; http://speeches.byu.edu/index.php?act =viewitem&id=1819; accessed October 5, 2009.

7. *Merriam-Webster's Collegiate Dictionary, Eleventh Edition* (Springfield, Mass.: Merriam-Webster, Inc., 2005), s.v. "yob."

"Stand in Awe . . . and Be Still"

Barbara Thompson

"Stand in awe . . . and be still"—spiritual receptiveness. I knew for eight months that this was to be my topic for BYU Women's Conference. I also knew that to speak about spiritual receptiveness and to be able to hear the whisperings of the Spirit, I would need to practice being still and have experiences listening and practicing what I planned to speak about. I asked Heavenly Father to help me learn how to listen and how to rely on His Holy Spirit to guide my life.

Well, that was the beginning of several very difficult months. They have been months that were filled with happiness and joy, but mostly those months have been filled with many challenges and experiences that have forced me to humbly approach my Heavenly Father in earnest prayer in hopes of receiving guidance and inspiration to get by from day to day.

There have been many challenges—personal challenges, challenges in my family and among my relatives and friends, the people I love. The list of challenges has included serious health problems, death, trouble with jobs, loss of employment, and financial reversals. Some have suffered with

Barbara Thompson is the second counselor in the Relief Society general presidency. Prior to her call, she worked as the executive director of an international charitable organization for abused and neglected children. She has worked in the social services field directing a number of state-level human and family services programs. She holds degrees in social work from Brigham Young University and the University of Utah.

addictions, marital problems, difficulties with children, and relationship problems—again, this is happening among those I love.

The Lord has blessed me with many opportunities to speak to various groups the past few months. Although joyous for the most part, it is just plain hard work to prepare for a talk, especially when called upon to speak in general conference. These opportunities are challenging and stressful. I know I need the inspiration of the Holy Spirit.

Of course, when we are the most stressed and feel the most pressure, it is then the most difficult to quiet our spirits, to be still and just listen. There are so many distractions and so many voices in our daily lives that it becomes increasingly difficult to hear the "still, small voice" unless we tune our hearts and listen carefully.

Revelation or inspiration from the Holy Spirit is probably the most powerful thing we can experience. It is the thing we can remember day after day, month after month, and year after year. We need to be able to recognize promptings and inspiration from the Holy Spirit.

Some of the ways the Spirit will speak to us are through the whisperings of the still, small voice (see Helaman 5:30), a thought or feeling in our minds and in our hearts (see D&C 8:2–3), an enlightenment of the mind (see D&C 6:15), a burning in the bosom (see D&C 9:8), peace to our minds (see D&C 6:23), a vision (see 1 Nephi 1:8), a dream (see 1 Nephi 1:16), or pure intelligence coming into our minds.[1]

The Holy Spirit can also speak to us through living prophets, the scriptures, an inspired priesthood leader, a parent, or a dear friend. Revelation from the Holy Spirit comes in many ways.

Are we sometimes guilty of not listening after we have asked the Lord for help? Do you sometimes accuse your husband, children, or work associates of not listening to you? How does that make you feel?

I have found that sometimes I get an answer to my pleadings only to then question if what I received was really an answer or if I just imagined it. Sometimes I think Heavenly Father might say, "Barbara, why are you asking about this again? I answered that. You need to listen. I won't be giving you two or three answers to a question I have already answered for you."

Sometimes, after feeling good about a decision, I think to myself, *Well, yes, I felt good about that decision, but it would have been better if I had heard a voice or if I had seen a vision. Then I would have been really sure.*

Elder Dallin H. Oaks said: "Most of the revelation that comes to leaders and members of the Church comes by the still, small voice or by a feeling rather than by a vision or a voice that speaks specific words we can hear. I testify to the reality of that kind of revelation, which I have come to know as a familiar, even daily, experience to guide me in the work of the Lord."[2]

Because revelation or the power of the Holy Spirit is so strong, Satan works very hard to tell us we didn't receive an answer. He works hard to deceive us, to tempt us, and to tell us it just isn't worth it to try to keep the commandments and live the gospel.

Once I was away from home attending some business meetings. I had a long lunch break and only needed a few minutes to grab a bite of food. I had some time before the meetings were to start up again. I noticed a card shop nearby and went in to read some cards. I enjoyed many of the humorous cards. Let me just apologize right now to any cat lovers—I don't really appreciate cats. I am allergic to cats. I try to stay as far away from cats as possible. Because of my allergy, I haven't been as sympathetic towards cats as I probably should be. (Please don't write me hateful letters. I am happy for those of you who love cats.)

I picked up a card with a drawing of a washing machine and dryer on it. The dryer door was open and there was a sign taped to it which said, "Cat food inside." There was an arrow pointing toward the inside of the dryer. Hiding next to the dryer, out of sight, was a dog. A cat was approaching the dryer, and the dog was quietly saying, "Oh please, oh please."

I think this is what Satan does to us. He tries to entice us with many things that seem exciting, fun, and look so good. He tells us that almost anything is okay if it feels good or looks good. He knows that if he can get us to let down our guard, desire that "cat food," step close to the dryer door, and then go inside, he has us. His heart delights that he has us.

Many years ago, when I was a young teenager, our family attended a movie. It was called *Butch Cassidy and the Sundance Kid.* This movie was about two men (two handsome men—Paul Newman and Robert Redford) who were bank robbers—that's how they made their living. The audience really liked the movie. We were cheering, laughing, and enjoying it. At the end of the movie, when the two main characters get shot as they rob their last bank, everyone was sad. My little brother was confused and asked me, "Were they the good guys or the bad guys?" That question caused me to stop and think. Well, we had been cheering for men who were robbing banks. That obviously was not a good thing to do. I had a hard time explaining this to my young brother.

This is exactly what Satan does to us. He tries to make the bad look good and he makes good seem unattractive or dull. He tells us that a little lie or a little sin is not a big deal. He slowly and carefully distracts us to the point where it becomes very difficult for us to feel the Holy Spirit and get the guidance we need to stay on the right path.

The Book of Mormon gives countless examples of good and evil people—both trying to win over the hearts of the people. The scriptures tell us of the joy of those who follow God and the misery of those who choose Satan's ways.

In Alma we read about the forces of evil fighting against the people of God. The people had experienced a time of happiness and peace. They were living the gospel. Then came Korihor, the anti-Christ, among the people. He preached many false and deceptive ideas. He told them their belief in God was foolishness. He told them exactly what Satan tells people today—that "whatsoever a man [does is] no crime" (Alma 30:17).

We read, "And thus he [meaning Korihor] did preach unto them, leading away the hearts of many, causing them to lift up their heads in their wickedness, yea, leading away many *women, and also men,* to commit whoredoms—telling them that when a man was dead, that was the end thereof" (Alma 30:18; emphasis added).

This is one of the few scriptures which singles out women specifically in connection with leading them away. The scriptures frequently say the people were led away, or that men were led away, meaning both men and women. But this phrase is specific about leading away many women. Women were falling into Satan's traps, believing a man who used flattering words, telling them the things they wanted to hear. I am fearful that this is beginning to be the norm today. Too many women are being deceived. We are being sold a pack of lies by Satan, the master deceiver.

Getting back to Korihor, he began to believe that his own lying words were true. Satan deceived him, even though he later admitted that he always knew there was a God (see Alma 30:52–53). Korihor's teachings had led away so many people that Alma's heart began to sicken because of the iniquity of the people (see Alma 31:1). These were his people, members of the Lord's Church. He desperately wanted them to repent and return to God. He pleaded with God in mighty prayer that he and his fellow leaders in the Church might be able to "[bring] them again unto thee in Christ" (Alma 31:34). Alma had hope that the people might be humbled and that he could help to bring them "without stubbornness of heart" (Alma 32:16) back to the Church and the safety it provided.

Alma's plea and hope for all the people was expressed earlier in Alma 13:27–29, "And now, my brethren, I wish from the inmost part of my heart, yea, with great anxiety even unto pain, that ye would hearken unto my words, and cast off your sins, and not procrastinate the day of your repentance; but that ye would humble yourselves before the Lord, and call on his holy name, and watch and pray continually, that ye may not be tempted above that which ye can bear, and thus be led by the Holy Spirit, becoming humble, meek, submissive, patient, full of love and all long-suffering; having faith on the Lord; having a hope that ye shall receive eternal life; having the love of God always in your hearts, that ye may be lifted up at the last day and enter into his rest."

Many people don't recognize the Spirit. They don't know what it is that they are feeling or experiencing—even some members of the Church. We need to learn to recognize the Spirit.

My mission president told us to remember that we needed to teach at every door; to every person to whom we spoke, we needed to teach them something to which we could testify. He said to tell them something about Christ, about His Church, about Joseph Smith, or the eternal nature of families and then testify to the truthfulness of that principle. Then the Holy Spirit can bear witness that you are teaching the truth. This works. I saw it happen many times.

I remember one day when it seemed the doors were slamming so fast that there wasn't any time to teach a sentence, let alone testify of anything. Finally we got to one of the last doors in the apartment building we were tracting. A lady came to the door. I told her we were representatives of Jesus Christ, that God loved her, and that He had a special message for her and her family. Then I testified to the truthfulness of this message. She hesitated for a moment. I could tell she felt something, but she politely told us she didn't have time and shut the door.

We finished at that apartment building and went outside to pack up our bags, get on our bikes, and leave. Moments later this woman came running after us and said, "I want to know why I felt so different when you were talking to me. I don't understand what was happening to me." This gave us the opportunity to explain what she was feeling and to tell her more.

Another day I felt impressed that we should ride our bikes out to a little village that was quite a few miles away and visit a family who had told us to come back sometime after they returned from vacation.

My companion said, "Don't you think we should try to call them to see if they're home?" I said, "Let's just go." So we rode all the way out to this little town. We parked our bikes out by the fence, then walked up the sidewalk to the front door. We knocked and waited. No answer. We knocked again. There was no one home. Everything was quiet.

I began to doubt the impression I had felt. Maybe, subconsciously, I had just wanted to go for a long ride to avoid knocking on doors. I felt bad. My companion was nice enough not to say "I told you so" about calling ahead first. We went back to our bikes, talking about what house we could go to next.

A man was walking by on the sidewalk in front of the house. He was a Lebanese man who spoke English. He was visiting his daughter and her husband who lived on the next block. He was just out for a walk.

He said to us, "I have been watching you. There is something different about you. Your eyes are shining. Who are you? What are you doing here? Please tell me." We told him that we were missionaries and we were there in Germany serving the Lord. He was very interested in our message. Of course, the Church was not allowed in Lebanon in those days. We spoke to him on the street for a while and explained about the Restoration and the Book of Mormon.

He told us that the next day he was flying to the United States on business. He would be in San Francisco for several weeks. We gave him an English pamphlet about Joseph Smith and the restoration of the gospel. On the back of the pamphlet there just happened to be an address in San Francisco where he could locate the Church. He said he was anxious to do so.

Do spiritual experiences only happen to missionaries? Why do they seem to happen to missionaries more than to some of us? Does the Lord love missionaries more? Well no, of course not.

He loves all of us. He wants to bless us. Think about what missionaries do. They study the scriptures daily. They pray, teach, and bear testimony often. And hopefully they live their lives in accordance with the gospel. Each of us who have been baptized and confirmed members of this Church have been told how we can always have His spirit to be with us.

The sacramental prayers remind us of how we can have the Spirit of the Lord in our lives. As we partake of the sacrament we renew our covenants with God and indicate that we are willing to take upon us the name of Christ, always remember Him, and keep His commandments (see Moroni 4:3). Then, as we do these things, we will put ourselves in a position to have His Spirit to be with us.

During the past year as I have done Relief Society auxiliary trainings, I have asked many sisters what they do to prepare themselves to receive revelation or what they do to get inspiration in their lives. They have shared many beautiful experiences. They have explained that they pray, fast, study the scriptures, go to the temple, read the general conference talks in the *Ensign* or the *Liahona*, listen to sacred music, repent, and they are still and quiet so they can hear when the Spirit whispers to them.

In Alma 8:10, we are told that "Alma labored much in the spirit, wrestling with God in mighty prayer, that he would pour out his Spirit." We have also been told to "counsel with the Lord in all [our] doings" so we can be directed for good (Alma 37:37). Prayer will be the source of much strength and will help us be receptive to the Holy Spirit.

We have been told in Isaiah chapter 58 that through fasting and giving offerings to help others, when we call, the Lord will answer and the Lord will guide us continually (see Isaiah 58:6–11). Fasting will help us to be humble and more receptive so we can hear the voice of the Spirit.

We have heard many times of the value of reading and studying the scriptures. "Feast upon the words of Christ; for behold, the words of Christ will tell you all things what ye should do" (2 Nephi 32:3).

Elder Dallin H. Oaks has given us some valuable insights into the importance of regular scripture study. He said, "Just as continuing revelation enlarges and illuminates the scriptures, so also a study of the scriptures enables men and women to receive revelations. . . . The idea that scripture reading can lead to inspiration and revelation opens the door to the truth that a scripture is not limited to what it meant when it was written but may also include what that scripture means to a reader today. Even more, scripture reading may also lead to current revelation on whatever else the Lord wishes to communicate to the reader at that time. We do not overstate the point when we say that the scriptures can be a Urim and Thummim to assist each of us to receive personal revelation."[3]

We have been counseled not only to attend the temple as often as possible but to worship in the holy temple.[4] Every latter-day prophet has stressed the importance of temple worship and the blessings associated with making and keeping sacred covenants.

Joseph Smith received by revelation the words to the prayer he offered at the dedication of the Kirtland Temple as recorded in Doctrine and Covenants section 109. One of the blessings mentioned in that section is that we can feel God's power (see D&C 109:13). In verse 22 it states: "And we ask thee, Holy Father, that thy servants may go forth from this house armed with thy power, and that thy name may be upon them, and thy glory be round about them, and thine angels have charge over them." What a great source of revelation we will find as we attend and worship in the holy temple.

I pray that we will each recommit to seek the Holy Spirit, live so the Spirit can be with us, listen for the answers, and then act upon the inspiration we have been given. I testify to you that our Heavenly Father lives and loves us. I testify that the Lord Jesus Christ is our Redeemer and that the Holy Ghost will be with us as we do the things we have promised to do.

NOTES

1. See *Teachings of the Prophet Joseph Smith,* comp. Joseph Fielding Smith (Salt Lake City: Deseret Book, 1976), 151.
2. Dallin H. Oaks, "Teaching and Learning by the Spirit," *Ensign,* March 1997, 14.
3. Oaks, "Scripture Reading and Revelation," *Ensign,* January 1995, 7–8.
4. See David A. Bednar, "Honorably Hold a Name and Standing," *Ensign,* May 2009, 97–100.

MAINTAINING THE TITLE OF LIBERTY

Elder L. Tom Perry

It is always good to search the scriptures for some assistance in developing an outline for the preparation of an assignment such as this. Since the time I had the opportunity to be the chairman of the Church's bicentennial committee during the United States's celebration of that milestone in 1976, one of my favorite accounts in the Book of Mormon has been the story of Moroni and his leadership over the people of Nephi.

The account begins with Amalickiah being a strong man and deciding to use his strength to rally support to become king over the land. He was able to persuade many to follow him. Moroni, the chief commander of the armies, became angry when he heard of the dissensions among the people:

"And it came to pass that he rent his coat; and he took a piece thereof, and wrote upon it—In memory of our God, our religion, and

Elder L. Tom Perry has been a member of the Quorum of the Twelve Apostles of The Church of Jesus Christ of Latter-day Saints since 1974. Prior to his call to the Quorum of the Twelve, he had served as an Assistant to the Twelve since 1972. Elder Perry has been a missionary, a counselor in a bishopric, a stake high councilor, a counselor in a stake presidency, and the president of the Boston Stake. He received a BS degree from Utah State University in 1949 and did graduate work there. His professional career was spent in the retail business where he served as vice president and treasurer in companies located in Idaho, California, New York, and Massachusetts. On July 18, 1947, he married Virginia Lee of Hyde Park, Utah, in the Logan Temple. She died December 14, 1974. They are the parents of two daughters and a son. He married Barbara Taylor Dayton on April 28, 1976, in the Salt Lake Temple.

freedom, and our peace, our wives, and our children—and he fastened it upon the end of a pole.

"And he fastened on his headplate, and his breastplate, and his shields, and girded on his armor about his loins; and he took the pole, which had on the end thereof his rent coat, (and he called it the title of liberty) and he bowed himself to the earth, and he prayed mightily unto his God for the blessings of liberty to rest upon his brethren, so long as there should a band of Christians remain to possess the land. . . .

"And when Moroni had said these words, he went forth among the people, waving the rent part of his garment in the air, that all might see the writing which he had written upon the rent part, and crying with a loud voice, saying: Behold, whosoever will maintain this title upon the land, let them come forth in the strength of the Lord, and enter into a covenant that they will maintain their rights, and their religion, that the Lord God may bless them" (Alma 46:12–13; 19–20).

Today, maintaining this title upon the land means we each dedicate ourselves to strengthening the image of the Church. We are among those who have entered into a covenant with the Lord to maintain our religion and to continue to establish His Church. We can also be certain we will have the strength of the Lord as Moroni did to carry our banner to the world as our witness and testimony of the restoration of the gospel of Jesus Christ.

We have covenanted with the Lord to go where He wants us to go; we will do what He wants us to do, and we will strive to become what we should and must become. "In the Strength of the Lord," and through His grace, I know that you and I can be blessed to accomplish all things.

"A city set upon a hill cannot be hidden from the world, but that doesn't mean it cannot be misperceived."—Gary Lawrence[1]

How Do We See *Ourselves?*

Imagine Latter-day Saints doing what Latter-day Saints do—attending church, helping their neighbors, fulfilling welfare assignments by canning food or assembling humanitarian kits, providing strong backs and able hands in the aftermath of a natural disaster. As we see this image of Latter-day Saints in our minds, there is so much we can tell the world about who we are and what we represent. We can and must present to the world this very positive image. We cannot let the world develop our image for us. These pictures surely tell us we are the happiest and healthiest people on earth. Statistics prove this statement to be true. The Word of Wisdom has given us a pattern which certifies to our health. Recently, a poll in the United States declared Utah to be the happiest state in the union.[2] We do not need to hide the blessings that gospel living has given to the members of the Church.

There are so many memories in these pictures which remind us of the blessings we receive from embracing the gospel of our Lord and Savior.

"Sometimes we members think that although the world may not be beating a path to our door, people generally respect us. Unfortunately, that is not the case. . . . For every person who strongly likes us, there are *more than four* who strongly dislike us."—Gary Lawrence[3]

How Does the *World* See Us?

"It's not what he doesn't know that bothers me, it's what he knows for sure that just ain't so."[4]

We have been looking at the image of the Church to better understand how to approach our missionary efforts. We have employed some professional firms to help us define and project our true image to the world.

Recent studies of U. S. non-members, conducted by Pew, Apco, and Gary Lawrence, found:

- 51 percent have little or no awareness of Mormon practices and beliefs.[5]
- 47 percent do not have a favorable view of Mormons.[6]
- 31 percent believe that Mormons are not Christian.[7]

These statistics clearly show the imperfect way we have communicated who we are and what we believe.

One- to two-word impressions of the Mormon religion included:

- Polygamy/bigamy,
- Family/family values,
- Cult,
- Different,
- Dedicated.[8]

Three out of five wrong impressions is not a good batting average for us.

Significant misperceptions shape the problematic side of the Church's image and standing in America.

IGNORANCE

First, those ont of our faith simply don't know much about us or our beliefs. It has been said that one recipient of humanitarian aid during the Katrina disaster remarked that there were two groups who really made a difference: the Latter-day Saints and the Mormons.

MISUNDERSTOOD DOCTRINES

"According to a new study, Mormon teenagers fare better than regular teenagers when it comes to staying out of trouble and doing well in school. Although, you would too if you had eight moms yelling at you."—*Saturday Night Live*[9]

Saturday Night Live had to twist a very positive statement about us into a very false one for an audience reaction. Again, some would say, "It's what he knows for sure that just ain't so" that is the problem here.

EXCLUSION

"I'd love to talk to my Mormon friends about their religion, but I wouldn't want to offend them, or threaten our friendship, and they don't seem to want to talk about it much."—Non-member in focus group[10]

Although eighty-four percent of Americans have seen our ads, been given our literature, and/or had missionaries approach them, less than thirty percent can identify our main claim—that we follow Jesus Christ, and are the reestablished original Christian church.[11] Seventy percent of the time we have missed declaring what this Church really is. We declare to the world that the priesthood of our almighty God has again been restored to the earth by the Prophet Joseph Smith. It contains the same keys which were given to the Apostle Peter on the Mount of Transfiguration by our Lord and Savior. We know by our study of the history of the former church, the priesthood was lost from the earth after the death of the Savior's chosen Apostles and the world went into a period called the Great Apostasy. It was necessary for a restoration of priesthood power to occur to bring the priesthood again to the earth. Peter, James, and John again returned to confer the keys of the priesthood on the head of the Prophet Joseph Smith, empowering him to effect the complete Restoration of the gospel of Jesus Christ.

"The many misunderstandings and false information about the Church are somewhat our own fault for not clearly explaining who we are and what we believe."—Elder M. Russell Ballard[12]

"[Many] are blinded by the subtle craftiness of men, whereby *they lie in wait to deceive,* and who are only kept from the truth because they know not where to find it."—Doctrine and Covenants 123:12; emphasis added.

"For we wrestle not against flesh and blood, but against principalities, against powers, against the rulers of the darkness of this world, against spiritual wickedness in high places."—Ephesians 6:12

How do we close the gap between how we see ourselves and how the world sees us? How do we let our light shine in a way that it is better understood by those who are not of our faith?

A person's view of the Church is the sum of personal experiences they have had which relate in any way to the Church organization.

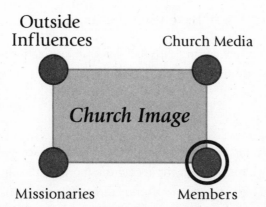

Most important of all, it is the members who build the image of the Church. There are several things we can do as members to help make people become more aware of our true beliefs:

LISTEN FIRST

Be willing to ask others about their own beliefs, concerns, and challenges.

We need to develop the art of learning to listen. As we establish common ground with our friends and neighbors, we then have a common base for a good solid discussion on religion.

KNOW THE DOCTRINE

Be prepared to explain what we believe and the facts of our doctrine and history.

We have been blessed with three very basic discussions used by our full-time missionaries from their mission training book that we all know as *Preach My Gospel*. The three basic discussions are:

- The Restoration;
- The Plan of Salvation;
- The Gospel: Faith, Repentance, Baptism, and the Gift of the Holy Ghost.[13]

All members of the Church should know the doctrinal base of these three topics and be able to discuss them.

LIVE THE STANDARDS

Strive to incorporate our beliefs and standards into our behavior.
Of course, we should be living what we preach!

BE EXEMPLARY CITIZENS

Serve our community and country. Put our faith into action to bless others.

There is a strong movement in countries north of the equator towards secularism. The United States tends to be following this trend. This nation was founded on Christian principles. Under such a banner, it was prepared to be the birthplace of the Restoration of the gospel of Jesus Christ. Citizens who understand the principles, values, and standards of our founding fathers must be able to strongly support and defend them.

Be Good Neighbors

Sharing the gospel is a natural outcome of our interaction with and love for our neighbors.

As basic as apple pie—or any other act of selfless service or kind interaction with our neighbors.

Open Our Mouths

Learn to have natural conversations about how living gospel principles has blessed your life.

The false image will not be changed unless we let people know who we are and what we believe.

Extend Invitations

Research indicates that, often, our friends and neighbors are simply waiting for an invitation to discuss faith with us.

Let's see you prove this statement to be right—that people are waiting to discuss our faith with them.

Use Technology

Explore ways to use technology to share your beliefs with others. The Church is creating tools that can help you do this—such as mormon.org, videos on YouTube, Facebook widgets, and other emerging technologies.

Two weeks before the April 2009 general conference we posted messages on YouTube entitled "Mormon Messages." The response has been almost overwhelming. Videos on the Church's new *Mormon Messages* YouTube channel have been viewed over 2,000,000 times.[14] Members are sharing these short, inspirational videos with their friends and family on blogs, Web sites, and Facebook. A video based on Elder Holland's Easter message recently went "viral" and became the number one most-popular video being shared and discussed on the Internet, with over 350,000 views.[15]

A message shared from our own Web site soon spans the world inviting two-way communication to explain our beliefs.

Be Bold, but Not Overbearing

Do not be afraid to speak up to others about how our beliefs and practices have blessed our lives.

Your personal experiences can be of comfort and a blessing to many.

"Hearken, O ye people of my church, saith the voice of him who dwells on high, and whose eyes are upon all men; yea, verily I say: Hearken ye people from afar; and ye that are upon the islands of the sea, listen together.

"For verily the voice of the Lord is unto all men, and there is none to escape; and there is no eye that shall not see, neither ear that shall not hear, neither heart that shall not be penetrated.

"And also those to whom these commandments were given, might have power to lay the foundation of this church, and to bring it forth out of obscurity and out of darkness, the only true and living church upon the face of the whole earth" (D&C 1:1–2, 30).

I have covenanted with the Lord to go where He wants me to go, I will do what He wants me to do, and I will strive to become what I should and must become. In the strength of the Lord, and through His grace, I know that you and I can be blessed to accomplish all things.

NOTES

1. Gary C. Lawrence, *How Americans View Mormonism: Seven Steps to Improve Our Image* (Orange, Calif.: Parameter Foundation, 2008), 20.

2. Lawrence, *How Americans View Mormonism*, 22.

3. Ibid.

4. Ibid., 38; this quotation has been misattributed over time to many individuals. See "Policing Word Abuse," Forbes.com, August 13, 2009; http://www.forbes.com/2009/08/12/nigel-rees-misquotes-opinions-rees_print.html; accessed November 17, 2009.

5. See http://pewforum.org/surveys/religionviews07/; accessed November 17, 2009.

6. See ibid.

7. See ibid.

8. See ibid.

9. *Saturday Night Live*, March 19, 2005; cited at http://www.ldsfilm.com/chars/lds_chars5.html; accessed October 13, 2009.

10. Focus group study, Missionary Department, The Church of Jesus Christ of Latter-day Saints.

11. Ibid.

12. M. Russell Ballard, "Faith, Family, Facts, and Fruits," *Ensign*, November 2007, 25.

13. See *Preach My Gospel* (Salt Lake City: The Church of Jesus Christ of Latter-day Saints, 2004), 29–70.

14. See http://www.youtube.com/mormonmessages; accessed October 5, 2009.

15. See http://newsroom.lds.org/ldsnewsroom/eng/news-releases-stories/mormon-apostle-s-easter-message-becomes-top-internet-video; accessed November 17, 2009.

INDEX

INDEX